Moving Pictures
Films Through a Psychoanalytic Lens

Moving Pictures
Films Through a Psychoanalytic Lens

Herbert H. Stein

IPBOOKS.net
International Psychoanalytic Books

Moving Pictures: Films Through a Psychoanalytic Lens
Copyright © 2016 by Herbert H. Stein

International Psychoanalytic Books (IPBooks),
30-27 33rd Street, #3R
Astoria, NY 11102
Online at: www.IPBooks.net

All rights reserved. No part of this book may be used or reproduced in any manner whatsoever including Internet usage, without written permission of the author.

Interior book design by Maureen Cutajar
www.gopublished.com

ISBN: 978-0-9969996-8-7

Preface

WE ENTER A MOVIE theater, find a seat and recline as best we can, waiting to be transported. Transported not only to another place and time, but to the perspective and sensibility of another person. It might be likened to a form of dissociation or, perhaps more positively framed, to a heightening of empathy. We not only roam the world in space and time, but we do it from a perspective only partly our own.

Filmmakers, assigned the task of pulling us in, appeal to our curiosity and our intellect, but also to our emotions, our desires and fears. The premise of the articles in this book is that in doing so they go beyond our conscious, surface desires and fears, finding access to our less conscious fantasies and distant memories. I won't attempt to say how they learn to do it, but hope to demonstrate their cunning in what follows. Who would have thought, for instance, that we could walk into a movie theater and experience subtle reminders outside our awareness of the experience of a parent teaching a baby how to walk?

These articles were written individually over the past eleven or twelve years for the Bulletin of the Psychoanalytic Association of New York, the *PANY Bulletin*, and published on-line at InternationalPsychoanalysis.net. I have loosely assembled them in groups with titles that could probably apply to any of these films, but clearly they can be read in any order as individual pieces, each probably best taken in a single bite. We do not usually think of psychoanalytic ideas as fun or of popular films as educational, but I hope you will find both to be true. Films allow us to see into the workings of our minds; but, above all, these were written to be fun, to tell a good story from an alternate point of view. Enjoy!

Contents

1: ATTACHMENTS

    Gravity 1
    The Wizard of Oz 12
    Pan's Labyrinth 20
    The Hours 30

2: MOODS

    The Grand Budapest Hotel 39
    Birdman: The Unexpected Virtue of Ignorance 50
    Black Swan 58
    Ex Machina 66

3: LOVERS

    Miracle on 34th Street 75
    High Noon 87
    Forbidden Planet 94
    The Artist (and A Star is Born) 106

4: BROTHERS

    The Road to Perdition 115
    The Prestige 122
    The Dark Knight 133

5: SELVES

    A Beautiful Mind 145
    Up in the Air 155
    About Schmidt 165

6: OUTSIDERS

King Kong *175*
The Lives of Others *184*
Capote, To Kill a Mockingbird, Breakfast at Tiffany's *194*

7: TRANSFERENCES

Slumdog Millionaire *207*
Eternal Sunshine of the Spotless Mind *218*
The King's Speech *228*

AFTERWORD *243*

1

Attachments

―――《◉》―――

Gravity

WE KNOW FROM DOING psychoanalytic work that people naturally use metaphor to connect ideas and experiences. In this case, hearing a very typical memory about a lost, frightened child suddenly associated in my mind to a film I had seen weeks before about astronauts stranded in space. Reexamining the film uncovered an even more basic childhood experience.

In an Ernie Kovacs skit, a boy sends in a question to Kovacs's eccentric answer man asking why people in South America, at the bottom of the world, don't fall off. Kovacs's answer: "Billy, people are falling off all the time."

My daughter told me that when she went to see the film *Gravity*, within a few minutes she was deeply regretting that she'd chosen to see it in 3D because she was feeling overwhelmed by a fear of heights and of falling. I didn't have to ask her at what point that was, because it obviously was at one of the opening scenes in which we are looking down from open space at a large Earth.

For me, the sense of being out in space was also frightening, but in an exciting way, much like you might experience an amusement park ride. The sense of fear was immediate, but tempered somewhat by my knowing that, unlike the astronauts in the film, I was in no real personal danger. I was sitting safely in a movie theater in normal gravity. And yet ...

The excitement of floating in space added an element of thrill that carried me to the point of involvement in the plot of survival. The strange sensation of floating in space gave *Gravity* an odd quality that we wouldn't usually get from a film. However, I did not give the slightest thought to using *Gravity* to demonstrate any psychoanalytic concepts.

Several weeks after seeing the film, I heard about someone with a memory of wandering away as a small child, searching for her parents, and getting lost. The memory carried feelings of being both frightened at suddenly being alone and chastened at having wandered on her own, a complex issue. Listening to it, I had the unbidden thought, "It's like *Gravity*," with the ambient fear of floating away on one's own, away from all contact and protection, like the child in the memory.

One of the miracles of art is its ability to evoke emotions and even sensations that have been repressed or dormant, at times from a much earlier period in our lives. Here is a film that gives us the visceral sensation of floating in space, aware that at any moment we could drift, losing all contact with Earth and with other people. It did, indeed, seem to mimic the emotional sensation of being lost as a small child, out of reach of any known adult, with possibly no hope of being found. With that in mind, I decided to revisit the film.

Before we enter the film itself, we see written large across the screen: "AT 600 KM ABOVE PLANET EARTH THE TEMPERATURE FLUCTUATES BETWEEN +258 AND -148 DEGREES FAHRENHEIT. THERE IS NOTHING TO CARRY SOUND. NO AIR PRESSURE. NO OXYGEN. LIFE IN SPACE IS IMPOSSIBLE."

If this was designed to create an atmosphere of anxiety, it probably succeeds, but is certainly unnecessary. Immediately, we are looking down at a section of the Earth that takes up our entire visual field. We soon see the two astronauts, Kowalski and Stone, small figures with the background of the Earth in one perspective, black space in another. Dr. Ryan Stone is tethered to a section of the shuttle, floating in space. Commander Matt Kowalski is untethered, floating in space. We will see that he has a jetpack for maneuvering.

It is really when we first see the small astronauts against the backdrop of a giant segment of Earth that we begin to feel giddy. Especially with 3D imagery, but even without it, the viewer can feel how small they are and how easily they could be lost in space.

As we watch the opening moments, in which the astronauts are going about their relatively routine business of space-walking, she attempting to fix a part of the Hubble telescope, he just standing by, chit-chatting and playing music, we are given just enough to understand their relative positions. Kowalski is calm, an old hand at this. We are told that he is only 75 hours short of the record for total time spent in "space walks." Ryan Stone is a medical engineer, not a trained astronaut, on her first mission in space after six months of training for this mission.

I had not noticed it particularly the first time around, but very near the beginning of the film, Kowalski tells a story with a theme quite close to the issues of loss and attachment that I was now pursuing.

"Houston, I have a bad feeling about this mission."

Mission Control responds, "Please expand."

"Okay, let me tell you a story. It was ninety-six. I'd been up here for forty-two days. Every time I passed over Texas, I looked down knowing that Mrs. Kowalski was looking up, thinking of me. Six weeks I'm blowing kisses at that woman. Then we land at Edwards and I find out that she's run off with this lawyer. So, I packed my car, and I headed to ..."

This is said lightly, a background accompaniment to the overwhelming scene we are viewing, but it is a tale of loss, a betrayal of love. Not long afterward, but after the traumatic event that sets the plot in motion, we hear a tale of loss from Ryan Stone that cannot be told or heard lightly.

"I had a daughter. She was four. She was at school playing tag. Slipped, hit her head, and that was it. Stupidest thing. I was driving when I got the call, so... ever since then, that's what I do. I wake up, I go to work, and I just drive."

After roughly 10 minutes of peaceful spacewalk, trauma propels the film's plot forward. We hear Mission Control in Houston in a not-to-worry type of message that a Russian missile has blown up one of their unused satellites, creating a mass of debris hurtling in orbit. Soon afterwards, Houston gives a more peremptory warning:

"Mission abort. Repeat. Mission abort. Initiate emergency disconnect from Hubble. Begin reentry procedure. ISS (International Space Station), initiate emergency evacuation."

When Matt asks what has happened, he is told:

"Debris from the missile strike has caused a chain reaction, hitting other satellites and creating new debris traveling faster than a high-speed bullet up towards your altitude. All copy."

Within moments, the debris hits them, creating chaos, cutting off communication with the Earth, and destroying the Explorer spacecraft, leaving Matt Kowalski and Ryan Stone alone in space. It was around this point that I began to see a further pattern related to attachment and fear of loss. As we watch, Ryan becomes detached from the structure she'd been working on and is spinning in space.

Ryan Stone is still connected to a robotic arm of the shuttle which breaks free and spins off, spinning her with it. We spin with her, while the following dialogue ensues. I cannot convey the voice qualities from the following dialogue, but keep in mind that Kowalski's voice is calm and firm throughout, with a persistent urgency. Ryan is anxious, as is the viewer. We start with Matt Kowalski:

"Astronaut is off structure! Dr. Stone is off structure! Dr. Stone, detach! You must detach! If you don't detach, that arm's gonna carry you too far!"

"No! No! I can-"

"Listen to my voice! You need to focus!"

"I can't! I can't."

"I'm losing visual of you. In a few seconds, I won't be able to track you. You need to detach! I can't see you anymore! Do it now!"

"Okay, I'm trying! I'm trying! I'm trying!" (Ryan detaches herself and flies off.) "Houston, I've lost visual of Dr. Stone. Houston, I've lost visual of Dr. Stone."

Attachments

(Ryan Stone is spinning out of control.)

"Dr. Stone, do you copy? Repeat, do you copy?"

"Yes, yes, yes. I copy! I'm detached!"

"Give me your position."

"I don't know! I don't know! I'm spinning! I can't -- I can't -- !"

"Report your position."

"GPS is down. I ca—It's down, I can't ..." (She spins and flips.)

"Give me a visual."

"I told you, nothing. I see nothing!"

"Do you have a visual of Explorer?"

"No. No."

"Do you have a visual of ISS?"

"No."

"You need to focus. Anything, use the sun and the Earth, give me coordinates."

"It's so fast. I can't breathe! I can't breathe!"

"Give me coordinates! Dr. Stone, do you copy? Repeat, do you copy? Give me your position! Report your position. Give me a visual! Do you have a visual of Explorer? Do you have a visual of ISS? I need you to focus. Anything. Use the sun and the Earth, give me coordinates. Give me coordinates."

(She continues spinning. Ryan glances about as she tries to calm down. The Explorer shuttle, a glowing light, is far off in the distance.)

"Kowalski? Kowalski, do you copy? Kowals—I have—have a vis— Kowalski, I have a visual. I have—have a visual of Explorer. With north at twelve o'clock and the shuttle is at the center of the dial. I can see—I can see the Chinese station. No—No, it's the International Space Station. ISS is at—ISS is at seven o'clock."

No wonder that I was reminded of this film while hearing a story of a lost little girl! The specific scene hadn't registered at that time, but the feeling of being small and lost and afraid of never finding my way back had to be indelible.

At this point, Matt tells Ryan to turn on her light so that he can spot her. She does this and he finally spots her and heads towards her using his jetpack. He crashes into her and they hold on tight. He tethers her to him, then tells her he needs to push her away. She is terrified, repeating, "No, no, no ...." He tells her he will "nudge" her away and she repeats screaming "No, no ..."

Finally he shows her that she is tethered to him. "Where you go, I go."

As this scene further unfolded, I discovered, or perhaps "re-discovered," another element of the theme I was seeking.

He is in control, she is terrified, and as they move back to the shuttle to find the entire crew dead, one man's head virtually taken off, we begin to see the pattern. He is taking her to the best chance for survival and in the process teaching her how to walk in space. On my second viewing, the analogy of parent and child was striking, and more particularly, a parent helping a frightened toddler to learn to walk, to learn to be more independent.

With the shuttle incapacitated, he takes her towards the International Space Station, where they hope to be able to use the Soyuz landing craft to get back to Earth. But when they get there, Matt sees that the only remaining Soyuz has deployed its parachute and is not viable for re-entry. His new plan is to use it to go to the Chinese space station.

But he is out of fuel in his jetpack and can't brake properly, they crash into the space station and he flies on. Ryan hits something and the tether snaps.

"The tether broke! I'm detached, I'm detached!"

"Grab hold! Grab anything!"

As she is flying off the station, her leg gets tangled in the ropes from the parachute, holding her loosely to the station.

We are, of course watching this, our hearts pounding as we experience the roller coaster ride and feel the fragility of attachment to the space station.

Finally, he flies close enough for her to attempt to catch him. She can't grab his hand, but she is able to grab onto the section of tether line that is attached to him. She says,

"Got ya. You just... hold on and I'm gonna start pulling you in. I'm gonna start ... "

"Ryan, listen. You have to let me go."

"No."

"The ropes are too loose. I'm pulling you with me."

"No."

Indeed, he is being propelled by his momentum away from the Soyuz, held back only by the tether line that she is holding onto. She is precariously attached, loops of rope from the Soyuz's parachute wrapping around her leg, keeping her attached to Soyuz.

Here we come to perhaps the most poignant moment of the film, and one with obvious significance in our parallel tale of attachment and autonomy.

Matt takes hold of the tether clip.

"No, no, no."

"You have to let me go, or we both die."

"I'm not letting you go! We're fine!"

Despite her protestations, he unclips the tether from his suit, and as he holds it, before releasing it, he says, "You're gonna make it, Ryan!"

As a story of two astronauts, one recognizing that he can't be saved, but that the other can, this is high drama and extraordinary courage. But as a story of parent and child, it takes on a new level of significance. The courage is still there, but it is now the courage of the parent who can let go and teaches the child to let go as well. When played out in life, this scenario is not usually a matter of life and death, and yet it probably often takes a quiet courage and reserve on the part of the parent as well as a mix of feelings on the part of the child. That is true at the moment of walking, during the stage of "rapprochement," in Mahler's words, and in later stages of childhood and adolescence.

At this point, Matt starts to drift away, still talking with Ryan, still with the same calm voice, very much in control. Ryan crashes into the station and is able to hold onto a railing.

"Ryan, do you hear me? Do you copy?"

"My CO_2 alarm went off. My CO_2 alarm went off."

"Look, you need to board the station. Do you see the airlock? Hey, Ryan, you copy? Look for the airlock. It's above you, next to the Zarya module. You see it?"

"Yes. Yes, I see it. I see it."

"All right, good. That's where you want to go. Now you're getting lightheaded, right?"

"Yeah. Yes."

"That's because you're breathing CO_2. You're losing consciousness. You need to board the station."

"Okay."

Holding on tight to the space station's railing, Ryan turns her body upside down and moves toward the station.

Matt says, "That second Soyuz is too damaged for re-entry, but it's perfectly fine for a little Sunday drive."

Ryan climbs upward.

"Sunday drive?"

"Look to the west. You see that dot in the distance? That's a Chinese station."

"Yes."

"You're gonna take the Soyuz, and you're gonna cruise over there. Chinese lifeboat is a Shenzhou."

"I've never flown a Shenzhou."

"It doesn't matter. Its re-entry protocol is identical to the Soyuz."

"Okay."

"You've never flown the Soyuz either?"

"Only a simulator."

"Well, then you know."

"But I crashed it."

"It's a simulator, that's what it's designed for."

"Every time. I crashed it every time."

"You point the damn thing at Earth. It's not rocket science. And by this time tomorrow, you're gonna be back in Lake Zurich with a hell of a story to tell. You copy? Ryan, you copy?"

She tells him that she's going to get the Soyuz and find him. He tells her, "Ryan, you've gotta learn to let go."

We go through another roller coaster ride as she opens the airlock door and has to hang on when it flies open. In fact, by the time she gets into the Soyuz craft, Kowalski is out of sight and not answering on the radio.

What is striking here is not only the paradigm of a parent and child involved in developing the child's autonomy, but that it also provides, in Kowalski, a model for parental behavior. This is a "parent" who is secure in himself and focused on helping the child to both survive and to develop confidence in its own survival skills. His relaxed, yet focused style fits the pattern described elsewhere (Main, 2000) of parents who promote secure attachment in their children. Although the film's limited plot clues suggest that he has detached from the world in what might seem some form of giving up, his actual interaction with Ryan suggests something else, an ability to persevere on the one hand, and yet also accept with relative equanimity what he cannot overcome. This is, of course, an ideal, but we must remember that this is, of course, a movie.

The ultimate success of Kowalski's "parenting" of Ryan Stone is demonstrated in a later sequence in the film. She has overcome more obstacles, including a fire that destroys the space station as she is separating from it and a parachute from the Soyuz that she must detach from the space station in another spacewalk with debris floating by in order to get free of the station. Finally, she is securely seated in the Soyuz, ready to jet her way towards the Chinese station, only to find that the thrusters are out of fuel.

She issues a Mayday call on the radio and hears a dim message, in a foreign language, with dogs barking in the background. In a plea to no one who will understand her, she says,

"Oh, I'm gonna die, Aningaaq. I know, we're all gonna die. Everybody knows that. But I'm gonna die today. Funny, that. You know, to know... But the thing is, it's that I'm still scared. I'm really scared. Nobody will mourn for me, no one will pray for my soul. Will you mourn for me? Will you say a prayer for me? Or is it too late? I mean, I'd say one for myself, but I've never prayed in my life, so... Nobody ever taught me how. Nobody ever taught me how."

She hears a baby crying.

"A baby. There's a baby with you, huh? Is that a lullaby you're singing? That's so sweet. I used to sing to my baby. I hope I see her soon."

At this point, giving up, she turns the dials to lower the oxygen in the cabin and begins to fade.

"That's nice, Aningaaq. Keep singing, just like that. Sing me to sleep, and I'll sleep. Keep singing. And sing, and sing."

Suddenly, a light shines from outside and Matt Kowalski appears, in his space suit. He opens the hatch and gets into the cabin with her.

"Check your watch. Thirteen hours and eleven minutes. Call Anatoly and tell him he's been bumped." (He is referring to the space walk record.) "It's a little gloomy in here, isn't it?"

She starts to ask him how he got there.

"Trust me, it's a hell of a story."

Now there is country music playing. He tells her he found a little extra battery power. He pulls a bottle of vodka out of somewhere and toasts Anatoly.

"All right. Let's get out of here. The Chinese station's about a hundred miles. Just a little Sunday drive."

"We can't."

"Sure we can."

"There's no fuel, I tried everything."

"Well, there's always something we can do."

"I tried everything."

"Did you try the soft landing jets?"

"They're for landing."

"Well, landing is launching. It's the same thing. Didn't you learn about that in training?"

"I never got to land the simulator. I told you that."

"But you know about it."

"And I crashed it... every time. But this ... "

"Listen, do you want to go back, or do you want to stay here? I get it; it's nice up here. You can just shut down all the systems, turn out all the lights... and just close your eyes and tune out everybody. There's nobody up here that can hurt you. It's safe. I mean, what's the point of going on? What's the point of living? Your kid died. Doesn't get any rougher than that. But still, it's a matter of what you do now. If you decide to go, then you gotta just get on with it. Sit back, enjoy the ride. You gotta plant both your feet on the ground and start livin' life."

"How did you get here?"

"I'm telling you. It's a hell of a story. Hey, Ryan?"
"What?"
"It's time to go home."

Suddenly, as an alarm sounds, we see that Kowalski is not there. Informed and re-energized by her hallucination, Ryan prepares to descend to Earth. Just before beginning the descent, she sends out a call to Matt on the radio, asking him to give a message to her daughter.

Here is a "live" depiction of that last intermediate stage between a parent/child interaction and complete incorporation of the parental attitudes and values. Ryan Stone can carry Matt Kowalski with her in her mind as a guide and comfort. We get to "see," perhaps "live through" vicariously, the proof that the parental figure has been incorporated into the child's mind and self identity.

Having taken the reader this far, I will not deny you the final spoilers.

Of course, Ryan makes it through re-entry, her pod landing in water just off a deserted shore somewhere on Earth. When she opens the pod, it fills with water, forcing Ryan to free herself lest she drown. We experience, vicariously, but intensely, the delicate line between death and birth.

We see Ryan push herself above the water, struggle to the shore and then propel herself on to her feet, her first experience of gravity in a week, with a look of determination, triumph, and relief.

We are left somewhat drained and relieved, saddened by the loss of the parental figure, Matt Kowalski, and thrilled by Ryan's victory, and his, as she slowly walks up the shore. And yet, I think we are also left with a touch of anxiety at having come so close to the experiences of early attachment and loss, relieved at this success, but perhaps aware that Ernie Kovacs was right,

"There are people falling off all the time."

Main, M. (2000). The organized categories of infant, child, and adult attachment. *Journal of the American Psychoanalytic Association*, 48:1055-1095

The Wizard of Oz

HERE IS ANOTHER FILM about attachment and independence, another skyward journey that takes us away from this world but also lands us back home on Earth.

My own interest in the film *The Wizard of Oz* started with a question raised by someone about L. Frank Baum's book, *The Wonderful Wizard of Oz*, from which the film was made. She had read the book, and wondered why Baum had chosen to make Dorothy an adopted child. The book describes Dorothy as an orphan whose laughter surprised a worn-out Aunt Em, beaten down by life on the lifeless prairie. It does not explain how Dorothy came to Aunt Em and Uncle Henry. The film tells us even less. We only know that Dorothy lives with a couple whom she calls Aunt Em and Uncle Henry. Harvey Greenberg in his book, *The Movies on Your Mind* (1975), says that Dorothy is "desperately trying to come to terms with her orphan-hood" as she enters the turbulence of adolescence. He accepts her orphan-hood as a given and perhaps implies that its purpose is to accentuate the problems of adolescence and the need to cling to an idealized parental image while breaking free of the parent-child relationship.

My own immediate reaction to the question was that placing Dorothy with an "aunt and uncle" planted a hint in our minds of a "family romance fantasy" by which a child imagines him or herself to secretly have parents who are noble or exalted in contrast to the actual parents. Family romance fantasies are used frequently in literature and film. *Star Wars* comes to mind. Like Dorothy, Luke lives with his worn down, pedestrian aunt and uncle, but, we come to learn, is the son of a princess and the powerful Darth Vader of "I am your father" fame. Putting Dorothy with an aunt and uncle makes it easier for us to question the parental bond and to imagine "idealized" parents, in this case in the form of good and bad witches and a powerful, but not so powerful, wizard.

Although Dorothy is a young adolescent in the film, her age is unstated in the book with hints (particularly from the accompanying pictures) that she is younger. I think that Baum's target audience was latency or pre-adolescent children. The film's opening prologue suggests a somewhat different audience when it says, in letters across a cloud-filled sky,

"For nearly forty years this story has given faithful service to the Young in Heart; and Time has been powerless to put its kindly philosophy out of fashion.

"To those of you who have been faithful to it in return

"...and to the Young in Heart ... we dedicate this picture."

It suggests an adult audience with a nostalgia for childhood. In fact, that shift in audience helps explain an important difference between the book and the film. Baum's book begins with a very short commentary on the dreariness of Kansas and the deadening effect it had had through the years on Auntie Em and Uncle Henry, then brings on the cyclone that takes Dorothy and Toto to Oz. There are no characters in the Kansas part of the book that correspond to the characters that Dorothy will meet in Oz. In the film, we see Dorothy with the three farm workers, Hunk, Zeke and Hickory who presage the scarecrow, the cowardly lion and the tin man. Ray Bolger's "Hunk" tells Dorothy that she should use her brains dealing with Miss Gulch and that her head's not filled with straw. Bert Lahr's "Zeke" is first very bold, telling her she has to have courage to deal with Miss Gulch then sinks into a panic attack after going into the pig pen to save Dorothy, who had fallen in. Margaret Hamilton's Miss Gulch is called a wicked old witch by Dorothy when she comes to take Toto. Auntie Em says of her that she owns half the county, much as the wicked witch of the East controls Munchkinland before Dorothy's house falls on her.

This sets up the famous final sequence in which Dorothy wakes from a dream and says, "I had a dream and some of it was terrible, but most of it was beautiful. And you were there, and you and you and you were there, too," pointing to the three farm hands who were matched with the scarecrow, tin man and lion and the traveling showman who was reprised as the wizard as well as some smaller roles in Oz. We have seen that "you were there, and you and you and you were there too" most famously in *Angels in America*.

The commentary that came with the DVD version I used quoted

sources as saying that the dream concept was added because they feared an audience would not accept the fantasy world of Oz without it. Clearly they meant the adult audience. It was done extremely well, utilizing the concept of "day residue" with good effect. I doubt that this was the first time a dream was used in this way, but it clearly was a most effective early application of a trope that has become a standard in film, the use of allusions to dreaming that casts ambiguity on the reality of a fantasy. It appears to add rather than detract from the effect of the fantasy, allowing it to exist in the intermediate space between real and unreal where it tends to reside in our minds. The book's very brief preamble to the cyclone emphasizes the emptiness and grayness of the landscape. Aunt Em and Uncle Henry are described as worn out, joyless, and "gray." The film captures this by showing the Kansas sequences in black and white, actually sepia tones, in contrast to the lush Technicolor of Oz. Technicolor was a relatively new process and it's clear that the filmmakers wanted to emphasize its power. But in addition to showing the grayness of Dorothy's real world and demonstrating this powerful new technique, the contrast captures the emotional intensity of dreams and fantasy.

The opening sequence in Kansas opens up nearly all the central themes and conflicts of the film. For those who do not recall, the film opens with Dorothy running home with Toto to tell Uncle Henry and Aunt Em that Miss Gulch had attacked Toto. The issue of parenting is present from the beginning. Dorothy is protective of Toto as she hopes Aunt Em and Uncle Henry will be of her and Toto. We hear, incidentally, that Miss Gulch attacked Toto because he had attacked her cat. The cat obviously links her with witches, but here, too, is the reaction of a protective parent. Following the same theme, Dorothy can't get Aunt Em or Uncle Henry's attention because they are busy caring for a large group of chicks taken from an incubator that had broken, much like an older child who must cede parental attention to a baby.

The issue of adequate parenting and protection is brought home more dramatically when Miss Gulch arrives with a sheriff's warrant authorizing her to take Toto. Dorothy pleads with her uncle and aunt to no avail. They are helpless to counter the power of the wealthy Miss Gulch. Aunt Em does confront her verbally when Dorothy has left the scene.

"Elvira Gulch, just because you own half the county doesn't mean you have the power to run the rest of us. For 23 years I've been dying to tell you what I thought of you and now, well, being a Christian woman I can't say it."

This brings us to a second theme. This is a world, both in Kansas and Oz, in which the women hold power and the men, well meaning on the whole, are powerless to confront them. The workmen, Zeke, Hunk and Hickory, want to help Dorothy, offering advice and support, but they are scolded by Aunt Em to get back to their work. When Miss Gulch comes to take Toto, Dorothy turns to Uncle Henry, who has appeared kinder and more accessible than Aunt Em. When Miss Gulch confronts Aunt Em and Uncle Henry with the sheriff's warrant to have Toto destroyed, Dorothy approaches Henry.

"Uncle Henry, you won't let her, will you?"

He answers, "Of course we won't." He looks doubtful and turns to his wife. "Will we, Em?"

In that subtle but obvious gesture, we are told where the power lies.

It is Aunt Em who tells Dorothy that they can't go against the law and instructs Uncle Henry to take Toto from Dorothy. He does her bidding, much as male characters in Oz will do the bidding of the fearful witch. This is a matriarchal world, one in which Dorothy, as a budding woman, must exert her own power.

In Oz, the seemingly powerful wizard has no power to confront the wicked witch himself, but sends Dorothy and her friends on a quest to get her broom. We see it again when the witch's fearsome male guards become benign once the witch is dead, revealing that they had been forced to do her bidding. In the straw man and the tin man, we see the vulnerable physical integrity of the male. Interestingly, Baum, who was very sympathetic to the feminism of his day, wrote another book in the Oz sequence in which the central character is a boy named Tip, initially under the spell of a witch, who is revealed to be Princess Ozma, the rightful ruler of Oz. This film is a good vehicle for expounding the rights and power of women except, perhaps, for the portrayal of the powerful witches as either evil hags or silly, frilly fairy tale princesses.

The Wizard of Oz is clearly focused on the mother-daughter relationship, but not in an Oedipal setting. There is no romance, no hint of sexual attraction. Baum, writing for a latency and pre-adolescent audience, believed that children were bored by romance. The filmmakers stayed true to that. We see a more dyadic mother-child relationship marked by hatred and rivalry as well as idealization, but not sexual rivalry.

This also pulls towards the earlier dyadic relationship and the wish that goes with it. The opening sequence in Kansas gives us only the faintest hint of the fantasy that encapsulates that wish. It is a line that we all know by heart.

"Somewhere over the rainbow, way up high, there's a land that I heard of once in a lullaby." It's hard to pin too much on a single lyric, written by a lyricist, E.Y. Harburg, not the director or a screenwriter, and barely noticed by the audience. Nevertheless, for the audience, the word lullaby has a clear association to a parent, in this case a mother, and a baby child. We will soon see Toto taken from Dorothy and Aunt Em helpless to stop it. We know that she is living not with her "mother," but with her aunt. In that context "a land that I heard of once in a lullaby" draws us to an image of a gentle, protecting mother at some earlier time in our lives. Remember the film's dedication to the "Young in Heart."

There is only one major character in Oz who does not have a counterpart in Kansas, Glinda, the Good Witch. Billy Burke, who plays her looking and sounding like an over-age debutante, does not appear in the Kansas sequences. Conversely, Aunt Em and Uncle Henry are the only characters in Kansas who have no counterpart in Oz.

When Dorothy's house lands in Oz and she opens the door to a beautiful scene, a land that she heard of once in a lullaby, the first person she encounters there comes from a bubble-like, shiny orb that materializes into the form of what looks like a fairy princess, dressed in white, wearing a crown and carrying a wand. She is Dorothy's benevolent good witch, Glinda. She is calming and positive and protects her from the Gulch-like wicked witch. If Dorothy is looking for her mother in her fantasies, is this not the embodiment of such an idealized mother?

There is also only one actual character from Kansas who is penetrated into the dream world and Oz, Auntie Em, who is seen in the witch's crystal ball. This, too, is a part of the "day residue." After Toto escapes from Miss Gulch, Dorothy runs away from home to protect her dog. She runs into Professor Marvel, a traveling showman, who looks into a crystal ball and says he sees Auntie Em. He'd sneaked a look at a picture of her among Dorothy's things. He kindly encourages her to go home, telling her that Aunt Em is worried about her. Whether in Oz or Kansas, home is associated with Aunt Em. In effect, she is torn between the idealized mother, the one who sang that lullaby, and her actual mother, Aunt Em.

It is not difficult for us to see the split maternal image in the wicked witch and the good witch, Glinda. The filmmakers actually had to cut out parts of the wicked witch's scenes because in trial runs children were too frightened. It should come as no surprise that Dorothy in her fantasy kills the wicked witch, not once, but twice, both "accidentally." It is almost trite to explain it in terms of a longing for an ideal mother and rage at the mother who has left her. In Baum's original book, the good witch appears as an old witch. The filmmakers decided to change that, implicitly encouraging that fantasy and merging it with what was beautiful in the land of Oz, the land of fantasy.

The witches allow Dorothy—and the audience with her—to indulge her fantasies about Aunt Em. These are fantasies embodied in Glinda about what she would like Aunt Em to be, a true protector. More importantly, Miss Gulch and the wicked witch give her a vehicle to legitimately express her rage at Aunt Em. Aunt Em has failed Dorothy, failed to listen to her about what had happened with Ms. Gulch (as she takes care of her chicks), failed to protect Dorothy and

Toto from the wicked witch, Miss Gulch, and her sheriff's warrant. This is the ultimate conflict that the film resolves as we hear it in Dorothy's final soliloquy.

"But it wasn't a dream. It was a place. And you and you and you and you were there." She is momentarily interrupted and Aunt Em tells her we dream a lot of silly things. Dorothy goes on, "No, Aunt Em, this is a truly live place, and I remember that some of it wasn't very nice, but most of it was beautiful, but just the same all I kept saying to everybody was 'I want to go home,' and they sent me home. Doesn't anybody believe me? But anyway, Toto, we're home, home, and this is my room and you're all here and I'm not gonna leave here ever again because I love you all. Oh, Auntie Em, there's no place like home!"

We have come to the spoiler—Dorothy and Toto do return to Kansas. (I won't tell how.) This is a common theme in children's books. The books appeal to a child's wish for escape and adventure, for power and freer expression of passions. But children, at least until they reach adolescence, do not want to simply escape. They must have their adventures and be able to return. To adventure forever is frightening. I remember my own favorite book of early childhood about a toy tugboat that excitedly sailed down a river and out to the ocean, but was rescued at the very end and taken back home to happily sail in the bathtub again. *Where the Wild Things Are* must end in a happy return home. Even *The Nutcracker* has such an ending.

The Wonderful Wizard of Oz was aimed at a somewhat older age group, but a latency-aged or pre-adolescent age group nonetheless. The child needs to return home. But this also answers the original question. Dorothy is an orphan, living with her Aunt Em because she must live out our fantasies of escape, our fantasies of leaving the drab parents and surroundings, the sepia tones of a dreary Kansas farm, much drearier, actually, in Baum's book. Dorothy's being an orphan quietly encourages us to remember the dissatisfactions and disaffections with our parents, the wish to go off on our own. It encourages vicarious family romance fantasies, a wish for better parents. But its primary effect is to allow us to feel the longing for maternal love and the reunion with the mother of childhood, now glorious in all her drabness and sepia tones. As Dorothy says, most of it was beautiful, "but all I kept saying was I want to go home....I love you all! Oh, Auntie Em, there's no place like home!" And if our eyes well up with tears at that point, it is because we can identify with her love for Aunt Em, the only real mother she has known, and like Dorothy we can vaguely recall and momentarily accept our own love for our mothers, imperfect but real, and endorse the feeling that there's no place like home.

There is an irony in this ending. Dorothy, who has made her way successfully through Oz, confronting the great and terrible wizard and killing two wicked witches, the rulers of the land, wishes to return to home to be with Auntie Em. The message is very clear when the wizard grants the scarecrow, tin man and lion their wishes: we must look to ourselves for the strength that we need to overcome difficulties, function independently without relying on an idealization of a parental image to save us. That is hard to reconcile with the film's other lasting image, "There's no place like home."

When Dorothy killed off her bad witches, she paved a road for herself, and us, to a more basic fantasy. In the last scene, she is lying in her bed surrounded by Aunt Em and all the male figures from both Oz and Kansas. The wish to return home is not just a wish to be with mother. It is a wish to be taken care of by mother, in this case by Aunt Em, Dorothy's true mother. A story whose message is that we have the wherewithal within ourselves to overcome great difficulties and to master the world around us ends with a regression.

Dorothy's story is not confined to the fictional world of Oz. There are real life Dorothies, people forced by circumstance to leave the comfort of home and childhood—perhaps their homeland—at an early age, who through resilience and talent were successful in the new world, slaying all the necessary witches and standing up to the wizards, but waking in the middle of the night with anxiety and an unconscious wish to return to the comfort of home and family, to be taken under mother's wing.

In life, this is a serious conflict between the wish to be strong and self-reliant and the wish to be back in the arms of a loving protective mother. But the film allows us to experience both wishes conflict free. It takes us to a once in a lullaby dreamworld, a fantasy that allows us to identify with the strength of a girl who can defeat witches, free Munchkins and help her friends achieve their dreams while also allowing us to return to the warmth and safety of mother's embrace while we close our eyes and say, "There's no place like home."

Baum, L. Frank (1900) *The Wonderful Wizard of Oz* in Oz, The Complete Collection (Kindle Edition) (2013). Maplewood Books.
Greenberg, Harvey (1977) *The Movies on Your Mind.* New York: Saturday ReviewPress/E.P. Dutton and Co.
Other sources for background information were the internet "Wikipedia" article on L. Frank Baum and the informational disk that comes with the DVD version of the film.

Pan's Labyrinth

THE THEME OF FAMILY romance fantasies leads us to a more recent film in which another young girl enters a fantasy world, leading to a very bittersweet ending.

Rarely, a filmmaker gives us a gift of a ready made demonstration of a well known psychoanalytic concept. We have recently been given such a gift by the Mexican director, Guillermo del Toro, whose film, *Pan's Labyrinth*, provides us with a complete family romance fantasy.

Freud (1909), like many of the authors who subsequently elaborated on the family romance, placed the emergence of such fantasies at pre-puberty. In his paper, Freud says that the child begins to develop dissatisfaction with his or her parents, partly out of sexual rivalry. He emphasizes that the provocation for this dissatisfaction comes from the child being slighted. "There are only too many occasions on which a child is slighted, or at least feels he has been slighted, on which he feels he is not receiving the whole of his parents' love, and, most of all, on which he feels regrets at having to share it with brothers and sisters. His sense that his own affection is not being fully reciprocated then finds a vent in the idea, often consciously recollected later from early childhood, of being a step-child or an adopted child. ... the child's imagination becomes engaged in the task of getting free from the parents of whom he now has a low opinion and of replacing them by others, who, as a rule, are of higher social standing." (pp. 237-238)

The film's central character, Ofelia, fits nicely into Freud's plan. She is pre-adolescent when we enter her life. Her father, a tailor, has died in the Spanish Civil War. He has been replaced by her mother's new husband, the very cold and cruel Captain Vidal, whom she will not accept as a father. Ofelia cannot feel that she is receiving all of the love of her remaining parent, having to share her with not only her stepfather, but also with the brother in her mother's belly. (When asked how he knows the child is a boy, Captain Vidal answers, "Don't fuck with me.") Ofelia's mother is dismissive of Ofelia's one true love, her books. She appears at times to value Ofelia as a prop to please her new husband. Her mother is further removed from Ofelia by her very painful and dangerous pregnancy. In addition, Ofelia and her mother have been summoned by Captain Vidal to a remote military outpost where the last remnants of the Spanish Civil War are being fought. There is much to turn her to a family romance fantasy.

The film begins with two prologues, one having to do with the outer world in which Ofelia will live, the other with the inner fantasy world.

The first is written on the screen, the style and content reminding me of the opening of Star Wars.

"Spain, 1944: The Civil War is over. Hidden in the mountains, armed men are still fighting the new Fascist regime. Military posts are established to exterminate the Resistance."

But instead of moving to a confrontation between the brave Resistance Fighters and the soldiers of the Evil Empire, the film next shows us a pre-adolescent girl breathing rapidly, with blood coming from her nose. A melody is being hummed in the background. The blood recedes and as the narration begins, we pan into one of her dark eyes.

"A long time ago, in the Underground Realm, where there are no lies or pain, there lived a princess who dreamt of the human world. She dreamt of blue skies, soft breeze and sunshine. One day, eluding her keepers, the princess escaped. Once outside, the bright sun blinded her and erased her memory. She forgot who she was and where she came from. Her body suffered cold, sickness and pain. And eventually she died. However, her father, the king, always knew that the princess' soul would return, perhaps in another body, in another place, in another time. And he would wait for her until he drew his last breath, until the world stopped turning … "

During this narration, we have seen a pictorial accompaniment, but at the end, we are back in the human world of Spain, 1944, with the focus on the same girl from the opening scene sitting with her mother in a touring car, reading a fairy tale.

The two prologues engage us in contrasts between the film's two parallel plots, between the world of fantasy and the world of reality, between a realm that is underground and inside and the one on the surface under the blinding light, between a place that is peaceful and timeless and one that is in the midst of bloody and tragic conflict.

There is some ambiguity about the narration. It seems to be told directly to the viewer, but the way that it is enclosed by the two images of the girl suggests that we are within the girl's fantasy world. The effect is that we experience the family romance as both the daydream of the girl, Ofelia and the mythic reality of the film. That tension draws us into the fantasy with Ofelia and creates a strange tragic-sweet effect at the film's end.

The film's dichotomies are brought home to us gently with Ofelia's mother's opening words as they drive through the woods.

"I don't understand why you had to bring so many books, Ofelia. We're going to the country, the outdoors. Fairy tales—you're a bit too old to be filling your head with such nonsense."

The mother is trying to coax Ofelia with the same enticements that lead the princess to leave her underground home, "blue skies, soft breeze and sunshine." Sunshine is usually presented as a positive force, for warmth and good humor; but here it enters into a different contrast, as part of a distant and somewhat threatening external world impinging on the world of introspection and inner fantasy. We shall see, as the film's fantasies develop, that there is also another reason for desiring the underground realm, away from the soft breeze and sunshine.

In fact, the world into which Ofelia enters is not all sunshine and breezes. Her new stepfather is a coldly efficient man who has no empathy for her introspectiveness and whimsy. His symbol is his pocket watch. He is obsessed with punctuality and order. He is controlling and sadistic, ordering Ofelia's mother to use a wheelchair, then squeezing the frightened girl's hand, reproaching her for extending the wrong hand to him. Ophelia has been told by her mother to call him Father, but when the kind Mercedes, who runs the Captain's household, refers to him as her father, she emphatically lets her know he is not her father, that her father was a tailor who died in the war.

Captain Vidal stands for both personal and institutional sadism in his desire to put down all rebellion. In an early scene we see him viciously murder a father and son picked up on suspicion, only minutes later making it clear that he knew they were innocent. The film is not subtle in its contrasts of the Fascists and the Resistance. The Resistance fighters are seemingly part of the world of nature as they appear in the forest, as if by magic. They and their collaborators within the camp, Mercedes and the local physician, are presented as brave and loyal in contrast to the sadistic Fascist soldiers, who appear out of touch with the people and the countryside.

Having lost her father, Ofelia is also missing some of her mother's love. Her mother is preoccupied with pleasing her new, demanding husband and with his baby in her womb. She is also very ill in her pregnancy, forcing Ofelia to take the role of caregiver. Ofelia's pain at being slighted in her mother's love is expressed in a short dialogue between them as they lie together in bed their first night in the country.

Ofelia asks, "Why did you have to get married?"

"I was alone too long."

Ofelia protests, "I'm with you. You weren't alone. You were never alone."

With all of Freud's requirements falling into place, Ofelia turns to fantasy. As they are driving through the woods in the opening scene, the mother becomes ill, stopping the car to get fresh air. Ofelia wanders off and finds a rock on the ground with some sort of engraving. She quickly sees that it is part of some ancient looking rune that stands close by. The piece she has fits into the rune, making the eye of a face with a hole for a mouth. An insect, perhaps a cicada, suddenly emerges from the hole. At first it startles Ofelia, but she tells her mother that she has seen a fairy. As she and her mother continue to drive on, we see the cicada following in the same direction.

The fantasy coalesces into the family romance. The cicada/fairy leads Ofelia to an ancient labyrinth in the woods in which she meets a large humanoid faun, who seems to come from the earth. He identifies her as the Princess Moanna, daughter of the king of the underworld. She protests that her father was a tailor (the second time she has insisted on this), but he tells her, "You are not born of man. It was the moon that bore you" and offers as proof the existence of a moon-shaped scar on her shoulder. He presents her with a series of tasks that she must perform to prove her true identity. Ofelia readily accepts the challenge.

The violence and cruelty of life surrounding the military outpost may also drive the viewer towards the fantasy. The magical underground world has its dangers, a giant toad that is eating the life from a tree, an ogre who kills and devours. Nevertheless, the fairy tale quality of this world offers us some reassurance of a happy ending and its monsters appear strangely tame compared with their counterparts in the human world. As viewers, we are relieved to retreat to the whimsical world of fairies and underground palaces.

The family in the underground realm is protected. In the "real world" we see glimpses of loving families endangered by the war around them. The father and son who are killed by Captain Vidal are affectionate and loyal to one another. They have been out shooting rabbits, attempting to maintain their normal existence.

Mercedes, the kind caretaker who befriends Ofelia, is separated from her (probably younger) brother who is with the resistance fighters in the woods. With every bit of news of fighting, we see her fear for him on her face. Mercedes and the doctor risk their lives stealing supplies under the nose of Captain Vidal, then sneaking into the woods to bring medicine and information under cover of night. Like Ofelia, Mercedes moves about in a hostile, treacherous world while her brother is in the womb of the woods, in nature. At the film's end, his resistance fighters move in on the outpost, reuniting brother and sister.

With Mercedes and her brother we see only filial affection. Ofelia's relationship with her brother is more complex and ambivalent. We enter it by returning to the scene in which Ofelia and her mother lie together in the dark of night. Ofelia is a little frightened of the noises. Her mother says that the country is different from the city where you hear the sound of cars and trams. In this quiet moment, she gently plays into her daughter's magical thinking, evoking the closeness of the country to nature and magic.

"Here the houses are old. They creak. As if they were speaking."

Within this closeness, Ofelia asks her, "Why did you have to get married?"

"I was alone too long."

Ofelia protests, "I'm with you. You weren't alone. You were never alone."

Her mother answers, "When you're older, you'll understand. It hasn't been easy for me, either."

We shall see in a moment that Ofelia may already understand.

At this point, the mother grimaces in pain and says, "Your brother's at it again. Tell him one of your stories. I'm sure he'll calm down."

Ofelia speaks to her mother's womb, "My brother, my brother" and lays her head upon her mother's belly as she begins her fairy tale. The story is of a "sad, faraway land" with a mountain of black stone atop which "a magic rose blossomed every night that made whoever plucked it immortal. But no one dared go near it because its thorns were full of poison. Men talked amongst themselves about their fear of death and pain, but never about the promise of eternal life. And every day, the rose wilted unable to bequeath its gift to anyone, forgotten and lost at the top of that cold, dark mountain, forever alone until the end of time."

If we take this as a sexual allegory, it tells of a feminine treasure, hidden away and protected by poisonous thorns, suggesting that unconsciously Ofelia is aware of the kind of loneliness of which her mother speaks. She lulls her brother to sleep with an ending in which the rose goes untouched.

But more interesting for our purposes than the story itself is the imagery that accompanies Ofelia talking to her brother. As she begins to speak to him, we see down into the womb, viewing the now quiet fetus. For Ofelia, the brother is present, inside her mother's womb, listening to her tale from the surface. It adds a shade of meaning to one of the film's dichotomies, between the underground world and the world of sunlight and human beings. Ofelia's brother is seen living in the equivalent of an underground realm.

Ofelia speaks to her brother one more time in the film. Her mother had hemorrhaged badly and was very ill, with a high fever. At this point the magic begins to enter into the mother's pregnancy. Hearing that Ofelia cannot complete her tasks because of her concern for her mother, the fawn gives her a magical cure.

"Look, this is a mandrake root, a plant that dreamt of being human. Put it under your mother's bed in a bowl of fresh milk. Each morning give it two drops of blood."

When Ofelia puts the mandrake root into milk and adds the two drops of blood it appears to come to life as a happy infant. The doctor is baffled by the mother's recovery.

It is at this point that Ofelia again speaks to her brother;

"Brother, little brother, if you can hear me, things out here aren't too good. But soon you'll have to come out. You've made Mama very sick. I want to ask you one favor for when you come out, just one: don't hurt her. You'll meet her, she's very pretty, even though sometimes she's sad for days at a time. You'll see, when she smiles, you'll love her. Listen, if you do what I say, I'll make you a promise. I'll take you to my kingdom and I'll make you a prince. I promise you, a prince."

Attachments

The fetus has taken on a life and a persona, animated by the image of the happy mandrake root lying in its bowl of milk. More importantly, it is the discontented baby brother who has been making Ofelia's mother ill. She sees him as a threat to her mother's life and in this dialogue she begs and bribes him to spare her. This fantasy is further brought to life when the captain finds the concoction under the bed and angrily accuses Ofelia of witch-like superstition, seemingly reacting as if she were trying to harm the baby. In response, Ofelia's mother throws the root into the fire. We hear its screams and instantly the mother falls ill again, as if attacked by the wrathful fetus inside her. Captain Vidal, who has originally instructed the doctor to care for the mother, now tells him that at all cost he must save his son. His primary interest in Ofelia's mother is as the bearer of his son. Mother and baby are at odds.

The angry brother does not satisfy Ofelia's one request of him, to spare their mother's life. In the end, he will not go with her into her kingdom to become a prince. Ofelia, now alone, hears that her mother has died giving birth to the baby brother as it is told to Captain Vidal. The brother is not only an intruder into Ofelia's family, but also an angry destroyer.

The stage is set for the resolution of the film's various plots and of the family romance fantasy. With the Resistance fighters gaining the upper hand, Ofelia is given one last task before she can take her place in the Underground Realm, that she bring her baby brother to the labyrinth. Amidst an armed battle, Ofelia carries the baby to the labyrinth with Captain Vidal in pursuit. Ofelia finds the fawn, who asks her to hand over the baby, but she sees a knife in his hand. "The portal will only open if we offer the blood of an innocent. Just a drop of blood. A pinprick, that's all. It's the final task."

Ofelia refuses to hand over the baby, telling the fawn,

"My brother stays with me."

Ofelia remains outwardly sympathetic and protective of her brother. The other side of her ambivalence, the frustration and anger that Freud alluded to is expressed by the fawn, who asks,

"You would give up your sacred rights for this brat you barely know? ... You would give up your throne for him, he who has caused you such misery, such humiliation?"

"Yes, I would."

"As you wish, Your Highness."

At this point, the captain catches up with her, takes the baby and shoots Ofelia. He is met at the entrance to the labyrinth by the victorious rebels, led by Mercedes, who takes the baby from him. He is shot as he is told that his son will never know of his existence. Mercedes and the rebels then race into the labyrinth where they find the dying Ofelia. Leaning over her, Mercedes sings the lullaby she has sung for her before. As we hear the melody and see Ofelia lying on the ground, we realize that we are back at the scene that began the film.

As Ofelia lies there a drop of her blood falls into the well of the labyrinth. A light shines and Ofelia rises in a great throne room to the words, "Arise my daughter." She looks up at a king sitting on a high throne.

"Father."

He answers, "You have spilled your own blood rather than the blood of an innocent. That was the final task and the most important."

We now see Ofelia's mother sitting on a throne next to that of her father. Her mother tells her, "Come here with me, and sit by your father's side. He's been waiting for you so long."

We return above ground where Ofelia's mouth momentarily forms a smile as she dies, with Mercedes weeping for her.

In this dramatic ending, we see the realization of the family romance, and more. Ofelia sacrifices her life for her brother. She dies and he remains alive. Her hatred of her brother is expressed by the fawn, who calls him a brat and speaks of the misery and humiliation he has caused her. But, within the film's mythology, Ofelia has traded places with her brother. He may have the kind Mercedes as a mother, but he will forever more be excluded from his mother's womb. Ofelia is in the "underground realm", back into the womb with her mother and father forever.

The narrator concludes, "And it is said that the Princess returned to her father's kingdom. That she reigned there with justice and a kind heart for many centuries. That she was loved by her people. And that she left behind small traces of her time on earth, visible only to those who know where to look."

The bittersweet ending is of a girl who dies, who goes underground; but in going into the underground realm, she returns to a blissful reunion with her dead parents in a magical womb. In this fantasy, there is a denial of death. This fantasy of denial also informs the film's other plot in which the brave resistance fighters overcome and kill the tyrannical captain. As we watch, we are certainly aware that the Fascists continued to rule Spain for over thirty years from that time. There was no general glorious and just victory until Franco died in his bed, but the film leaves us with a momentary sense of victory and denial of the death of a free Spain for an entire generation.

But *Pan's Labyrinth* offers us more than an escape from the reality of death. I called attention earlier to the ambiguity of the narrative concerning the Underground Realm. We are made to feel simultaneously that the narrator is speaking directly to us, creating a fictional reality, and that we are hearing the fantasy of a girl reading a fairy tale. As we approach the film's end, we are again given the opportunity to experience that ambiguity, to experience death as a reality and its denial in fantasy simultaneously, as we experience the tragic death of a young, bright, creative girl and the fantasy in which her spirit lives forever basking in the light of her parents' love.

I suspect that each viewer is aware of a different mix. I felt a great sadness combined with a strong pull to the reassuring fantasy. I found myself moving back and forth within the figure-ground emotional illusion in which I was seeing a dying girl's last fantasy and a poetic vision in which her spirit will never die. I take this as a gift of awareness of an internal conflict, for me and perhaps for many viewers, between an acceptance of the reality of inevitable and irrevocable death and the wish for a return to a blissful reunion in a magical womb "where there are no lies and no pain."

Freud, S. (1909) Family Romances. *The Standard Edition of the Complete Psychological Works of Sigmund Freud,* Volume IX (1906-1908): Jensen's 'Gradiva' and Other Works, 235-242.

The Hours

THE IDEA OF DEATH as a return to the womb leads us to another, very different film which also brings us full circle with attachment, painful separation, and a desire to return to a beautiful moment.

The Hours has very much to do with death and suicide. It begins and ends with the suicide by drowning of Virginia Woolf. In between, we witness one other suicide and a suicide attempt. Based on Michael Cunningham's book, the film focuses on a day in the life of three women, separated by decades and miles. Virginia Woolf is feeling trapped in her suburban home in 1923, where her husband tries to shelter her from the stimulation of London life that was believed to have contributed to her psychosis, suicide attempts and hospitalizations. She is beginning to write a new book, *Mrs. Dalloway*, about a woman who plans her suicide, then decides against it. Laura Brown is a housewife in 1951 L.A. She is baking a cake for her husband's birthday, reading Mrs. Dalloway, and leaving her son with the baby sitter so that she can go to a hotel to kill herself and the fetus she is carrying. Like Mrs. Dalloway, she will change her mind. Clarissa Vaughan is living in New York in 2001 with her woman partner, preparing a party to honor her old friend and one time lover, Richard, who has won a prestigious poetry prize. Richard is living alone in a seedy building, dying of AIDS.

Each of the three women—as well as Richard, the dying poet—is trapped in her life. Virginia Woolf is described as an eccentric, brilliant young woman who is clumsy, like a recently arrived immigrant to ordinary human society. She is bored living in their suburban home with her printer husband and their two servants. She longs to get back to the excitement of the city, even as she retreats into the book she is writing. Laura Brown is a housewife doing her duty to her husband, recently returned from the war, trapped in the life that fulfills his dream but not hers. She is clumsy in her attempts to bake a wedding cake, appears not to fit the role she has been assigned in pre-sixties suburbia. Clarissa Vaughan feels a constant ache of unhappiness, yearning to get back to a moment, a morning in the country with Richard many years before. She sees her confinement in a more depersonalized way, through Richard's eyes. "He gives me that look ... to say, 'Your life is trivial, you are so trivial.' Daily stuff, you know, schedules and parties and details." In this, she appears to recreate the plight of Mrs. Dalloway, herself, capable, like Clarissa (who shares her first name) of making a grand party and organizing other people's lives, but caught in a world of details. It also links her with Laura caught in her own world of trivial events. Finally, Richard is dying painfully of AIDS, with obvious brain involvement as he struggles with painkillers and "voices". For him, the life remaining is just a succession of painful hours. He is confined in life itself.

Virginia Woolf is direct and articulate about her confinement as she confronts her anxious husband at the suburban train station. He is very caring, and wishes to keep her protected from the dangers of psychotic relapse and repeated suicide attempts. She convinces him with her determination and her eloquence.

"My life has been stolen from me. I'm living in a town I have no wish to live in. I'm living a life I have no wish to live. ... I'm dying in this town. ... If I were thinking clearly, Leonard, I would tell you that I wrestle alone in the dark—in the deep dark—and that only I can know, only I can understand my own condition. You live with the threat, you tell me, the threat of my extinction, Leonard. I live with it, too. It's my right, the right of every human being. I choose not the anesthetic of the suburbs, but the violent jolt of the capital. The meanest patient ... is allowed some say in the matter of her own prescription. Thereby she defines her humanity. ... If it is a choice between Richmond and death, I choose death."

I think more is suggested than geography. She suffers the confinement of a creative woman who does not react to things like other people. She appears to have less of the protective, defensive covering (Freud's stimulus barrier) of those of us who manage to go through our days cushioned from the full emotions of what we experience. She cannot dissemble, to others or to herself. She appears strange to her sister, Vanessa, and her three children, with her dreamy removed states. Vanessa explains to her daughter, "You're aunt's a very lucky woman, Angelica, because she has two lives. She has the life she's leading, also the book she's writing. It makes her very fortunate indeed." We get a sense that Virginia feels some communion with the young girl, Angelica, who unlike her hyperactive brothers, feels true empathy and curiosity about a dying bird that she and Virginia lay to rest. After the girl leaves, Virginia lies her head on the ground, looking at the bird, as if trying to imagine what it is like to be dead. The film does not shout out about this particular form of confinement, the creative artist's "difference." Her thoughts and feelings, so out of place amidst the commonplace events of daily life, can be expressed fully in her writing, where they appear not odd, but important, where they can touch others, like Laura Brown.

Mrs. Dalloway's ambivalent longing for escape obviously touches a chord in Laura Brown. She is not an artist, as far as we know, but clearly experiences the same confinement in the world she inhabits. She could echo Virginia Woolf's words, "My life has been stolen from me. ... I'm living a life I have no wish to live." On that day, she is living a life chosen for her by her husband, who explains to their son at the dinner table about the girl he thought about while he was in the South Pacific, "the sort of girl you see mostly sitting on her own. ... I used to think about bringing her to a house, to a life, pretty much like this. And with the thought of the happiness, the thought of this woman, the thought of this life, that's what kept me going. I had an idea of our happiness." Towards the end of the film, we learn that Laura left her family, on another day, and explains it. "There are times when you don't belong, and you think you're going to kill yourself. ... It would be wonderful to sense you regretted it. It would be easy. But what does it mean? What does it mean to regret when I had no choice? It's what you can bear. ... It was death. I chose life."

There are hints that the confinement is related to homosexuality. We see the day in 2001 New York through the perspective of a homosexual community. Clarissa has been living with her partner, Sally, for ten years. We meet Richard's former long time lover, Louis Waters, and are probably to presume that Richard's AIDS is the result of homosexuality. Homosexuality is expressed fleetingly in Virginia Woolf and Laura Brown. At the end of her sister's visit, Virginia hugs her sister, Vanessa, and then kisses her with feeling on the lips. Nessa appears to be upset, although we are not told how. This is repeated with Laura. She has a visit from her friend, Kitty, who is to go into the hospital for exploratory surgery of a mass in her uterus. Kitty becomes tearful and Laura comforts her, then kisses her full on the lips. I have been told (no written source) that the director, Stephen Daldry, has said he put these passionate kisses into the script (along with one other towards the end in which Clarissa kisses her lover, Sally, in the same way) because he thought they fit, with no stated purpose. However included, they become an important part of the film, not easily ignored. They suggest a passion that overcomes convention and, in Laura's case, an underlying unfulfilled homosexual passion that is buried in her straight, exaggeratedly ordinary life.

But *The Hours* transcends this one particular form of entrapment. Clearly, this is a film that offers a channel of expression for those who ache, perhaps without having been aware of it, for something beyond the daily routines of modern life, for those who feel stifled in their role and place in time even if they find it satisfying, those who feel that somewhere there has been something more fulfilling, something lost, possibly to be regained.

Loss is implicit in the central themes of the story. Suicide is an escape and escape is freeing; but both also confront us with painful separation. The film alludes to fears of death and separation when Laura's friend, Kitty, tells her about the tumor in her uterus, alluding to both fears of death and fears that she will never be able to bear a child. We touch upon death in a bittersweet way in the fall of the sparrow (ornithologists forgive me if my literary allusions have gotten me to the wrong bird) lying peacefully on its bed of leaves. Virginia Woolf's suicide note alludes to that separation even as she explains the need for it. "To look life in the face, always to look life in the face and to know it for what it is. At last to know it, to love it for what it is, and then to put it away. Leonard, always the years between us, always the years, always the love, always the hours." Laura Brown has also ultimately found that she had to leave those who loved her. She expresses it as survivor guilt after the last of them, her son, Richard, has died. "It's a terrible thing, Miss Vaughan, to outlive your whole family. ... Obviously, you feel unworthy. It gives you feelings of unworthiness, that you survived and they didn't."

Although the film appears to focus on those who leave their loved ones behind, it also shows us the desperation of those who are left. We see it earliest when Virginia Woolf's husband, Leonard, panics, first in the opening scene when he sees her suicide note in 1941 and a little later in the film when he discovers that she has suddenly left the house in the middle of the day in 1923. He races after her, fear evident on his face, and ultimately confronts her angrily at the railroad station. We experience it late in the film when Clarissa Vaughan watches helplessly as her friend, Richard, dives out the window, having just expressed his love for her.

We sense it in Clarissa's daughter, Julia, who hints at being jealous of her mother's attachment to her lover and fears being seen as a burden or an afterthought. We momentarily share a moment in which they are together, mother and daughter, lying on the bed as Clarissa shares the shining memory of her life, the bond broken by the ring of the doorbell. That pain of separation from her own mother explains a warm hug she gives to Richard's mother, whom she meets after his death.

We even get a sense of that longing for union from the maternal side, through Laura Brown's friend, Kitty, childless, presumably because of her uterine tumor, who tells Laura how much she envies her ability to have children, and even through the older Laura, seen in 2001, who tells Clarissa that she envies her for both having "so wanted a child" and been able to gratify the wish.

We experience the pain of loss and separation most poignantly through the eyes of Laura Brown's little boy. We see Laura fill her purse with pill bottles from her medicine cabinet along with her copy of *Mrs. Dalloway*. She takes her son, Richie, to the babysitter so that she can go on her errands.

The boy protests, and protests with intensity. We see him screaming at the separation, pulling himself from the babysitter to chase after his mother's car as she drives off. This is one of the beauties of film and of fiction. We might easily detach ourselves from the separation pains of a four or five year old boy being taken to the baby sitter. We could look at it clinically.

But the film creates an ambiguity that allows us to empathize fully with the boy's fears and pain. We know that his mother is not just leaving him for a couple of hours with the baby sitter. She intends to kill herself. From what he ostensibly knows, this is only a fantasy on his part; but, we suspect that he suspects the truth.

We have seen that Laura is very gentle with her son, keeping close to him, sharing her whole day with him, calling him pet names, like "Bug". She appears to be much closer to him than to her husband, and on her return from her aborted suicide attempt, she tells him, "You're my guy."

Yet, we know that she intends to kill herself, abandoning him and killing his soon to be baby sister. Richie has also seen her passionately kiss her friend Kitty as he sat there, a primal scene of unknown effect upon him. Through Richie, we can feel a painfully intense attachment and fear of separation.

The Hours has an important secret, trick if you will. We see little Richie screaming for his mother in 1951 and then fade to her black and white wedding picture being touched by Richard, the dying poet, in 2001. Little Richie is the poet, Richard Brown, abandoned after his sister's birth by the loving mother who shared so much with him, who called him "My guy," an abandonment he had anticipated on that day in 1951.

This turns the entire film on its head. Now, we can experience these three days not through the eyes of the women, but through the eyes of Richard, the little boy who became a famous poet and a tortured dying man. We can suddenly experience this film as a story of a young boy holding desperately to his beloved and hated mother. Throughout the film, he calls Clarissa "Mrs. Dalloway." We see that it is not a coincidence, that he was aware of the book that his mother was reading and of its significance for her. We more fully understand his suicide as he turns, himself, and dives out of his window with

Clarissa watching. There is an element of revenge for his mother's abandonment as well as an escape from his pain of eternal separation.

Through little Richie's screams, we re-experience being torn from our mother, however or whenever we first experienced it. This is what is felt as so unbearable; a sense, not even a memory, of having had something wonderful once and lost it. It is a feeling evoked by this film that our lives are a trap, keeping us from what we most desire.

The film gives us a glimmer of that fantasied bliss. Clarissa describes her remembered moment of happiness. "I remember one morning, getting up at dawn. There was such a sense of possibility. You know that feeling? And I remember thinking to myself, 'so this is the beginning of happiness. This is where it starts, and of course there'll always be more.' It never occurred to me, it wasn't the beginning, it was happiness, the moment right then."

Richard recalls it as well, sharing the moment with her, just before he plunges to his death. "Like that morning when you walked out of that old house and you were 18 and maybe I was 19. I was 19 years old and I'd never seen anything so beautiful. You, coming out of a glass door in the early morning still sleepy. Isn't it strange, the most ordinary morning in anybody's life. I'm afraid I can't make it to the party, Clarissa. ... You've been so good to me, Mrs. Dalloway. I love you. I don't think two people could've been happier than we've been."

What does it mean when we long for a return to some particular moment of happiness, a screen memory seemingly emblazoned with light? In this context, it suggests a fantasy of return to a blissful reunion with mother, to that moment (surely not one moment, but a series of moments coalesced into a platonic ideal of happiness) which we seek over and over, a moment we cannot return to that leaves us feeling locked in our world of detail, a moment sought in a passionate kiss on the lips, or a descent into the water.

Suicide, death, is both an escape and a return. Whether we see *The Hours* as depressing, as simply well done or as liberating a deep hidden pain may depend on how we have each dealt with the loss of the loving bond with our mother at the moment we view the film.

The Hours has the potential to evoke in us a particular pain, a frustration at the confinement and lack in our lives. It reminds us of something wonderful that has been lost and that we long to regain; and, through death it offers both that terrible loss and the fantasy of reunion.

In *The Hours*, that reunion through death is also represented as a return to the womb. When Laura contemplates suicide, she sleeps and dreams that the room is filling with water. She touches her belly, evoking an identification with the baby in her womb. She is thinking of her own unborn child that she will not kill while imagining that she is re-entering the watery womb. The film begins and ends with Virginia Woolf's suicide. At the end, we see her methodically walk into the river about to drift beneath the surface. In the film's opening, she half floats, half sinks under the river, in the quiet that also evokes fantasies of the womb. Her words that accompany her descent into the water complete the fantasy of reunion: "... Always the years between us, always the years, always the love, always the hours."

2

Moods

The Grand Budapest Hotel

HOW DOES A FILM evoke our emotions? Here it is accomplished with an odd mix of a horrifying truth and the manic defenses used to escape from it.

The first time I saw the film, *The Grand Budapest Hotel*, I left the theater with a particularly good, buoyant feeling. On the way out, I saw a colleague waiting on line to get in. He later told me that he had had a similar reaction to it, that he left the theater feeling very good. Two or three weeks later, I went again with a friend who hadn't seen it. I was particularly looking forward to seeing it a second time, and, if anything, I enjoyed it more, with that same somewhat buoyant feeling.

There's nothing intrinsic about the film's style that would necessarily draw me to it. Although the madcap quality is appealing, the predominant humor is something I would call verbal slap-stick, a child-like play with language. There are several uses of funny sounding made-up German phrases, lightly mocking the use of such terms by 20th century intellectuals. In line with that the characters in the film are often dressed in exaggerated period costumes for comic effect, and the film liberally makes fun of people's looks. All of that can be amusing if done well, but hardly something that would cause me to keep returning.

There are familiarly pleasing plot lines of a developing father/son relationship, a coming of age story and a gentle love story, all told in comic fashion. The film has a host of recognizable and sometimes tantalizingly almost recognizable actors, often in cameo roles. It was clearly fun to try to place them through their disguises. The amusements mount, but don't really explain my reaction.

As I began to think about the film and to examine it more closely, I realized that the answer to my question lies in the structure of the film and its humor.

The film starts with a descending series of flashbacks, the temporal equivalent of a Russian doll, with one time period looking back on a second earlier time period which looks back on a third time period. We begin with a scene that is presumably close to the present in which a woman devotedly goes to the memorial of a great writer. We immediately flash back a number of years, to 1985, and see the writer, himself, speaking to a camera while partly off camera a little boy squirts him with a water pistol. The author's somewhat pompous speech moves us back many more years to the time when he was a young man visiting the over-the-hill Grand Budapest Hotel, in 1968. With the author, now a young man, we meet the then current owner of the hotel, who tells his story, from his own youth, pulling us much further back in time to the period just before World War II for the main action of the story.

In effect, we feel the passage of time, moving backwards stepwise, while also getting a sense of a story that has been told and retold by different people until it is handed down to us. We are continually reminded that even as we get caught up in the action on the screen, it is not immediate reality, but a story being told in a particular style about a time long ago. We are intrigued by the colorful telling of the story, and also assured at crucial moments that what we are seeing is far removed from our current world. The little boy with the water pistol squirting the pompous author sets a tone of self-ridicule. The implicit message is that this is all a joke, not to be taken seriously.

As we move from the older author to his younger version, we get our first view of the Grand Budapest Hotel and his description of it, "... a picturesque, elaborate, and once widely celebrated establishment. I expect some of you will know it. It was off-season and, by that time, decidedly out-of-fashion; and it had already begun its descent into shabbiness and eventual demolition."

There, the narrator comes across the eccentric, elderly owner of the hotel, Zero Moustafa, described as "A small, elderly man, smartly dressed, with an exceptionally lively, intelligent face, and an immediately perceptible air of sadness. He was, like the rest of us, alone, but also, I must say, he was the first that struck one as being deeply and truly lonely."

This somewhat serious statement is immediately followed by a scene, an interruption, which uses a defensive style, a form of denial that trivializes what is frightening and disturbing. (I've taken the verbal description from the published screenplay, in italics):

The author says in voice-over, "At that moment the curtain rose on a parenthetical, domestic drama which required the immediate and complete attention of M. Jean. ..."

Jean frowns. The fat businessman, sitting at a table in the middle of the lobby drinking hot chocolate and eating biscotti, appears to be choking to death.

We see a flurry of activity around the choking man, replete with a hiker and a Saint Bernard with a flask.

"... but, frankly, did not hold mine for long."

While the others are huddled around the choking victim, the author calmly enters the elevator.

There is something frightening, yet comic about this scene. It is scary to see someone choking. The author's indifference appears cold and unempathic, and we may feel that; yet, the comic, slapstick elements in the scene cause the viewer to see it as amusing, the frightening elements pushed from the surface. It skirts the divide between tragedy and comedy.

The author, indifferent to the choking scene, is left intensely curious about Moustafa, "*gespannt wie ein Flitzebogen,* that is, on the edge of my seat, where I remained throughout the next morning until, in what I have found to be its mysterious and utterly reliable fashion, fate, once again, intervened on my behalf."

He meets the mysterious Mr. Moustafa in the baths at the hotel. They are discussing how Moustafa came to own the hotel, when their dialogue is momentarily interrupted by a bizarre, comic scene, as described in the screenplay:

"*At this moment, one of the matrons of the hammam blasts the fat, now naked, businessman with a jet of icy water. He hollers as he is sprayed down.*"

The author and Moustafa exchange a little smile and go on with their story. This episode, involving the same fat man who had been choking in the last, is not as frightening as the previous one, but along with it's comic quality is a clear dose of sadomasochism, with a heavyset woman spraying this naked man who is naked, his back to her, leaning against the wall and screaming.

These two scenes, the choking man and the same man screaming as he is sprayed down in the baths, are not part of the story. They appear to be superfluous, added for comic effect. We are explicitly being told, this is unimportant to our story. We are in each instance given a glimpse of something disturbing while being told that it is a joke, incidental, to be disregarded.

Moustafa is the narrator of the final flashback, the primary story, set in the period just before the Second World War. It focuses immediately on the film's central character, M. Gustave, "the beloved, original concierge of the Grand Budapest."

M. Gustave is a somewhat effeminate, decadent, charming and forceful man, played by Ralph Fiennes. In his first scene, we have another of these subtle movements from the serious and painful to the superficial detail. Gustave is preparing an aristocratic octogenarian's departure from the hotel. She insists that she cannot go home and begs him to come with her because she fears if she leaves alone, she will never see him again.

Gustave tries to calm her: "You've nothing to fear. You're always anxious before you travel. I admit you appear to be suffering a more acute attack on this occasion, but, truly and honestly ... (*Suddenly taken aback.*) Dear God. What've you done to your fingernails?"

He goes on to express his horror at the color of her nail polish, then gets her on her way as she ponders the new problem of her nails.

Here, one of the film's characters, the very elderly Madame du T., is distracted from her mortal fear, a fear we will later learn was justified, by having her attention turned to something superficial, her nail polish. There is a neat reversal, the ominous trivialized and the superficial brought to our attention.

We soon come to a more striking and pointed example of this same defensive style. Some time has passed, and Zero Moustafa has become established as a "lobby boy" at the hotel under the personal tutelage of M. Gustave. We see him walking into town in the snow to get the morning papers. On his way back, he glances down and sees something in the papers that pushes him into a run back to the hotel and Gustave. He interrupts Gustave (who was finishing a tryst with one of the hotel's elderly female patrons), knocking furiously on a room door, to show him the paper. We see the headlines, "WILL THERE BE WAR? TANKS AT FRONTIER." Momentarily, we are struck by the imminent danger of a world, a civilization, about to undergo terrible changes as World War II and the Nazi advance are onrushing; but, that is not what has caught Zero's attention or that now catches the attention of Gustave. It is a tease. Below that article is another, "DOWAGER COUNTESS FOUND DEAD IN BOUDOIR," with a dramatic photograph of Madame du T's body sprawled on a carpet.

Once again, our attention is called to a disturbing event, but then we are pulled away to a lesser tragedy framed in comic presentation. The countess's death has a comical quality in this context, in part because she has been presented as a caricature, an overly dramatized figure, playing at being beautiful and seductive while appearing quite the opposite. There is something absurd about the image of her lying on that rug, playing a tragic diva. But what is more striking when we take a closer look is the contrast between what we know to be real

Nazi tanks at the border and this scene from a dramatic telling of a light fiction. It is as if the filmmakers are telling us, "Don't worry about the Nazi invasion, it is peripheral to our story."

As viewers, we may quickly become accustomed to this repetitive technique, and even accept it as a form of humor. The sense of danger is much more trenchant when we see Gustave and Zero on a train heading to Madame du T's estate for the funeral. The train stops abruptly and grim-faced, dangerous looking soldiers barge into their compartment, speaking with authority with Germanic accents. They want to pull Zero off the train because he does not have the proper papers. When Gustave objects, he and Zero are violently grabbed and pushed up against the wall, blood trickling from their noses. Suddenly, rescue comes in the form of an officer who has fond memories of M. Gustave from his family visits to the Grand Budapest when he was a boy. Once again, the mood shifts with the light banter between Gustave and the grateful officer. We are relieved of having to witness the kind of scene that we might have expected if this were not a comedy.

And what would that scene have been? At the end of the scene in the train, after the soldiers have left them, M. Gustave says to Zero,

"You see? There are still faint glimmers of civilization left in this barbaric slaughterhouse that was once known as humanity. Indeed, that's what we provide in our own modest, humble, insignificant— Oh, fuck it."

What are we spared here? We have been told that we are witnessing the end of a civilization, a civilization embodied by M. Gustave and the hotel. We have seen the ominous headlines about tanks across the border. Now we see thuggish looking soldiers boarding a train and threatening to remove helpless passengers, handling them violently. These are images of a new world order in which powerful, totalitarian forces obliterate the personal life. The "civilization" represented by the Grand Budapest is itself a myth of a peaceful time in which people could focus on the joys and problems of everyday life. It is presented as a caricature. But it is a welcome escape from the realities the film alludes to and then hides.

Although it is somewhat disguised, this could be viewed as a holocaust film, and my hypomanic response a result of the film's defensive style that continually distracts the viewer towards the trivial, humorous fictions, while presenting disconnected images suggestive of the real horror. The artistry of the film allows us to briefly hold those images, not fully formed, just long enough, it seems, to allow us to feel that we have successfully escaped them.

With this in mind, we can now see evidence of another defensive technique, one sometimes seen in dreams[1] and in the associations of analytic hours. We are presented with disconnected images, each faintly suggestive of the hidden, disturbing content, but displaced and out of context so that we can keep it just beyond recognition.

As the central action of the film evolves, Nazi brutality is embodied in a character named Jopling, played with brilliant sadistic effect by Willem Dafoe. Jopling is not ostensibly a Nazi or even a soldier. He is a thug working for Madame du T's greedy and ruthless son, Dmitri. Nevertheless, he commits a series of violent and horrendous acts that are similarly disguised in humorous form.

We see him in a family meeting with "Deputy Kovacs," who is the executor for Madame's estate. As Kovacs is telling Madame's son, Dmitri, that there are questions about the will, a missing document which must be investigated, Jopling is petting Kovacs's pet cat. At the end of the meeting, when Kovacs has refused to squash the investigation, saying that he is an attorney and must follow the rule of law, Jopling abruptly throws the cat out the window. We see it flattened on the ground below like a cartoon character. Kovacs says, unbelieving, "Did you just throw my cat out the window?" There is no response. We are left with the disbelief of brutality intruding upon ordinary events and the rule of law.

Jopling follows Kovacs as he leaves the estate. Kovacs's fear obviously mounts as he gets off a bus and runs into a museum that is near

---

[1] I was reminded of Freud's (1900) dream of Irma's injection in which both he and, later, Max Schur (1972) found evidence of denial of disturbing thoughts and memories.

closing time. Kovacs tries to elude Jopling, listening to his boots as they follow him through the museum, but finally opens a door to a street where he sees the bicycle that Jopling has used to follow him. This is the script's description of what follows.

There is a bicycle leaning against the wall across the alley behind the museum. Deputy Kovacs grabs the doorframe and takes one last, quick look back into the darkness behind him. Insert: Deputy Kovacs' hand on the knob. A second hand, wearing brass knuckles, gently enfolds it.

Cut to Deputy Kovacs' face. He gasps.

The door hammers shut with a bang. Four of Deputy Kovacs' fingers, gripping the doorframe, pop off at the knuckles all at once and fall down into a shallow puddle. On the other side of the door, there is a scream of bloodcurdling agony, then a thump, a thwack, and, finally, a wallop. Pause. The door opens again. Jopling comes out in his stocking feet. He puts on his boots. He takes out a handkerchief, leans down and collects the four fingers off the ground, wraps them up, slips them into his pocket, and walks away down the alley.

This is a terrifying image to anyone, but what we see once again reminds us that it is just a farce. On the ground, we see what are supposed to be the fingers, but they look like cartoon fingers, not real ones, lifeless sausage-looking fingers that Jopling can easily collect. Even the screenplay emphasizes the comic, unreal quality of the events with the words, "thump", "thwack", and "wallop," although we actually hear only the scream. We hear that Kovacs has disappeared. But even that ominous fact is blunted because Kovacs, like most of the characters in the film, is a comically drawn figure from a past that we know to be somewhat unreal and overly dramatized, a world, a "civilization," that in this context is itself more fantasy than real.

In a later scene, a policeman opens a basket and pulls from it a severed head, clearly Jopling's work. The image is frightening, but leaves us relieved that it is not the head of Zero's beloved girlfriend, Agatha, as we had been lead to fear.

There are additional images that in themselves are further disguised, but in context add to the impressions of Nazi atrocities: scenes in a prison in which an odd assortment of misfit prisoners wear ill-fitting uniforms and are fed mush that might suggest the camps, a mock underground consisting of hotel managers, "the society of the crossed keys," that hides and moves Gustave and Zero as they escape from the police (who have been falsely led to believe that Gustave killed Madame du T.) and, more importantly, Jopling.

Casual murders, dismembering of bodies, prison uniforms, an escape from mortal danger with the aid of an underground, all images that suggest the terrible times that underlie this story, but told with just enough remove, discontinuity and comic disguise to spare us the impact.

We come closest to full disclosure of the sense of tragedy through Zero, himself. We know that he comes from some form of impoverished background. After Gustave has escaped from the prison, with the help of Zero, who with the help of his girlfriend who works in a pastry shop near the hotel has smuggled in tools inside pastries, Gustave is horrified to learn that Zero has not only failed to bring all the necessaries for a disguise, but has also forgotten to bring Gustave's favorite perfume.

Angrily, he says to Zero, "Precisely. I suppose this is to be expected back in Aq Salim al-Jabat where one's prized possessions are a stack of filthy carpets and a starving goat, and one sleeps behind a tent-flap and survives on wild dates and scarabs, but it's not how I trained you. What on God's earth possessed you to leave the homeland where you very obviously belong and travel unspeakable distances to become a penniless immigrant in a refined, highly cultivated society that, quite frankly, could've gotten along very well without you?"

Zero replies, "The war."

"Say again?"

"Well, you see, my father was murdered, and the rest of my family were executed by firing squad. Our village was burned to the ground. Those who managed to survive were forced to flee. I left-because of the war."

Even here, we are successfully distracted. M. Gustave abandons his comical pose and becomes genuinely sympathetic and apologetic, but then they move on to their madcap escape. We are happily distracted, watching the exciting antics. Jopling and the dynamic duo of Gustave and Zero chase each other up and down snowy mountains, culminating in a harrowing scene in which Jopling stands over Gustave, who is hanging by his fingers at the edge of a cliff. Zero comes seemingly from nowhere to push Jopling over the edge and save his mentor. There is a scene in the hotel with bullets flying back and forth in oddly comic fashion. And finally there is the discovery of Madame's last will, leaving everything to Gustave.

But the film's true dynamic artistry comes at the end, in a series of scenes that both provoke images of trauma and help us defend against them in a pattern that presents them in a disordered manner that keeps them just out of consciousness, much like the defensive structure of a good dream.

Once again Zero and M. Gustave are on a train, this time accompanied by Zero's girlfriend, Agatha. Throughout the film, in light form, we have observed this love affair between two poor innocents in the midst of the tumultuous events surrounding them.

The older version of Zero Moustafa tells us in a voice over: "On the first day of the occupation, the morning the independent state of Zubrowska officially ceased to exist, we traveled with M. Gustave to Lutz."

They toast with wine while M. Gustave tells them about his own humble beginnings. It looks like a happy ending. But in a reprise of the earlier scene, the train suddenly stops in the middle of nowhere with tanks and soldiers in black uniforms seen through the window.

Once again, the soldiers enter the compartment and ask for papers. Seeing special papers that had been written for Zero, unfortunately by the officer of the now defeated army, the chief officer tears them up. This leads to a scuffle, in which Gustave is taken away by the soldiers, angrily throwing epithets at them.

We hear another voice-over from Moustafa, echoing Gustave's words, "There are still faint glimmers of civilization left in this barbaric slaughterhouse that was once known as humanity. ... He was one of them. What more is there to say?"

"He was one of them." In this context, it suggests a second meaning. Gustave was one of *them*, one of the many victims.

As we move up to the young author and the older Zero sitting in the dining room of the dying hotel, the author asks,

"What happened in the end?"

Zero Moustafa answers, shrugging, "In the end, they shot him. (Pause.) So it all went to me."

He goes on to explain that he kept the hotel not for the memory of M. Gustave. "No, I don't think so. You see, we shared a vocation. It wouldn't have been necessary. He's always with me. (Pause.) No, the hotel I keep for Agatha. ... We were happy here. For a little while."

This set of scenes is more suggestive of the underlying horror, but it is still disguised. Once again, the film has successfully planted the seeds of the disturbing content just out of reach. It is before the scene in the train, before we learn that Gustave has been shot, at a point when it is poignant but not so pointed, in a coda, an add-on to a comment about Gustave's fate, that we learn about Agatha. By breaking up the pieces of the story, the film allows us to ignore the magnitude and full meaning of the tragedy.

Moustafa: "He (Gustave) did not succeed, however, in growing old—nor did my darling Agatha. She and our infant son would be killed two years later by the Prussian grippe (pronounced almost like 'group'). An absurd little disease. Today, we treat it in a single week; but, in those days, many millions died."

Many millions, indeed, died of "the Prussian grippe." It is told in an off-handed manner before the scene in the train car, with the reassurance that "today we treat it in a single week." It carries the weight of his grief, but also disguises the grief and tragedy of a survivor of a series of events that were not fictional and certainly not amusing. We are reminded here of our introduction to Zero Moustafa: "A small, elderly man, smartly dressed, with an exceptionally lively, intelligent face, and an immediately perceptible air of *sadness*. He was, like the rest of us, *alone*, but also, I must say, he was the first that struck one as being *deeply and truly lonely.*" I have added the italics. We learn by the end of the film that our hero, Zero Moustafa, is a lone and lonely survivor of world events that affected millions, events that the film evokes mostly at an unconscious level, while granting us permission to focus our attention on the concerns and pleasures of our private lives without dwelling on the terrible things happening in the world around us; and, by doing so, allows us to feel very good, if only for a time. Such is the magic of artistic creativity.

Anderson, Wes (2014) *The Grand Budapest Hotel: The Illustrated Screenplay* (Opus Screenplay) (Kindle Locations 112-114). Opus Books. Kindle Edition.
Freud, S. (1900) *The Interpretation of Dreams. The Standard Edition of the Complete Psychological Works of Sigmund Freud,* Volume IV (1900).
Schur, M. (1972) *Freud: Living and Dying.* New York, IUP.

Birdman: The Unexpected Virtue of Ignorance

AS WE ALL KNOW, manic defenses do not always work so well. They can lead us into dangerous territory, ultimately creating more stress than relief. These next two films take the viewer into the mind of someone struggling with psychosis.

In the spirit of full disclosure, I must tell you that I may have a particularly subjective view of the film *Birdman*, as I set about commenting on it. Obviously, all examinations of film have some subjectivity assumed, but in this case I seem to be outside the mainstream. I say it because I was totally baffled to learn that the film is widely considered to be a comedy. It is described as such in reviews and, as if to codify the point, it was nominated for a Golden Globe award for comedy.

I did not experience it as a comedy at all. I found myself in rapt attention in a continual state of tension, anxiety, anticipation, even worry over what would happen next. When it was over, I texted that I had just seen it and didn't know if I loved it or hated it.

Much later, as I was writing this discussion, I recalled that this had happened to me once before, many years ago, with the film, *Dr. Strangelove*. As a young man who had grown up with the fear of a nuclear attack, reinforced by television warnings and duck and cover exercises in school replete with instructions about leaving to go home after the nuclear attack we had somehow survived, the comedy of a madman directing the launching of weapons and of an accident that resulted in the destruction of the world did not strike me as funny. I learned then that humor often plays upon an edge of anxiety, relieving us if it remains within bounds we can tolerate, but only feeding on our fear if it comes too close to being real. The difference between my reaction to *Birdman* and my reaction to *Strangelove* is that even as I was watching *Strangelove,* I could see the intended humor. With *Birdman* I cannot to this moment see what in it was intended as humor.

That difficulty may have to do with my training and profession. *Birdman* thrusts us, the viewers, into a mind that is struggling with psychosis, violence and suicidality. The character is Riggan Thomson, an actor turned director who has written and is directing a serious drama based upon a short story by Raymond Carver which is about to go into previews on Broadway. He is trying to resurrect his career and his image with this play after his movie career has typecast him as a cartoonish superhero, Birdman.

But the problem for the film, as for me, is that he is also struggling internally with this identity issue. From the outset, we hear him arguing with a voice presumably coming from within himself, the voice, we gradually learn, of his alter ego, Birdman. What is more, we see that at times he appears to believe that he has Birdman's special powers, particularly the powers of telekinesis and flight. That, along with a heightened irritability and tension, strongly suggests that he is in a manic state and is moving in and out of psychotic thinking. As a clinician, it's hard for me to laugh at his illness, particularly since his mania is fraught with so much tension, rage, anxiety and depression. I could easily see him as a patient, like some I've seen, who is on the verge not only of falling into complete psychosis, but also of violence and potential suicide. That alone would have me on the edge of my seat and holding it tightly as the plot advances and we see Riggan standing at the edge of a roof of a building, seemingly ready to jump.

We do not experience Riggan's struggle with psychosis from the outside, with sympathy and concern for a fellow human being. The film thrusts us *into* his mind. It does not present his psychotic thinking in the third person. In fact, as the film opens, we see a man hovering above the ground—not a man who thinks he is hovering above the ground—his back to us, naked except for his jockey shorts, cross legged, back straight, in quiet contemplation in what we will soon learn is his dressing room. And, we are not told that he is hearing a voice, we hear the voice, the first words spoken in the film, a gravelly voice coming from the screen, saying, "How did we end up here? This place is a fucking dump. Smells like balls. We don't belong in this shithole."[2]

We soon see Riggan's telekinetic power. Sitting in his dressing room, he makes a motion with his hand sending an object from his dressing table flying across the room, smashing against the wall. At one point, the voice says, "They have no idea."

Sure, we can make the assumption that this is Riggan's fantasy. But we are in a movie theater, a place where people can fly, where they can have superhuman powers. It gives us just enough ambiguity to create that kernel of uncertainty about what is real, an uncertainty that must infect the mind of someone like Riggan, struggling on the edge of psychosis. Adding to that sense of uncertainty are "coincidences" that feed the psychosis. There is a strong suggestion that through his telekinesis, Riggan can unleash a dangerous rage. We see him in a rehearsal in which four people are seated around a kitchen table, engaged in a dialogue which is a rough reproduction of the main scene in Carver's story. He is frustrated by the poor acting of the other man in the scene, Ralph, something which has been brewing. Riggan looks up at a heavy piece of machinery, which moments later comes crashing down on Ralph's head, leaving him unconscious and bleeding. In the excited aftermath, Riggan makes a comment that it wasn't an accident, and talks about the man's terrible acting and the

---

[2] Dialogue from the film is taken either directly from the audio or from the screenplay published online.

fact that his incapacitation (we later see him crippled) is a good thing for the play.

As if to further emphasize Riggan's powers, he and his attorney and co-producer talk about finding a new actor for the play when Riggan suggests that the door may open at that moment and such an actor will step in. That doesn't happen, exactly, but one of the actresses comes in just then and tells them that a well known stage actor, Mike Shiner, is available to take the role.

Add to that a manic quality that infects the entire film. It starts with the soundtrack, marked by steady, although slightly uneven drum beats. At a couple of points we see the drummer as Riggan walks past him on the street or even in the hallways of the theater.

Events quickly get out of control, driven in part by other characters, particularly the new actor, Mike Shiner, who replaces Ralph. He creates a diversion in the first preview in front of an audience, complaining in the middle of the kitchen scene that the gin in his glass is watered down and that the entire set is phony. Mike starts throwing things, bringing the entire set down in a crash. In a later scene in which he is supposed to be under sheets making love to a woman, he proposes that they really make love and develops an erection, bringing laughter from the audience moments later. His extreme form of method acting gives increasing tension to the production.

There is Riggan's daughter, Sam, recently out of drug rehab, who sits on the edge of a balcony overlooking the street and plays truth or dare with Mike, at one point acting out his dare to lean over and spit on the head of someone down below. Their flirtation adds another level of excitement and tension as they kiss and embrace above the set while her father and others are rehearsing.

Riggan and Mike get into a wrestling match in between performances. Riggan is accidentally locked out of the theater in his underwear during a performance and enters the theater practically naked to assume his role in the final scene of the play while the audience watches in bewilderment. All to the intermittent beat of the drum.

And through all this, we go through highs and lows, rages and suicidal behavior with Riggan. In a later scene, which seems a mix of reality and fantasy, he stands at the edge of a roof of a building while a worried young man tries to ease him down from the edge. Suddenly, he does jump off, but instead of falling to his death, he flies down the street, seemingly moving from depression to mania. At times we see him flying, at times we look down through his eyes. Perhaps more gullible than the average viewer, I was momentarily confused, unsure if the film was suddenly bursting into fantasy or depicting his fantasy, and, if so, was he actually hurtling towards the ground? This double focus is momentarily resolved when we see him landing in front of the theater and walking in and then see a cab driver chasing after him, demanding his fare. At least for the moment, we have a structure, a reality. He has been imagining himself flying, but was actually in a cab headed to the theater. For that moment, we are watching *his* delusion from a safe distance.

But that resolution is temporary, and not totally reassuring. The play within the play ends in a scene in which Riggan's character points a gun at his head and fires. In the last version of that scene, we see him fire a live bullet at his head, with real blood spurting as he falls, only to see him awaken in a hospital bed in what appears to be a happy ending. Left alone in the room by friends and family (the psychiatrist in me was going crazy at the incompetence of leaving a suicidal man alone in a hospital room with an open window), he calmly goes out the window. Moments later, we see his daughter look out the window with concern, only to smile as she looks upward, presumably seeing her father hovering above. Through the ambiguity of perspective along with the multiple events and special effects, *Birdman* does not merely allow us to witness a man in a mental crisis, but puts us inside his head. As we watch the film, we are thrown into a state of uncertainty about the film's reality and in effect of our own at that moment. We are as close as we can be through art to experiencing ourselves moving in and out of psychosis, with a strong awareness of at times exhilaration, agitation and a sense that we might be driven to something cataclysmic.

What are we to make of all this?[3]

---

[3] I want to be clear that I am not suggesting that the formulation offered for this film is an explanation of the underlying causes or dynamics of bipolar disorder.

The film takes us through certain key scenes in Riggan's play in rehearsals, previews with live audiences, and the play's official opening on Broadway. The final scene, in which Riggan's character, Eddie, enters a motel room to confront his former girlfriend and her new lover, is repeated three times in the film. With each repetition, we hear Riggan say, "I don't exist. I'm not even here. I don't exist. None of this matters," before putting a gun to his head and pulling the trigger.

Grinstein (1956) and Balter (2006) have shown that like a dream within a dream (Freud, 1900), a play within a play can give direct expression to a central disturbing idea while disguising it as a bit of fiction. In this case, we have not only the repetition to support that, but also earlier dialogue from the film in which Riggan's sense of unimportance and non-existence is affirmed by another character in the film, his daughter, Sam. She tells him that his play is aimed at "a thousand rich, old white people whose only real concern is gonna be where they go to have their cake and coffee when it's over," and finishes, "*You're the one who doesn't exist.* You're doing this because you're scared to death, like the rest of us, *that you don't matter.* And you know what? You're right. You don't. It's not important. You're not important. Get used to it." (my italics)

Sam announces not simply that Riggan is "scared to death ... that you don't matter," but says that in this he is "like the rest of us," implicitly including "us," the audience. We also feel the desperate fear that we don't matter. It helps explain the continual turning to fantasy, delusion, throughout the film to regain a sense of importance.

And whence comes this fear? We go back to the scene, to the dialogue just before Riggan expresses his existential hopelessness. He is a woman's former lover, Eddie, barging in upon the woman he still loves and her current lover, who are making love in a motel room. Pointing a gun threateningly, he says, "What's wrong with me? Why do I end up having to beg people to love me?"

Leslie: "Ed. Eddie. Please... Give me the gun. Just look at me. I was drowning. I was not capable of—You deserve to be loved. You do."

Riggan: "I just wanted to be what you wanted. Now I spend every fucking minute praying to be someone else. Someone I'm not. Anyone..."

Mike: "Put down the gun, Ed. She just doesn't love you anymore."
Riggan: "You don't, do you?"
Leslie: "No."
Riggan: "And you never will..."
Leslie: "I'm sorry."
Riggan: "I don't exist. I'm not even here. I don't exist. None of this matters."

The play within a play tells us that the desperation comes from seeking a love that isn't there. In an earlier part of the play, Leslie's character describes Eddie as being possessed by a passionate, violent love.

"Okay, well, he did beat me up one night. He dragged me around the living room by my ankles, yelling "I love you, I love you, bitch."

This, too, is reinforced elsewhere in the film, in dialogue between Riggan and his ex-wife, Sylvia, who we come to see he still loves. In answer to his question, "Why did we break up?" she tells him. "You threw a kitchen knife at me... and one hour later you were telling me how much you loved me." She adds, "Just because I didn't like that ridiculous comedy you did with Goldie Hawn didn't mean I did not love you. But that's what you always do. You confuse love with admiration."

Through these bits and pieces scattered amidst the riot of the film, we are given hints of an existential despair based upon a basic sense of futility at getting love and admiration (mirroring?) from the one person from whom we need it.

The play within a play even gives us a fleeting hint of the importance of the infant's gaze upon the mother. Riggan (playing a different role here) delivers a monologue about an elderly couple badly injured in an auto accident, lying in the hospital in body casts.

"The husband was depressed. Even when I told him his wife was gonna pull through, he was still depressed. So, I got up to his mouth hole and asked him, and he told me it was because he couldn't see her through the eyeholes. Can you imagine? I'm telling you, the man's heart was breaking because he couldn't turn his goddamn head and see his goddamn wife."

This need to win the love and approval of an unaffirming, indifferent mother is expressed directly in the film. Riggan's attempt to redeem himself through the play, to be someone other than a cartoon character, to be someone, comes down to his winning the approval of the *New York Times* theater critic, Tabitha. She is seen in a Broadway bar, a cold, imperious figure who admires the method actor, Mike Shiner, who is devoted to the theater, but despises Riggan, the Hollywood actor. She tells him that there is nothing he can do, that she will kill his play. She is clearly the embodiment of the unattainable mother whose love and admiration are so desperately needed.

In the end, Riggan wins her admiration, if not her love, by shooting himself on stage. In the sequel to his on stage suicide attempt, he hears her approving review of his act of heroic realism under the title, "The Unexpected Virtue of Ignorance," the alternate title for the film. Only self destruction can get the attention of such a mother.

And what of the ending? We see Riggan shoot himself and we seemingly lose consciousness with him, the screen melting into confused frozen images, only to awaken to a "reality" in which he has seemingly survived. But in his survival, he has shot off his nose and had it replaced with a more beak-like nose, subtly blending him with the Birdman of his fantasy life. We see him, left alone in his hospital room *(by a totally irresponsible hospital staff and administration)*, opening the window and stepping out, not to be seen by us again. As the film ends, his daughter, Sam reenters the room, looks out the window, first glancing down—we half expect a look of horror on her face, but no—she finally glances upward and smiles, suggesting that she sees her father hovering above, with all the power of the Birdman. Ultimately, the film gives us a delusional fantasy as the only alternative to existential despair and self-annihilation. No, I was not laughing.

Balter, Leon (2006) Nested ideation and the problem of reality: dreams and works of art in works of art. *Psychoanalytic Quarterly* 75:405- 445.
Freud, S. (1900) *The Interpretation of Dreams. The Standard Edition of the Complete Psychological Works of Sigmund Freud,* Volume IV (1900).
Grinstein, Alexander (1956)The dramatic device: a play within a play. *Journal of the American Psychoanalytic Association* 4:49-52.

Moving Pictures: Films Through a Psychoanalytic Lens

Black Swan

BLACK SWAN IS A film about the ballet, adolescence and psychosis. It is a "psychological thriller," a "suspense thriller," a "horror movie" and a tragedy. It blends psychological insight with theatrical melodrama, myth with personal story. It depicts a mother/daughter relationship that is loving and protective at the same moment that it is rivalrous and destructive.

The story concerns the adolescent conflicts of a young ballerina, Nina Sayers, who is vying for the starring role in a production of *Swan Lake*. We are never told her age, but her conflicts are clearly those of a young adolescent. She is torn apart by intense conflicts between ideals of innocence and kindness and sexual and aggressive passions. Her conflict is reified in the form of the twin swan princesses, the innocent White Swan, Odette, and her seductive, aggressive twin Black Swan, Odile.

That story is laid out for us by the ballet company's director, Thomas (pronounced in the European style) Leroy: "We all know the story. Virginal girl, pure and sweet, trapped in the body of a swan. She desires freedom, but only true love can break the spell. Her wish is nearly granted in the form of the prince, but before he can declare his love, the lustful twin, the Black Swan, tricks and seduces him. Devastated, the White Swan leaps off a cliff, killing herself and in death, finds freedom."

At its surface, *Black Swan* is about the soaring and grinding world of ballet, which one analyst, referring to this film, described as misogynistic. Even before the film's major conflicts are apparent, we see Nina attending to her bruised and bleeding feet and hear loud, crunching noises as she tries to manipulate them or to dance upon them. But the physical punishment is secondary to the psychological demands of pursuing technical perfection and artistic expression. We will see that Nina is driven and tortured by her own ambition and by the ambition of her director, Thomas.

Black Swan is a psychological drama that can take us out of our usual exterior clinical perspective and into the experience of increasing psychosis. There are hints early in the film that Nina has a longstanding habit of compulsive scratching to go along with the self-destructive exercises that the rigors of her career demand. Under the strain of her new role, she will begin to hallucinate and to experience paranoid fears, and we with her. We experience them with confusion and some loss of reality, but also with fear and, at times, shock as the film uses techniques of timing and sound effects borrowed from the genre of the horror movie.

The film accomplishes all of this by throwing us into the maelstrom of an adolescent transformation contracted into what feels like a few days. Under the strain of this precipitous change, the cracking of reality feels almost inevitable.

The opening scene portends this transformation. We see a young beautiful ballerina, Nina, dressed in white and dancing beautifully and freely. Suddenly, a dark male figure approaches and seems to attack her. Terrified, she attempts to dance out of his clutches, but is transformed by him into a swan. As the scene ends, we see Nina lying in her bed, awakening from this dream, which she explains to her mother is the prologue to *Swan Lake* in the Bolshoi version.

Nina appears to be locked in childhood in symbiosis with her adoring single mother, Erica, herself a former ballet dancer. As she sits for her breakfast and looks at the half grapefruit in front of her, she smiles at it and says "pretty." As she does so, her mother joins her in the refrain and they laugh and smile together at what is obviously a standard shared exchange that gives us the feel of a mother/child relationship at a much younger age. In keeping with this, we will see that Nina's room is filled with light, fluffy, airy stuffed animals, making it seem like a child's room. Her mother, Erica, lovingly calls her "sweet girl."

There is a hint of conflict when Erica sees scratch marks on Nina's back and questions her about them. We experience a further vague sense of danger on the subway train that takes Nina to the ballet company at Lincoln Center. Nina first sees her reflection in the train window, then turns the other way to see a young woman in another train who looks like her, suggesting another reflection, or, perhaps, her double.

There are two catalysts for the rush into adolescent conflict. The first is Thomas, the middle aged, accented company director. We are told by various characters that he is ruthless, a bastard, a womanizer and user of women. He tells Nina that she is perfect for the role of the White Swan, innocent, beautiful, perfect and cold, but that to dance the role of the Black Swan, she must be able to let go. That role requires sexual aggressiveness and a capacity for ruthless competitiveness.

Having slipped while dancing for him and afraid that she won't get the role of the Swan Queen, Nina goes to Thomas to tell him that she had completed the routine afterward. He tells her that he knows she has the technical skills, but lacks the ability to unloose the emotions needed for the role of the Black Swan. He suddenly grabs her and kisses her on the lips and is surprised when she bites him, drawing blood. For that show of spirit, he reverses his decision and awards her the role of the Swan Queen.

The second catalyst is Lily, a new girl to the company, "straight off the plane from San Francisco." Lily will play a complicated role in this psychological drama. She is what Nina is not, relaxed and unafraid to be sexual. As the story develops, she will become a real life version of Nina's "evil" double, the Black Swan to Nina's White Swan. Nina will be both drawn to her as her other half and fearful of her as a rival for the part. But Lily serves another, equally important role. She represents the seduction of peer pressure that helps to move the young adolescent away from the protection of home and the child's role that she plays there.

Pulled by the seductions of the older man and the freer girl, as well as by her own ambition to conquer the role of the Black Swan, Nina is suddenly jerked into conflict, long suppressed with her mother's help, between innocence in a comfortable but confining dyad with her mother and the freedom to express and explore her own sexuality and aggressiveness.

There is a third character who plays a role in this conflict, the aging star, Beth McIntyre, Thomas's former "little princess" who is now losing her appeal and is being forcibly retired. Just as Lily is Nina's double, Beth doubles for her mother, as a displaced older rival, jealous and angry at her successor. It is through Thomas and Beth that Nina will, as an adolescent, play out her Oedipal drama.

Early in the film, Nina defends Beth. The other young women in the company are talking about declining attendance and blaming it on Beth, saying they need "someone new," "someone who's not approaching menopause." Nina shows her admiration and sympathy, saying that it's sad because "Beth is such a beautiful dancer." Shortly afterwards, she hears Beth throwing a tantrum in her private dressing room. After Beth leaves in a huff, Nina sneaks into the dressing room and steals a lipstick. Later in the film, she is put into Beth's dressing room and steals a few other small items. It is clear that she is looking for totems from the admired older dancer.

But Beth does not reciprocate the sympathy. She sees Nina as a rival and usurper. After a fundraising dinner at which Thomas has announced Beth's upcoming retirement and presented Nina as his new Swan Queen, Beth approaches Nina angrily, finally drawing an angry response.

Beth: "What did you do to get the role? He always said you were a frigid little girl. What did you do to make him change his mind? Did you suck his cock?"

Nina: "Not all of us have to."

Beth: "You fucking whore! You fucking little whore!"

We soon hear that Beth has suffered an accident, hit by a car. Thomas tells Nina that he thinks she ran in front of the car on purpose. With obvious guilt, Nina visits Beth and is horrified to see under the covers that her legs are badly damaged.[4]

Her relationship with Beth reflects her relationship with her mother. Unlike Beth, Erica's ballet career was apparently unsuccessful. In small

---

[4] This is a reminder of and possible homage to the dramatic closing scene in *The Red Shoes*, in which the camera shows the bruised, broken legs of the heroine, a ballerina, who has thrown herself under a train.

interactions, it becomes clear that Nina sees her mother as a failure as a ballerina. With Erica and Beth, we have the Oedipal rivalry, one the mother she is surpassing, the other the successful ballerina she is replacing as Thomas's "little princess."

Winning the role and feeling the pressures upon her to let out her feelings, Nina begins to show signs of rebelling against her mother's attempts to keep her as her "sweet girl." After she wins the role, Erica brings her a gift of a large stuffed bear. Nina clearly does not want it. Later, she will throw out all of her stuffed animals. Her mother has made her a cake, which she does not want to eat. When Erica starts to take the cake to the garbage can, Nina relents and tries to make peace, but the movement towards growth and independence has started.

Thomas gives it further impetus in an attempt to get Nina to allow her sensuality to come to the fore. After the fundraiser, he takes her to his apartment, but instead of seducing her, he sends her home with a homework assignment, to masturbate. We see Nina in her bed beginning to excite herself. She rolls over in an orgasmic frenzy, then sees her mother sleeping on the chair beside her bed. Afterwards, she finds a board in the garbage room and uses it to block the door to try to establish some privacy, attempting to set a boundary with her intrusive mother.

As this develops, we can begin to notice an ambiguity in Erica's attitude. She clearly gets vicarious pleasure from hearing about her daughter's success, pumping her for information about the fundraiser at which Nina was brought out by Thomas. On the other hand, it is not clear if her ready acceptance earlier of Nina's not getting the role—discouraging her from approaching Thomas to try to change his mind and telling her about the good lesser roles she'll probably get—is an attempt to comfort or a hint at her unconscious jealousy of her daughter's success. As the story develops, there is a continued obvious ambiguity about Erica's attempts to hold her Nina back, ostensibly in an attempt to protect her. The fact that Nina increasingly needs protection adds to the ambiguity, but when Erica tells Nina she wants her sweet girl back, the attempt to arrest her development is palpable.

Their conflict comes to a head. Questioning Nina about whether Thomas has made any advances, Erica goes on to say that she doesn't want Nina to repeat the mistake that she had made with her career.

Nina: "What career?"

Erica: "The one I gave up to have you."

Nina: "You were 28."

Erica: "So?"

At this point, Erica becomes controlling. Her face hardens and she angrily questions Nina about her skin, demanding that she take off her shirt. Nina angrily refuses.

With Thomas pushing her to let go of her inhibitions—dancing with her and physically seducing her—Nina is unable to contend with her unrepressed sexuality and aggression. She begins to project her impulses, hallucinating with more intensity, and we, the viewers hallucinate with her.

Up to this point, there have been ambiguous occurrences—seeing her double on the train, passing a woman in the dark who appears to be her double—made ominous by the film's sound effects and lighting. But as the genie of sex and aggression is let out of the bottle, the hallucinations become more definitive and frightening. Nina tries masturbating in her bath. As she does so, we see drops of blood landing on the bath water above her body. She lies down under the water and with her we see the view as she looks up from beneath the surface. Suddenly, a young woman, her double, is leaning over her. We experience it with her with horror movie shock. This is one of several times that Nina will suddenly and shockingly be confronted by another woman, sometimes real, sometimes an apparition.

There are other images as well. An older man in the subway makes obscene gestures with his face and mouth. It might be real, might be a hallucination. We are losing our own grip on reality along with Nina.

To Thomas's push is added Lily's pull. On the heals of Nina's confrontation with her mother, Lily offers her the alternative of a peer, asking Nina to join her for drinks. Against her mother's wishes, Nina grabs her coat and joins Lily for a night out that turns into an encounter with men and drugs in a club. We see her leave the club with Lily, who accompanies her home.

Nina taunts her mother with her escapade, locking her out of the room, saying "It's called privacy. I'm not twelve any more," with Erica shouting, "You're not my Nina right now." With the room effectively locked with the wooden board, Nina and Lily have an intense sexual encounter.

But the next morning, Lily is not there and the room is boarded shut. We begin to suspect that the scene was a hallucinated fantasy as a puzzled Nina goes to the dance company. Lily is dancing the part of the Black Swan, arousing Nina's suspicions of rivalry and a deliberate attempt to usurp. She confronts Lily, who says that they were separated at the club and that she never went home with her. Lily, in a friendly teasing voice says, "Did you have some screwed up Lezzy wet dream about me? Oh, my God, you did, you fantasized about me!"

The drugs at the bar and hallucinated sex magnify the rate of transformation. As Nina morphs into adolescent rebellion and pleasure seeking at an accelerated pace, we are drawn into a psychosis that we are made to experience with confusion and terror, the lighting and sound adding a sense of threat. In a sequence with the artistry of a good horror movie, Nina becomes frightened when left alone in the ballet studio. At first she sees strange things in a subtle way, her mirror image seemingly separating its movements from hers. The lights go out and she anxiously pursues a possible shadow and noises, finally peeking in on Thomas having sex with Lily, then with Nina's double, who stares back at her with an eerie smile.[5] Thomas becomes a grotesque swan figure from the ballet.

Frightened and horrified, she flees and goes to the hospital to see Beth, to return the things she has taken from Beth's dressing room and to apologize, telling Beth, "I know how it feels now. She's trying to replace me." But Beth rebukes her for stealing her things and begins to stab her own face with an emery board. As Nina runs from

---

[5] For me, at least, reminiscent of a very similar scene in Bernardo Bertolucci's *The Conformist*.

the hospital room, she is holding the bloody emery board. We may tell ourselves that we are watching a psychosis, but we feel the effects of horror, experiencing the dread of the psychosis ourselves, directly.

This sets us up to careen towards the film's finale. Back in her apartment, the horror continues as we and Nina see apparitions and hear voices. When her mother tries to intercede, she slams the door on her mother's hand to force her out, finally blocking the door, setting a boundary with new-found violence.

But when she wakens, Erica is with her. Nina soon realizes that this is the night of her debut in Swan Lake. Erica tells her that she has called Thomas to let him know that she is too ill to perform.

As they grapple, Erica asks, "What happened to my sweet girl?"

Nina answers, "She's gone."

With Erica telling her she can't handle the role, Nina's parting words are, "I can't? I'm the Swan Queen. You're the one who never left the corps."

Adult viewers who were once adolescents may be caught up in the ambiguity of Erica's attempt to protect her daughter by thwarting her ambitions, but Nina sees it unambiguously as a threat to her success and independence,

When she arrives at the theater, Lily is prepared to fill in as the Swan Queen. Now, she clearly sees Lily as the jealous rival who wishes to take her place, the evil double. Nina convinces Thomas to let her do the part. From this point, the action is backed by the sound of Tchaikovsky's music.

After the first act, in which Nina has danced as the White Swan, Lily appears in her dressing room, aggressively demanding to take the role of the Black Swan and morphing into Nina's double, choking her in a grotesque manner and saying, "It's my turn." Nina says. "It's my turn," and stabs the double/Lily with a piece of broken glass, leaving her for dead.

Now she dances the challenging Black Swan role with intensity and perfection, the audience responding. When she goes back to her dressing room and realizes what she has done, mopping blood from the floor, there is a knock on the door and Lily appears, alive and well, congratulating her on her amazing performance.

Nina looks around the room and sees no blood and no body. But putting on her White Swan costume, she sees in the mirror that she is bleeding. Pulling a shard of glass from her belly, she goes out to do the final dance as the distraught White Swan, eventually jumping off a balcony onto a mattress on the stage, ending the performance to thunderous applause.

With Thomas leaning over her admiringly, the others, Lily first, see that she is bleeding, now copiously. Through her vision, we see the screen turn white and then black for the credits.

It is only at this point that we can separate ourselves from Nina and her psychosis, wiser in our first-hand knowledge of adolescent conflict, ambivalence and violence directed inward, coming both from the passions of sexuality and competitive violence directed at the child being left and from the rage of conscience against the violation of that child-like ideal.

Ex Machina

"THE FIRST TIME I saw the film, *The Grand Budapest Hotel*, I left the theater with a particularly good, buoyant feeling." I wrote that for the Fall, 2014 issue of the *PANY Bulletin* (and internationalpsychoanalysis.net) and added that a colleague later told me he had the same reaction after seeing the film. After seeing the film, *Birdman*, I wrote that I "found myself in rapt attention in a continual state of tension, anxiety, anticipation, even worry over what would happen next. When it was over, I texted that I had just seen it and didn't know if I loved it or hated it." I again left the theater with the mood of the film lingering.

Neither of those experiences was as striking as my reaction to *Ex Machina*. I saw it originally alone, and on leaving the theater, I found myself totally caught in the mood the film had created, walking homeward on familiar streets, but feeling oddly disconnected from the world and the pedestrians around me. I was totally conscious and aware of my surroundings. Cognitively and visually, my contact with reality was intact; but, my feeling state was as if I was still in the world of the film. The "real" people I was passing in the street were strangers, of course, but now they felt strange. A colleague described her reaction after seeing *Ex Machina* as being dissociated.

I decided rather than analyzing myself that I would try to analyze *Ex Machina* to better understand its effect.

If we are looking for elements that might lead to a sense of strangeness and estrangement, we may easily start with the setting. The body of the film takes place in an extremely remote area, a vast wilderness surrounding a closed-in, spare complex with a minimum of comforting images. The doors open to key cards and many are locked to all but the proprietor. There is little that is warm or familiar.

I am reminded of the enchanted isle of Shakespeare's *The Tempest*, which I saw in Central Park around the same time. Like that island, this isolated place is populated with strange creatures, adding to our sense of unfamiliarity. It is the living space of Nathan Bateman, a child prodigy who has chosen to live in this state of extreme isolation, pursuing his interest in the magic of cyberspace while living off his childhood creation, the world's most powerful search engine.

This Prospero shares his island with his creation, in effect his child, an "AI," artificial intelligence, named Ava. She has the face and the shape of a beautiful woman in a wire mesh and carbon body and a brain made of some sort of gel. Nathan also has a servant, an enigmatic, mute attractive Asian woman named Kyoko.

We, the viewers, are left on this virtual island in the company of an innocent looking young man, a computer programmer from Nathan's company, named Caleb Smith. Caleb has won a prize of one week with Nathan. He is left by helicopter in the middle of nowhere and told to follow the river to Nathan's "building." The pilot has never seen Nathan, only dropped off supplies and people at a clearing. That pilot is the last normal person that Caleb, or we, will see for the next two hours.

Already thrown into this strange party, we are next given a task that pushes us to question the minds and motivations of its inhabitants. After getting Caleb to sign a non-disclosure agreement, which also gives Nathan access to all Caleb's electronic devices, Nathan asks Caleb,

"Do you know what the Turing Test is?"

"Yeah. I know what the Turing Test is. It's where a human interacts with a computer. And if the human can't tell they're interacting with a computer, the test is passed. "

"And what does a pass tell us?"

"That the computer has artificial intelligence."

From Wikipedia: "The Turing test is a test of a machine's ability to exhibit intelligent behavior equivalent to, or indistinguishable from, that of a human." It is named after Alan Turing, the father of the computer age. Many of us saw him recently depicted in film uncovering the German code and facilitating victory in World War II. As Alan Turing conceived of the test, the rater does not see the subjects, human and artificial intelligence, so that the test is not influenced by the obvious physical differences.

The film presents us with a different type of Turing test. Caleb will meet with Ava, separated by a glass wall, and will attempt to determine if there is anything about her mind that distinguishes her from an intelligent human being.

Immediately, almost at its outset, the film throws us into the task of trying to understand someone else's mind. In effect, this variant of Turing's test becomes an exercise in and a test of mentalization, the ability, again taken from Wikipedia, "to understand the mental state of oneself and others which underlies overt behavior." Caleb, knowledgeable about such matters, questions this variation of the Turing test and is told by Nathan, "I think we're past that. If I hid Ava from you, so you just heard her voice, she would pass for human. The real test is to show you she is a robot, then see if you still feel she has consciousness." Nathan wants to see if Caleb will *respond* to the AI as if it was a human being.

Ex Machina will challenge our ability to make sense of someone else's mind, something we as analysts are challenged to do daily. Already thrown into a very strange place with strange people, we are now going to try to solve a mystery, not of actions or events, but of motivations.

Caleb meets with Ava daily through a clear partition. She is limited to her small set of rooms. In some ways, these meetings have the structure of analytic or therapy sessions in that the interviewer knows about the other's life only from their words. If we follow the analogy, this will turn out to definitely be a "two-person analysis." At the first meeting, they both admit to being a little nervous at meeting one another. She explains that she has never met anyone other than Nathan. He tells her that he has never met anyone like her before. She tells him her age is "one," that she never learned how to speak, which she knows is unusual, that she likes to draw. They agree that they'd like to meet and talk again.

In the second interview, Ava turns the tables. After getting him to agree that they are "friends," she points out that their conversations have been one sided, in effect asking him to tell about himself. He talks about his background, his parents' death in an auto accident. She asks if he's single and he says he is. At some point, she turns the conversation to Nathan.

Ava: "Do you like Nathan?"

Caleb: "Yes. Of course."

Ava: "Is Nathan your friend?"

Caleb: "Sure."

Ava: "A good friend?"

Caleb: "Well, a good friend is ... We only just met. It takes time to get to know ..."

At this point, there is a power shutdown. We've seen one in the scene before. Nathan doesn't know what is causing them. There is momentary darkness and then a dimmer light as the emergency power goes on. Before full power is restored, with Nathan's ability to view them presumably cut off, Ava speaks to Caleb.

"Caleb. You're wrong."

"Wrong about what?"

"Nathan."

"In what way?"

"He isn't your friend."

"Excuse me? I'm sorry, Ava, I don't know what you're ..."

"You shouldn't trust him. You shouldn't trust anything he says. Trust me."

Power is restored. Ava resumes her seat and her former demeanor, continuing the conversation as if nothing unusual had happened.

As viewers, seeing this world through Caleb's eyes, we suddenly find ourselves in the middle of a dangerous triangle. Who do we trust? Who do we believe? Where do we ground our reality?

As we all know, films can give us a clear sense of a character's intentions. But that is not the case with Nathan Bateman. When we first meet him, he doesn't come out to greet Caleb on his entry into his home. Instead, Caleb comes upon him as he is ferociously punching a heavy bag on his terrace with bloodied fists. He then comes across warm and buddy-like, calling Caleb "Dude." But we also see that he drinks heavily at night and can mock his own friendliness, as when he explains why Caleb doesn't have access to the phones, "You understand. Given Ava. And you being kind of an unknown. I mean—a great guy, and so on. Instant pals. But ... ."

Ava's warning forces Caleb to make a decision, in a sense to choose between them. Nathan has been monitoring the interviews and has seen everything except what transpired during the break in power. Caleb can tell him what she said, betraying Ava, or lie to Nathan, betraying him. Sometimes, I suspect, the choice of action determines the trust rather than the other way around. Caleb lies to Nathan, in effect distrusting him.

I said that there was a fourth inhabitant, the servant girl, Kyoko. She is somewhat peripheral to the plot; yet she plays a very important role in setting the tone and mood of the film. She appears without explanation on the morning of Caleb's second day at Nathan's compound. We see Caleb awakening in his room, apparently in the morning, as an attractive Asian woman enters to leave a tray with coffee and food. She says nothing and walks out.

Nathan later apologizes, "Hey. Sorry to send Kyoko to wake you, man. I just didn't want too much of the day to slip by," a moment later adding, "She's some alarm clock, huh? Gets you right up in the morning."

That last comment will prove telling. Kyoko, always silent, is seen first as an obedient servant, cutting food for their meal, serving food as they relax in the evening. When she spills some wine, Nathan yells at her. Caleb is upset at what borders on abuse. Nathan later shows Caleb that Kyoko is a good dancer, putting on loud music and watching her dance, then joining her. We see her lying naked in Nathan's room, and then see him appearing to have intercourse with her. In all of this, she is eerie in her lack of emotion, the stereotypy of her reactions. Finally, we see that she is a robot, as she demonstrates for Caleb that she can remove sections of her skin, revealing a metallic surface.

At the same time, Caleb finds a series of closets with other robotic women, all inanimate. In a state of clear confusion, he seems to question his own identity, taking a razor and attempting to cut the skin on his forearm. As a viewer, not quite knowing the limits of the film I was watching, it crossed my mind that he, too, might turn out to be one of Nathan's creations[6]; and, I was as relieved as he was to see human tissue and blood beneath the surface. *My sense of the reality of what I was seeing was distorted as I immersed myself in the plot and tone of the film.* But even this misses a dimension of the film. Part of the artistry of this film is that it presents images hidden in plain sight. We see Kyoko as a strange, seemingly automated creature, and eventually we learn that she is a robot. But we should distinguish between what we understand from the plot and what we *see*.

We see a powerful man, powerful in body and in position, abusing a female employee. The actual images are of a man screaming at his young female servant for spilling some wine. We see him turning on music so that she will dance with him. We see her lying naked in his room, seemingly waiting. We see him having sex with her, and she impassive. This is a clear image of an abuse of power, gender abuse, sexual abuse, and interracial abuse. We do not register it fully, but we cannot be immune to it. *At some level, we react to what we are seeing rather than what we are being told.*

---

[6] In fact, Caleb was severely injured in the auto accident that killed his parents and underwent surgical repairs.

And what of Ava? One of the complicating factors for this film is that it fails what I will call the reverse Turing test. When we look at Ava, we do not see a robot. We see a woman playing a robot. Again, there is a discrepancy between what the film tells us we are seeing and what our eyes see, what we inevitably perceive.

What we see is a man holding a woman captive. Caleb is able to steal Nathan's key card when he is drunk at night. He goes on his computer and finds images of past AI's, a series of attractive women that Nathan has created and discarded. Poignantly, one of these women pounds violently on the glass partition in a fury of frustration at being unable to escape.

We are easily reminded of images of an abusive home in which the man of the house plays God, controlling and using the women, a nightmarish scene that we sometimes hear about from traumatized children and adults.

It is in this context that Caleb decides to save Ava. He visits her the next morning. By this time, he has learned that she controls the power shutdowns that have been occurring.

Caleb: "Don't talk. Just listen. You were right about Nathan. Everything you said."

Ava: "What's he going to do to me?"

Caleb: "He's going to reprogram your AI. Which is the same as killing you."

Ava: "Caleb, you have to help me."

Caleb: "I'm going to. We're getting out of here tonight."

Ava: "What? How?"

Caleb: "I get Nathan blind drunk. Then I take his keycard, and reprogram all the security protocols in this place. When he wakes, he's locked inside, and we've walked out of here. I only need you to do one thing. At ten o'clock tonight, trigger a power failure. Can you do that?"

When we enter a movie theater, we make a decision to enter the world of the film, temporarily, so that we may experience something that will move us, perhaps transform us. We know that we can act only through the characters on the screen, but how can we not respond to this rescue fantasy? How can we accept this abuse and allow this intelligent, responsive, emotionally sensitive woman to be killed?

In a prior meeting, Caleb and Ava had fantasized about going out in the world together, mingling with people, "a date." Now, he is going to make that happen. And he does. Through duplicity and counter-duplicity, he allows Ava to escape her prison.

But not all rescue fantasies play out smoothly. We are witness to a violent confrontation in a hallway in which Ava charges the threatening Nathan knocking him down, only to have him gain the upper hand, knocking off one of her metallic hands with an iron bar he is wielding. As he stands over Ava, Kyoko stabs him in the back with the kitchen knife she has been holding for much of the film. He turns and knocks off Kyoko's head, leaving her inert. Ava pulls the knife from Nathan's back and stabs him in the belly as he turns to face her. He stumbles down the hall and sinks down against the wall. Ava pulls the knife from his belly as we see him dying.

This scene of graphic violence is given a slight remove by being set in this eerie, sci-fi setting. Earlier in the film, Nathan has speculated that this new form of intelligence would one day replace the humans that had spawned it. It is intended as an ominous message, a sort of warning to those who play God. But it is far less ominous than the message hidden in what we see.

What we witness here, transposed to a hallway in an ordinary house or apartment, could easily be a final episode of extreme domestic violence, the battered wife's revenge.

As she heads to prepare herself for her escape, Ava tells Caleb, "You stay here." He remains where he is, recovering from a punch to the solar plexus from Nathan, while she replaces her missing hand and covers her artificial body with "skin" from the inanimate robots in the closets. Finally, she walks past him, opening a door with Nathan's keycard and leaves the startled Caleb behind, trapped in the prison that she is escaping, presumably to die.

This last betrayal leaves us helpless, with no one to trust, perhaps feeling somewhat like the children born into homes of mutual abuse. For us, for me, it was a temporary state, one in which we cannot trust our own feelings of love and faith in another.

It was a temporary state, but it lingered beyond the limits of the movie as I walked my way home, briefly knowing what it is like not to know that I can rely on the humanness of other people. Examining it leaves me—momentarily because that is all I can tolerate—aware of another horror, that *there are people who have endured enough abuse early in life that they experience most or all of the time what I went through for a brief period on an isolated evening.*

3

Lovers

Miracle on 34th Street

FOR THE PAST FEW winters, my teaching schedule has me reading Anna Freud's monograph, *The Ego and the Mechanisms of Defense* at around the same time that I come across the Christmas classic, *Miracle on 34th Street*. One wouldn't think that they have much in common, but each year I am re-reminded of passages in the book that come to life in the film.

Miracle on 34th Street is a light, beautifully constructed story about a bearded, white haired portly gentleman (Edmund Gwenn) who insists, and clearly believes, that he is the real Santa Claus. Although he gives as his address an old age home in Great Neck instead of the North Pole, he does go by the name of Kris Kringle. From the outset, the film pulls at us to disregard our "common sense" and join in the collective fantasy that this is truly Santa Claus.

The first "proof" of Santa is a public and superficial one, but it does enlist our sympathy, forcing us to choose sides. The story follows an arc that begins on Thanksgiving Day and ends on Christmas

Day. We are first introduced to Kris as a likeable oddball who attempts to correct the arrangement of reindeer in a storefront window. The fellow putting up the exhibit clearly thinks he's addled, but we are charmed, and since we are watching a movie, our expectations are flexible. As the story progresses, there are little bits of evidence that he may be Santa Claus. He knows all about toys and where they can be found, he speaks fluent Dutch to a refugee girl who has been adopted by an American family. Above all, he is kind and loving, the way we might expect Santa to be. We come to want him to be Santa.

Kris happens into the role of Santa in the Macy's Parade, replacing the hired Santa who is dead drunk by parade time. From there, he becomes the store Santa for Macy's where he wins over Mr. Macy himself by establishing an entire new ad campaign around sending parents to other stores for toys that Macy's doesn't have, winning Macy's a large quantity of good will.

There are suggestions throughout the story that Kris is concerned that the spirit of Christmas is being lost to commercialism. The tension is set up between idealism and cynicism and over the value of fantasy.

In an early scene, Kris talks with a teenager, Alfred, who sweeps floors at Macy's. Alfred tells him that he plays Santa at the local Y in Brooklyn.

Kris: "You enjoy impersonating me?"

Alfred: "Yeh."

Kris: "Why?"

Alfred: "I don't know. When I give packages to the little kids, I like to watch their faces get that Christmas look all of a sudden. It makes me feel kind'a good and important."

At this point, a Macy's employee comes in to give Kris a list of toys "that we have to push. Things that we're overstocked on." Kris is instructed that when a child is undecided, he should suggest one of those items. Kris is incensed. He tells Alfred, "Imagine. Making a child take something it doesn't want just because *he* bought too many of the wrong toys. That's what I've been fighting against for years, the way they commercialize Christmas."

It is no surprise that Kris is very upset when Macy's store psychologist, Granville Sawyer, "analyzes" Alfred, telling him that his desire to please children is based upon deep-seated guilt. He also has told Alfred that he hates his father. Kris has had his own problems with Sawyer, a grumpy man who has declared Kris psychotic and dangerous. By questioning Alfred's kindness, Sawyer forces us to choose sides not only over belief in fantasy, but over belief that people are capable of being kind and good.

In his confrontation with Mr. Sawyer, Kris gets so angry that he bops him on the head with his cane, giving Sawyer evidence that Kris is not only crazy, as he has contended, but also dangerous. Sawyer convinces one of the executives at Macy's to have Kris committed, bringing matters to a head and forcing us to choose sides between the kindly Santa who is being threatened with being held in a locked psychiatric unit and the mean, duplicitous Sawyer, who believes only in greed, aggression and personal advantage.

In the commitment trial, Kris's attorney, Fred Gailey (John Payne), first establishes that there is a Santa Claus by bringing the state's attorney's son to the stand to say that his father told him that there was a Santa Claus, then that Kris is Santa by showing that a huge pile of letters to Santa Claus have been directed to Kris in the courtroom by the post office. The judge, who wants no part of the political fallout from committing Santa Claus on Christmas Eve, declares that the United States Government has decided that Kris is Santa, throwing out the commitment. We have little choice other than to be drawn into the fun of Fred and Kris's victory.

But as a proof of Santa, this has a superficial quality. We enjoy the fun, but we can see the trickery. Kris, himself, sets the test on a more personal level. This "proof" revolves around a little girl and her mother who Kris sets as his test case. He has chosen them because they are kind people who have chosen not to accept fantasy in their lives.

This is where Anna Freud came into it. In Chapter six of *The Ego and the Mechanisms of Defense*, Ms. Freud (1936) talks about the use of fantasy as a normal childhood function. Starting with Little Hans and moving to examples of her own and other analysts who treat children, she demonstrates that children use fantasy to defend against realities with which their child-like egos could not otherwise contend. Little Hans ultimately solved his dilemma of being unable to compete with his father by developing a fantasy of a plumber who removes his genitals and replaces them with bigger ones. Ms. Freud points out that the fantasies exhibited by the children she and others have treated are "by no means peculiar to these particular children: they are universal in fairy tales and other children's stories." (p. 77)

The little girl in *Miracle on 34th Street*, Susan Walker (Natalie Wood), pointedly does not believe in fantasies or fairy tales. We first see her watching the Thanksgiving Day parade with her neighbor, Fred Gailey.

Fred: "Looks like they're having a little trouble with the baseball player."

Susan: "He was a clown last year. They just changed the head and painted him different. My mother told me."

Fred: "He certainly is a giant, isn't he?"

Susan: "Not really. There are no giants, Mr. Gailey."

Fred: "Well maybe not now, Susie, but in olden days there were a lot of …"

Susan shakes her head knowingly.

Fred: "Well, what about the giant that Jack killed?"

Susan: "Jack, Jack who?"

Fred: "Jack, Jack … Jack and the beanstalk."

Susan: "I never heard of that."

Fred: "You must have heard of that. You've just forgotten. It's a fairy tale."

Susan: "Oh, one of those. I don't know any fairy tales."

Fred: "Oh, your mother and father must have told you a fairy tale."

Susan: "No. My mother thinks they're silly. I don't know whether my father thinks they're silly or not. I never met my father. You see, my father and mother were divorced when I was a baby."

Fred: "Well, that baseball player certainly looks like a giant to me."

Susan: "People sometimes grow very big, but that's abnormal."

Fred: "I'll bet your mother told you that, too."

Susan comes across as precocious, a caricature of an adult. The lack of a capacity to fantasize looks odd in a child that age. A little later in the film, as she talks with Kris, we see that it is interfering with her ability to play with other children her age.

Kris: "What sort of games do you play with the other children in the apartment building?"

Susan: "I don't play much with them. They play silly games."

Kris: "They do?"

Susan: "Like today. They were in the basement playing zoo and all of them were animals! When I came down, Homer, he was supposed to be the zoo keeper, he said, 'What kind of animal are you?' And I said, 'I'm not an animal. I'm a girl.' He said, 'Only animals allowed here. Goodbye!' So I came upstairs."

Kris: "Why didn't you claim you were a lion or a bear?"

Susan: "Because I'm not a bear or a lion."

Kris: "Yes, but the other children were only children, but they were pretending to be animals."

Susan: "But that's what makes the game so silly."

Kris: "Oh, I don't think so. It sounds like a wonderful game to me. Of course, in order to play it, you've got to have an imagination. Do you know what the imagination is?"

Susan: "Oh, sure. That's when you see things, but they're not really there."

Kris: "Well, that can be caused by other things too. No, to me imagination is a place all by itself, another country. You've heard of the French nation, the British nation. Well this is the Imagi-nation. It's a wonderful place. How would you like to be able to make snowflakes in the summer time, eh? Or drive a great big bus right down Fifth Avenue? How would you like to have a ship all to yourself that makes daily trips to China or Australia? How would you like to be the Statue of Liberty in the morning and in the afternoon fly south with a flock of geese?"

He clearly has her astonished attention as she nods vigorously, her eyes wide. He goes on to teach her how to act like a monkey and has her dancing around the room grunting and scratching her side.

Here is the heart of the story, the importance of imagination and fantasy. We see Susan as lacking something vital. The beautiful and skillful child star, Natalie Wood, enlists us in her conflict over the wish to indulge in fantasy and the need to stick to reality.

The film, of course, while intended to engage children, engages adults as well. Without succeeding in that, I suspect it would be relegated to occasional showings on Nickelodeon or some suitable children's venue rather than being watched each year by nostalgic adults. Anna Freud was less sanguine about adult fantasy. She makes a slight concession at one point: "We know that in adult life, daydreams may still play a part, sometimes enlarging the boundaries of a too narrow reality and sometimes completely reversing the real situation. But in adult years a daydream is almost of the nature of a game, a kind of by-product with but a slight libidinal cathexis; at most it serves to master quite trifling quantities of discomfort or to give the subject an illusory relief from some minor unpleasure." (p.81)

But she adds a few lines later: "At any rate, it is certain that in adult life gratification through fantasy is no longer harmless. As long as more considerable quantities of cathexis are involved, fantasy and reality become incompatible; it must be one or the other. We know, too, that for an id impulse to make an irruption into the ego and there to obtain gratification by means of hallucination spells, for an adult, psychotic disease. An ego which attempts to save itself anxiety and renunciation of instinct and to avoid neurosis by denying reality is overstraining this mechanism." (p. 81)

We could speculate that the store psychologist, Sawyer, had read this passage before passing judgment on Kris. Anna Freud (circa 1936) might well have been brought in as an expert witness for the prosecution in Kris's commitment trial.

Susan's adult counterpart is her mother, Doris, who also lacks the ability to tolerate fantasy. In fact, it is Doris who has taught Susan to distrust her imagination. She and Fred have an ongoing dialogue about this aspect of child rearing.

Fred: "I see she (Susan) doesn't believe in Santa Claus, either. No Santa Claus, no fairy tales, no fantasies of any kind. Is that it?"

Doris: "That's right. I think we should be realistic and completely truthful with our children and not have them growing up believing in a lot of legends and myths like Santa Claus, for example."

They resume the conversation later when Doris takes Fred to task for taking Susan to meet Santa at Macy's.

Fred: "I'm sorry, but I couldn't see any harm in just letting her say hello to the old felluh."

Doris: "But I think there is harm. I tell her Santa Claus is a myth and you bring her down here, she sees hundreds of gullible children, meets a convincing old man with real whiskers. This sets up a very harmful mental conflict within her. What is she going to think? Who is she going to believe? And by filling them full of fairy tales, they grow up considering life a fantasy instead of a reality. ..."

It is through this subplot that the film wins us over. In Kris's words, we see how the public issue of the Christmas spirit and idealism is translated into a personal story: "You see Mrs. Walker, this is quite an opportunity for me. For the past fifty years or so I've been getting more and more worried about Christmas. It seems we're all so busy trying to beat the other fellow in making things go faster and look shinier and cost less and Christmas and I are sort of getting lost in the shuffle." She tries to reassure him that "Christmas is still Christmas." He responds, "Oh, Christmas isn't just a day. It's a frame of mind. And that's what's been changing. That's why I'm glad I'm here, maybe I can do something about it. And I'm glad I met you and your daughter. You two are a test case for me. ... Yes, you're sort of a test case in miniature. If I can win you two over, there's still hope."

When Fred Gailey offers to take him in as a roommate, he accepts, seeing it as an opportunity to have more time with Susan. He enlists Fred as an ally. Kris will work on Susie and Fred on Doris. In fact, when Kris is taken to Bellevue, he deliberately fails the psychiatric exam because, he explains, he thought that Doris had collaborated in his commitment. Fred convinces him that she didn't know about it and that he should not give up.

Kris is right, of course, because it is through Susan and Doris that he will win us over, the audience. Susan is taken with this kindly grandfatherly figure who sings her nursery rhymes at bedtime and blows bubble gum bubbles with her. She is also slowly won over by the fatherly Fred Gailey. A turning point comes at the time of Kris's commitment hearing.

Hearing about the commitment trial, Susan tells her mother that she has a feeling Kris is Santa Claus. "He's so kind and nice and jolly. He's not like anyone else. He must be Santa." To our surprise, Doris answers, "I think perhaps you're right, Susie." This is the first time she has called Susan by her diminutive name as Fred and Kris have. She is beginning to accept her as a child.

Susie decides to send Kris a letter to cheer him up. It reads: "Dear Mr. Kringle, My mother says you are sad now. I am writing to you because I want you to be happy again and to tell you that I believe all you told me and everything will turn out fine. I even believe you will get me the present I asked for. I hope you are not sad."

Seeing the letter, Doris adds, "I believe in you, too."

It is this letter directed to Kris Kringle at the court that starts the men in the post office thinking about sending their Santa letters to Kris at the courthouse.

Susie's present that she had asked for is a house, a two story colonial with a back yard and a swing in the back. Kris has told her that Santa can't give everything that every child wishes for, but he will try. After his case is dismissed, on Christmas Eve, Kris invites Doris, Susie and Fred to a Christmas party the next day at the old age home in Great Neck. There are presents under the tree, but Susie is bitterly disappointed that Santa has not given her the house she had wanted.

She tells Kris, "You couldn't get it because you're not Santa Claus. You're just a nice old man with whiskers, like my mother said. I shouldn't have believed you."

Doris says, with concern, "I was wrong when I told you that, Susie. You must believe in Mr. Kringle and keep right on doing it. You must have faith in him."

She goes on to tell her daughter that "Faith is believing in things when common sense tells you not to. I mean, just because things don't turn out the way you want them to the first time, you've still got to believe in people. I found that out."

Doris has been given a second chance, a chance to believe in people. I will return now to the dialogue between Fred and Doris over his taking Susan to see Santa.

Doris: "I tell her Santa Claus is a myth and you bring her down here, she sees hundreds of gullible children, meets a convincing old man with real whiskers. This sets up a very harmful mental conflict within her. What is she going to think? Who is she going to believe? And by filling them full of fairy tales, they grow up considering life a fantasy instead of a reality. They keep waiting for Prince Charming to come along. When he does, he turns out to be …"

Here Fred interrupts with a pointed interpretation, "We were talking about Susie, not about you."

We never do get to hear what Doris's Prince Charming, her ex husband, turned out to be. We are left to assume that he was not what he appeared to be, but turned out to be a cad who betrayed her love and her trust and left her clinging to "reality." Doris has been disillusioned in love and has decided that she won't be fooled again.

We have sensed that Doris's distrust of fantasy is extreme and pathologic. We are obviously concerned at her engendering that distrust in a child. But now we can see that she is trying to protect her daughter from later disappointment and, as Fred points out, is attempting to undo her own traumatic relationship through Susan.

But we are also led to suspect that Doris is trying to shut herself off from love. Her distrust of fantasy and imagination is itself a defense designed to protect her from the disappointment that we can feel if we allow ourselves to love. It points up to us that we depend upon some level of fantasy to allow us to enter into some of the most important relationships in our lives. It is likely that unconscious fantasy is closely tied to some of our strongest and most important emotions. Without such fantasies, how would we subvert our own interests to those of a beloved, a child or lover? In this sense, the film takes issue with Ms. Freud's dismissal of the importance of fantasy in adult life.[1]

---

[1] With the qualifier that she appeared to be talking about conscious fantasy.

Doris has been given her second chance through one of the most subtle romances in film history. It begins with Fred Gailey romancing the child to get to the mother. When Doris returns from the parade, she finds Susan in Fred's apartment, watching the ongoing parade from his window. They have been having their chat about the "giant" that we saw earlier and have a cozy relationship when Susan's mother enters. They tell each other that Susan has told them a lot about the other.

Serving her coffee, Fred makes a confession after Doris has thanked him for being so kind to Susan. He answers, "I must confess it's part of a deep dyed plot. I'm fond of Susie, very fond. But I also wanted to meet you. I read someplace that the surest way to meet the mother is to be kind to the child." While this sounds forthcoming, he has held back his trump card. As Susan and Doris are leaving the apartment, Susan asks her mother to invite Mr. Gailey to share their Thanksgiving turkey. Their scheming comes to light when she asks him, "Did I ask right?" Despite the duplicity, Doris good-naturedly tells him that dinner is at 3.

As significant as the words is the setting. Fred makes his pitch serving Doris coffee in his kitchen. This will be a domestic courtship. After their little tiff at Macy's over Fred taking Susan to see Santa Claus, we next find him in her kitchen, helping prepare dinner and even telling her it's time to take the meat out of the oven while Kris is in the dining room teaching Susan to be a monkey. He is wearing an apron and carrying a glass of milk when he goes out to see Kris and Susan. It is then that he gets the idea of inviting Kris to stay at his place. When Doris's phone rings, Fred answers it. He is winning his way into her home on the way to her heart.

The next time we see them together, they greet each other with smiles at her door and he kisses her on the cheek, telling her he reserved "our regular table at Luigi's." It is in this scene that he tells her he quit his job rather than drop Kris's case.

She says to him, "Look, darling, he's a nice old man and I admire you for wanting to help him, but you've got to be realistic and face facts. You can't just throw your career away because of a sentimental whim."

He tells her he will open his own law office, defending "people like Kris that are being pushed around. That's the only fun in law anyway. But I promise you, if you have faith in me and believe in me, everything will ... You don't have any faith in me, do you?"

She answers, "It's not a question of faith, it's just common sense."

He tells her the words that she will repeat back to Susan on Christmas Day. "Faith is believing in things when common sense tells you not to." He goes on to state the film's credo, "It's not just Kris that's on trial, it's all the things he stands for. It's kindness and joy and love and all the other intangibles."

Frustrated, she tells him to grow up. They begin to argue, and she says, "These last few days we've talked about some wonderful plans, and then you go on an idealistic binge." She looks lost and disturbed as he walks out the door.

In just a few short scenes with no more than a kiss on the cheek, Fred and Doris have begun to look like a married couple, calling each other "darling," having a regular table at the restaurant, making "wonderful plans," quarreling relatively gently about child rearing and career ambitions. There are never any dramatic turnings, any statements of love. As the film progresses, we see them drawing closer, closer in domestic ways, working in the kitchen together, discussing his career, talking about Susie.

That is because this is a love affair seen through the eyes of a child. Fred is fatherly before he is a suitor. He works his way into the lives of mother and daughter, setting the table, helping with the meal. This is a domestic romance. What is more, the issues of faith and idealism not only have to do with Kris being Santa Claus. Now, there is a second tension. Doris believing in Kris is tied to her believing in Fred, and that is tied to the prospect of their forming a family for Susie.

All of this comes together at the film's climax. At the end of the Christmas party at which Susie has been disappointed at not getting her present, Kris gives Fred specific directions for driving back to the city. As they are driving, following Kris's directions, they already look like an intact family with Fred driving, Doris beside him and Susie in the back, trying to convince herself to have faith.

Susie suddenly tells "Uncle Fred" to stop the car. She runs into a house with a "for sale" sign on the lawn. Running in, she announces that this is her house from Santa, the one she had asked for. Excitedly, she sees that there is a swing in the back. She tells Fred that her mother had told her that if things didn't work out the first time you still have to believe.

He turns to Doris. "You told her that?" They embrace and kiss. "The sign outside says it's for sale. We can't let her down."

"I never really doubted you. It was just my silly common sense."

Then, Fred and Doris see Kris's cane propped up near the fireplace, the final proof.

Susie's house is the miracle that gives conviction that Kris is Santa, but Santa's gift to Susie, Doris and Fred is much more than a house. His true gift, the one that reaches our hearts and makes us want to believe, is an intact family.

As psychoanalysts we focus on the conflicts within the family, the Oedipus complex, clumsily alluded to by the store psychologist to Alfred when he tells him he hates his father. But we all know that there is also a very powerful, ubiquitous wish on the part of every child, and every adult who was a child, to have an intact family. It is that wish that finally pulls us in. We know that whatever the circumstances of our lives when we happen to see *Miracle on 34th Street*, we still hold a place in our minds for the comforts and loving of family, the loving relationships of parents and children and parents and parents. If Santa Claus can give a fatherless child a loving father, then we have to believe. That is the fantasy that the film uses to comfort and warm us and that allows us for that moment to want to believe in Santa Claus.

Freud, Anna (1936) *The Ego and the Mechanisms of Defense*. (English Translation; 1966 Edition) New York; International Universities Press.

Lovers

High Noon[2]

ANOTHER COUPLE TRYING TO start a family discovers that sometimes a train isn't just a train.

We cannot literally put Marshal Will Kane on the analytic couch, but he has much in common with a young man who was analyzed by Dr. Jacob Arlow.

Post 9/11, the idea of a town under threat from psychopathic killers reverberates with our personal fears. *High Noon* is a film about coping with dangerous bullies, about terror and its effect upon a community. Its pertinence to our current situation is one example of its universal appeal. In its own time, it was a statement about the McCarthy era and the need for courage. The outer dangers change in form from generation to generation, while the inner dangers with which they reverberate are more constant.

High Noon was released in 1952. Along with *Shane*, it was heralded as a mature, psychological western. It won awards at the time and quickly became established as a "classic". Most readers have probably seen it, but not in many years.

The story is about a small town marshal, Wil Kane, who discovers on the morning of his wedding day, as he is about to retire and leave town, that a vicious killer, Frank Miller, has been pardoned and is returning to town on the noon train to exact vengeance on the marshal who arrested him. At first, Wil heads out of town with his new bride as originally planned, urged on by his friends, but he turns back to face Miller and his three cronies. They wait for Miller at the train station while Wil tries to recruit deputies to help him. As he goes through the town, he gets no takers. Most turn him down out of cowardice and practicality. They argue that Frank Miller's only interest is Kane; so that it is in their best interest and Kane's if he would leave. Kane's deputy, Harvey, backs out because he feels slighted that

---

[2] With much thanks to the members of the NY chapter of the Psychoanalytic Study of Film who discussed this film in June, 1999.

he was not chosen to replace Kane as marshal. The only ones to offer help are a middle-aged drunk and a boy.

Kane's bride, Amy, became a Quaker after her brother and father were killed in a gunfight. She wants no part of more violence and waits at the hotel near the train station, ready to leave on that same noon train while the film's recurrent theme song keeps wailing, "Do not forsake me, oh, my darling, on this our wedding day."

The story has been generally understood as a psychologically minded tale of a man who has the courage of his convictions. He will not accept somewhat reasonable rationalizations to skirt what he sees as his responsibility, and he knows that running, once begun, can never stop. He is afraid, but knows he must face his fear. One of the powers of the film is that we can easily identify with the fear that Kane and the townspeople feel. The gunmen waiting at the train station look frightening. There are few of us who would not be very tempted to accept the rationalizations to avoid this fight, and at some level we know it.

The film begins with contrast, the ornery gunmen preparing to enter the town and the smiles on the faces of the townspeople at the wedding of Wil and Amy Kane. When it is realized that Frank Miller is arriving on the noon train, bent on revenge, Wil and Amy are rushed out of town on a wagon.

Wil is barely out of town when he realizes that he must go back to face the threat, against his wife's pleas. He explains his reasons over time. He feels a sense of responsibility. The new marshal won't be arriving until the next day. He also feels that if he runs now he will have to run for the rest of his life. "What's a hundred miles? They'd come after us. We'd never be able to keep that store, Amy. They'd come after us and we'd have to run again, as long as we live." We have all known the fear of a confrontation, the conflicting urges to flee and stay.

A patient described in the psychoanalytic literature a few years after *High Noon* appeared similarly had to face a man who could hurt him.

"'I went to see Ms. X, the secretary, at the University. ... This time I got the word. 'The financial officer wants to see you.' I had sent a letter of complaint regarding a delay in getting paid. Now, two weeks later I was told, 'Mr. P. wants to see you about the letter.' I had the thought, 'I'll be punished.' I felt scared." (Arlow, 1959 p. 616)

As he waited in the outer office, he betrayed the urge to flee with his gaze:

"Suddenly, I looked out the window at the fields and the surrounding landscape."

He, too, was contemplating a "wedding day."

"The patient at this time was engaged to an attractive young woman of his own faith and found himself in a serious conflict over whether to have intercourse with her." (Arlow, 1959, pp. 615-616)

Kane's "serious conflict" over Amy appears to have nothing to do with sex, but with his fear of losing her if he confronts Frank Miller. The song tells us that that is his greatest fear. "I'm not afraid of death, but, oh, what will I do if you leave me?"

Amy is a Quaker. Her father and brother were killed defending what was right. Now, she is against all violence. She cannot understand why her husband would stay to fight and decides that if he will she cannot stay with him. She cannot tolerate a violent image of her husband and will not allow herself to be re-traumatized with another violent death of a loved one. She leaves Wil with the intention of taking the noon train out of town. Her abandonment of her new husband is particularly painful as he prepares to face his deadly enemy.

Amy Kane is an innocent. One of the first things that we notice about her is that she (Grace Kelly) is much younger than her husband (Garry Cooper). We are not even sure, at first, if this difference is intended or merely an artifact of casting. But, Wil is not merely older looking; he is more experienced than Amy in the ways of the world. His former lover was the sophisticated Helen Ramirez.

When Kane goes to the town hotel to warn Helen that Frank Miller is coming, he finds Amy there, seeking harbor away from the lecherous gunmen at the train station.

As he starts up the stairs towards Helen Ramirez's room, the hotel clerk asks, with dripping sarcasm, "Think you can find it all right?"

The comment is meant as much for Amy as for Wil, and Wil looks back at Amy as he continues up the stairs.

After Kane leaves the hotel, Amy approaches the hotel clerk.

"Who is Miss Ramirez?"

"Mrs. Ramirez? She used to be a friend of your husband's a while back. Before that she was a friend of Frank Miller's."

Arlow's patient does not describe a former lover, but there is another woman, with whom he is less conflicted about his sexuality:

"I went to Mr. P's office and saw Miss X, his secretary. I've had lots of sexual thoughts about her. I'd often watch her walk down the halls and would have the thought, I'd like to climb into bed with her." (1959, p. 616)

Arlow has told us that (like Wil Kane) this man's former lover was of an ethnic background different from his own, presumably further from the image of his mother or sister.

Sex is brought in subtly in this fifties film. Frank Miller's younger brother, Ben, leers at Amy at the train station. We are given a hint of sexual danger to come. Ben says to the other two gunmen, "Hey, that wasn't here five years ago." One of them answers with a surly, "So what?", to which Ben replies, "Nothing, yet." For the gunmen, Amy is a sexual object. If Kane cannot defeat Miller's gang, the innocent Amy is in danger of sexual attack. Amy Kane's fear and abhorrence of violence takes on an additional, sexual meaning.

On the surface, Kane's confrontation with Frank Miller has nothing to do with sex, and yet it does. When Kane goes to warn Helen Ramirez, she greets him with hostility, although we have seen her admiring him in front of others, particularly her young jealous lover, Harvey, the deputy. When Helen sees Kane enter her room, she stares at him, then snaps,

"What are you looking at? You think I have changed? Well what do you want? You want me to help you? You want me to ask Frank to let you go? You want me to beg for you? Well, I would not do it. I would not lift a finger for you."

Hell hath no greater fury than a woman scorned. Clearly, Kane left her.

He explains that he came to warn her that Frank Miller was coming:

"I think you oughta get out of town. I might not be able to ... . Well, anything can happen."

"I'm not afraid of him," she answers.

"I know you're not, but you, you know how he is."

"I know how he is. Maybe he doesn't know."

"He's probably got letters."

In this brief dialogue we see the artistry of the filmmakers. Without saying anything explicitly, the film has planted in us the seed of an idea that Frank Miller's hatred of Kane goes beyond the arrest. There is a sexual rivalry. Kane has slept with Miller's woman after sending Miller to jail. Miller's younger brother has been eyeing Kane's bride and Kane has taken Miller's woman after defeating him.

It is in the context of that sexual rivalry, not quite fully in our awareness, that we wait for the noon train. With mounting tension, we see the clocks in the town advancing towards noon, almost in real time as we watch the film. Someone in our film study group wisely raised the issue of the meaning and significance of that train. It certainly focuses us on the issue of time and the inevitability of that confrontation as it approaches with Mussolinian ruthlessness. In that sense, it gives us a sense of death and all the other inevitabilities that we know we will one day have to face. It is a deadline.

But the train has another meaning, another inevitable collision, in the language of our unconscious fantasies. A train is a powerful, heavy machine that carries enormous momentum as it speeds towards its destination. Children, particularly boys, are drawn to the phallic image of trains speeding through tunnels, down tracks towards their inevitable destinations. This train will penetrate the town and bring with it seemingly unbridled violence when it plants its evil seed in the form of Frank Miller.

The phallic image of the train approaching the town to deposit its violent passenger creates a complementary image in the town, which becomes a passive female receptacle ready to be violated. There stands Wil Kane, forced to do battle with the frightening intruder, much like another of Arlow's patients who entertained an unconscious fantasy of doing battle with his father at the entrance to the vagina. (Arlow, 1991) The patient we have been following had a similar fantasy.

"As the conflict over whether to have intercourse with his fiancée was becoming more intense," (p.619) the patient's associations linked thinking about having intercourse with her with dreams of snakes attacking him from a woman's vagina and thoughts of crashing his car into another in a tunnel and having fistfights with a man, there. (Arlow, 1959)

"Let us compare the objective situation [in the waiting room outside the treasurer's office] with the patient's unconscious fantasy. In reality, the patient found himself with a sexually tempting woman while waiting to enter the inner office. In the office was an authority figure, an adversary, with whom he might quarrel over money. This configuration corresponds to the elements of his unconscious fantasy—namely, an encounter with the father and/or his phallus within the body of the mother." (Arlow, 1969, p. 12)

Like Arlow's patient (in his unconscious fantasy), Wil Kane is anticipating a violent confrontation, "an encounter with the father and/or his phallus within the body of the mother." But, as an older brother (to Ben), as the seed deposited by the phallic train, as a contemporary of Kane, almost his antithesis, Frank Miller can also be seen as a brother, perhaps an evil twin, who enters into a life and death battle with Kane in the womb.

Arlow's patient gives us a clue as to how that battle is to be won. While waiting with the secretary outside the treasurer's office, he experienced a *dejas vu*. Looking out of the window at the surrounding landscape, he had the uncanny feeling that he had seen it before and been through it before. The analysis traced that symptom to a defense against his anxiety connected to his memory of the bible story of Jacob stealing his father's blessing with his mother's help. The patient's mother had often reassured him when he had been afraid that he had been through it before and survived.

Like Arlow's patient, like Jacob in the bible, Wil Kane needs the support and approval of the woman to be successful in his encounter. Wil is upset at the failure of the townspeople to help him, but he is most deeply troubled by Amy leaving him, a theme hammered home repeatedly through the song. He needs her to defeat his rival, but there is more.

He also must have her support to overcome her fears. As we have seen, Amy's pacifism is not just a wish for peace and brotherly love; it has a sexual meaning. Amy is an innocent, a virgin. Her fear of violence extends unconsciously to a fear of the aggressiveness of sexuality.

Similarly, Kane is conflicted about deflowering his new virginal bride. This is a film about a wedding day. Frank Miller does not only represent a powerful, aggressive rival. As was quite rightly pointed out by a member of the study group, Miller and his gang, train and all, also represent the aggressive sexual urges that the groom is struggling to come to terms with on his wedding day as he draws closer to the conjugal bed. ("High noon" becomes midnight.) This adds meaning to the opening scene in which he attempts to ride off alone with his new bride. He turns around—he is not ready. Can he tame the violent, sadomasochistic passions in himself without compromising his proper role as a sexual aggressor? These are the conflicts and demons he must face before he can properly ride off with his bride. It is the similarity between Kane and Frank Miller—they are both gunmen—that frightens Amy.

For this reason, despite our wish for Wil to recruit help from the townspeople, this is a conflict that Wil and Amy must confront themselves. Like Arlow's patient, unconsciously unable to complete intercourse without the woman's approval and support, Kane needs Amy's acceptance, support, and ultimately collusion with his violence in order to consummate the marriage.

This is the key to the film's resolution. Through clever tactics, daring maneuvers and good marksmanship (as well as the bad guys' inability to hit him with their first shots), Wil succeeds in paring down the gang. At a crucial moment, Amy, who has left the train at the first sound of gunfire, thinking Wil has been shot, overcomes her own scruples and fears and shoots one of the gang members. In the final confrontation, Frank Miller grabs Amy and tries to use her as a shield, but she scratches his face and struggles free long enough for Wil to shoot him. Together, Wil and Amy have overcome the wedding night jitters. Amy Kane's participation in the violence has not only molded them as a family, but has also given Kane tacit approval to do the loving violence that we know will come as they ride off to begin their new life.

Arlow, J.A. (1959). The Structure of the Déjà Vu Experience. *Journal of the American Psychoanalytic Association.*, 7:611-631.
Arlow, J.A. (1991). Methodology and Reconstruction. *Psychoanalytic Quarterly* 60:539-563.

Forbidden Planet

SOME DAY YOU CAN tell your grandchildren (it might even be now) that there was a time (1956) when psychoanalysis was so prominent in the popular culture that it was used as the basis for the plot of a glossy, high budget science fiction film with flying saucers and a powerful humanoid robot. I'm referring to the film, *Forbidden Planet*, which brought us the tagline, "Monsters from the Id."

Before analyzing the monsters, it's worthwhile going over some other interesting points about this relatively forgotten "sci-fi classic." Gene Rodenderry reportedly took ideas from *Forbidden Planet* in his construction of *Star Trek*. A modern viewer will, in fact, feel very comfortable with the opening scenes onboard a flying saucer whose interior will easily remind us of the inner workings and crew of the Starship Enterprise. One notable exception, which is important for the plot of the film, is the absence of women aboard ship. In fact, although it will undoubtedly be common in the 23rd century, it would have seemed out of place in 1956 to have women aboard a military expeditionary ship. One little detail that Rodenderry may have co-opted directly is the presence of cylindrical compartments in which the men stand to be put into some form of alternate existence to help them tolerate the gravitational effects of slowing down from hyperdrive (from speeds well beyond the speed of light). Although these are not used to beam anyone down or up, they will also be familiar to the modern viewer.

This film was also a debut performance for "Robbie the Robot," who went on to have a successful Hollywood career. He looks halfway between a mechanical man and an R2D2 type of robot, with rotating parts and fiery lines that we would associate with digital or wave imagery. Also of note, is that the film uses electronically produced music to create an odd otherworldly effect.

There are aspects of *Forbidden Planet* that betray broad ambition. It was unlike most, if not all, its science fiction predecessors in its budget and style. Internet sources, including Wikipedia and the IMDb website point out that until that time, science fiction films were low budget, in black and white, with ensemble actors. Science Fiction was primarily relegated to the "B" movie category.[3]

Forbidden Planet was made with a respectable budget. It was in color and presented in "cinemascope," a wide screen effect. Perhaps more significantly, it featured Walter Pidgeon as Dr. Morbius and Ann Francis as his daughter, Altaira or Alta. Pidgeon was a very well known and well respected actor with classic theater skills and Ann Francis was a hot young starlet. We will also recognize the other male lead, Leslie Nielsen as Captain Adams, although I don't think he was of the same stature as the other two at the time.

Perhaps of even more interest in terms of the film's artistic ambitions is the fact, noted in several internet sites, that the plot was taken from Shakespeare's, *The Tempest*. In fact, the Wikipedia article about the film states prominently that "The characters and setting were inspired by Shakespeare's *The Tempest* and the plots are very similar." It is easy to line up corresponding characters—Prospero/Morbius,

---

[3] I don't know if the term "B" movie had this exact connotation, but keep in mind that in the '50's, double features were common and the science fiction was often relegated to the second feature role.

Miranda/Altaira, Ariel/Robbie the Robot, Ferdinand/Captain Adams and Caliban/the Monster. *The Tempest* takes place on an island under the control of a powerful magician, Prospero, who lives there with his beautiful daughter. Prospero causes a shipwreck, stranding a group of travelers (well known to Prospero) on the enchanted island. In *Forbidden Planet*, the island is an isolated planet (the fourth planet of the star Altair, or Altair 4) with an earth-like atmosphere and the magician is a scientist whose magic rests on the powerful equipment left behind by a superior, extinct race, the Krell. Nevertheless, the plot details diverge from that point.

The film may have been based on *The Tempest*, but I think we could make a closer comparison with *Oedipus Rex*. For all the sci fi distractions and the somewhat wooden romance between Captain Adams (Nielsen) and Alta (Francis), this is the story of a powerful king (Pidgeon) who is aware of a terrible hidden murderer in his kingdom only to find that the murderer is himself. In fact, it is a particularly interesting variation on *Oedipus Rex* because here we see Oedipus not as a son but as a father caught up in much the same tragic dynamics with his daughter. For this purpose, Pidgeon plays his part beautifully until the very end, reciting his lines with a beautiful baritone voice and with elocution and pacing worthy of Shakespeare or Sophocles.

At the outset, Dr. Morbius (Pidgeon) makes his appearance as either a threatening presence or a prophet of doom as he warns the expeditionary force circling over his planet that they must turn away lest something terrible happen to them. Captain Adams has orders to explore the planet in order to find out what happened to the colonists who arrived on Altair 4 twenty years earlier. He is a simple straightforward man who obeys his orders.

Dr. Morbius reluctantly gives them landing coordinates and sends a high speed land transport device driven by Robbie the Robot. The robot conveys Morbius's invitation to take their leaders, Captain Adams, Lieutenant Farman and Dr. Ostrow, to his home. His greeting to them could be from the classic theater.

"How ironic, that a simple scholar with no ambition beyond a modest measure of seclusion should out of a clear sky find himself besieged by an army of fellow creatures all grimly determined to be of service to him." After Adams apologizes, saying, "We do have our orders," Morbius continues, "But of course you will stay for lunch and do forgive the ill manners of an old recluse."

Clearly he feels he must satisfy their curiosity, but if we pay close attention, we may hear signs of his ambivalence as he objects to the visit with subtle sarcasm while inviting them in for lunch. Since his objective should be to get them in and out, we might also wonder as he brags about his creation, the powerful robot that he "tinkered together in the first few months here," opening the door for greater curiosity. But if we have any doubts about his ambivalence or the film's underlying tension, we are given clearer evidence as he gives a demonstration of Robbie's (and his own) peaceful nature.

Wishing to demonstrate that Robbie is not dangerous, Morbius has the robot point a blaster at Captain Adams and instructs him to shoot. Robbie's circuits begin to sizzle as he cannot respond to the command, having been programmed with "his basic inhibitions against harming rational beings."[4] But as we see Robbie pointing the weapon at the captain, we are struck by the sense of menace conveyed under the guise of demonstrating an attitude of peace. We are being prepared for the presence of unconscious conflict.

In answer to their questions, Morbius explains that the members of the Bellerephon party all succumbed to some dark, incomprehensible planetary force that literally tore them limb from limb. "Only my wife and I were immune." He attributes this immunity to their love for the planet and describes how heartbroken they were when the vote was taken to return to Earth. "How could we have foreseen the extinction of so many co-workers and friends?" He explains that his wife had died a few months later of natural causes.

In answer to questions about the strangeness of his never having seen further evidence of the force, Morbius answers ominously and

---

[4] Science fiction aficionados of that era will recognize this as a basic rule of robotics created by Isaac Asimov.

with prescience, "Only in nightmares of those times, and yet always in my mind I seem to feel the creature is lurking somewhere close at hand, sly and irresistible and only waiting to be re-invoked for murder."

As if in association to these last words, a new voice appears on the heels of his invoking "murder." "Father, ..." It is, of course, Alta, a beautiful young woman dressed provocatively and bearing an innocent smile for the men.

What follows could be taken for a typical interchange between a doting father and a sly teen who knows how to get around him.

"Alta, I specifically asked you not to join us for lunch!"

"But, Father, lunch is over. I'm sure you never said a word about not coming in for coffee. Did you or did you?"

It is obvious that Morbius didn't want the men to know about his daughter, but curiously he has a pleasant smile on his face as she flirts with them.

"I've always so terribly wanted to meet a young man and now three of them at once. You're lovely, Doctor. The two end ones are unbelievable."

Alta's presence immediately creates conflict amongst the officers. Lieutenant Farman flirts with her and warns her away from the captain, telling her that he's notorious in seven planetary systems. When Morbius explains that his daughter has never seen a man other than himself, Doc Ostrow explains in kind that the young men on the ship have not seen a woman in over a year.

Despite Morbius's attempts to keep Alta away from the ship, she circumvents him with the same childish tricks. "He told me to stay away from the ship, but he didn't say how far away." Just as Morbius appears to be unable to control Alta, Captain Adams implies that he cannot control his men. He catches Lieutenant Farman teaching Alta how to kiss, sends him away and angrily rebukes Alta for her scanty dress and for provoking his men. By the next scene, he is kissing her himself.

Now the pattern of violence escalates. A mysterious unseen force enters the ship and destroys an important piece of equipment. Knowing that this must be connected to Morbius, Captain Adams and Doc Ostrow go to confront him.

Hearing about the sabotage on the ship, Morbius decides to let the captain and the doctor in on his secret, leading them into his laboratory, a large room filled with strange devices and flashing lights and meters all around the walls. It is now that we learn that he has come upon the fantastic scientific achievements of a superior, extinct race, the Krell. Morbius shows them a pad (we would think of it as a large IPad or Kindle) from which he was able to learn the history and wisdom of the Krell. Another device attaches to the skull, allowing Morbius to use his mind to create from his thoughts a temporary sculpture of his daughter. When Adams wants to try to use it, Morbius warns him that when he first tried that, he was shocked into a coma for over a day, but woke up with a dramatic increase in his intelligence that had allowed him to begin to use and understand the Krell technology.

He takes them into a giant atomic generating system 20 miles wide and 80 levels down, providing the potential for the enormous power of the Krell machinery. Morbius explains that the Krell had achieved fantastic heights to their civilization, living in a peaceful state for generations; but, as they approached some new level of achievement, something went wrong and the entire population was wiped out by some terrible, mysterious force.

While Captain Adams and Dr. Morbius argue over Adams's plan to turn the Krell information and equipment over to the United Planets, a new invisible intruder enters the ship, this time bearing enough weight to bend the steps and create large footprints in the sand. This time a crew member is killed in the brutal style of the murders of the Bellerephon crew described by Morbius. As Morbius and the captain are talking, Alta runs in to say that she has had a frightening dream about something terrible attacking the ship.

Once again, there is violence attached to dreams. We are being led to the film's psychoanalytic secret. The captain sets up a perimeter at night to fight off the unseen attacker. They wait as their radar picks up movement of a large force coming towards them, but still they see nothing. As the force approaches their perimeter, they begin to fire at it. The glow of the weapons fire meeting resistance outlines a terrible monster of no clearly definable shape, something like a cross between a large animal and a genie, which has no form of its own, and only takes form from the impact it has and reflects from its surroundings, unnatural footprints in the sand and shapes defined by the bouncing of the weapons fire. I have used this image in classes to try to describe the relationship of the drives to the ego, the drives having no form, only force that is given form by the ego that gives it expression through attempts at gratification and defense.

Now, we see glimpses of Morbius, asleep with his Krell machinery, the lights of the Krell apparatus flashing wildly. As he wakes up, the monster disappears. We now have enough to know what is happening and await only its elucidation in words. The captain and the doctor return to Morbius's laboratory. While Captain Adams is comforting Alta, the doctor sneaks in and boosts his intelligence with the Krell equipment, throwing himself into a terminal state, but giving himself the enlightenment that escaped Morbius. As he lies dying, Doc Ostrow tells Captain Adams, "Morbius was too close to the problem. The Krell had completed the project. Big machine. No instrumentalities. True creation. But the Krell forgot one thing, monsters, John, monsters from the id."

Doc Ostrow dies before he can explain the id to the captain. He must turn to an angry Morbius for an explanation. "Id, id, id, id. It's an obsolete term, I'm afraid once used to describe the elementary basis of the subconscious mind."

Now the captain understands it all. The giant Krell machinery is designed to create and transport matter and energy throughout the planet under the control of the Krell mind. "Creation by mere thought. But like you, the Krell forgot one deadly danger, their own subconscious hate and lust for destruction. ... And so those mindless beasts of the subconscious had access to a machine that could never be shut down. The secret devil of every soul on the planet all set free at once to loot and maim and take revenge, Morbius, and kill."

Morbius laments, still unaware of the significance, "My poor Krell. After a million years of shining sanity, they could hardly have understood what power was destroying them."

Now, like an analyst, Adams must interpret Morbius's resistance to the idea that his own subconscious has been committing the violent crimes that they had witnessed. As they hear the beast approaching them from outside, Alta clings to Adams.

Morbius: "I feel sorry for you, young man."

Adams: "Feel sorry for your daughter, Morbius."

Alta: "It's listening."

Morbius: "Alta go into my study."

Adams: "You still refuse to face the truth."

Morbius: "What truth?"

Adams: "Morbius, that thing out there, it's you."

Morbius: "You're insane. How else would you have led it here where Alta must see you torn to pieces?"

Adams: "You still think she's immune? She's joined herself to me, body and soul."

Alta: "Yes, and whatever comes, forever."

Morbius: "Say it's a lie. Shout! Let it hear you out there. Tell it you don't love this man!"

Alta: "Not even if I could."

The meaning is obvious. The force outside the door is the father's jealous rage directed at the loving couple.

Robbie can't shoot at the force, prompting Adams to say, "It's no use. He knows it's your other self." From a technical point of view, we might argue that Adams has committed an error, allowing Morbius to dissociate from his id by calling it "your other self." On the other hand, he provides Morbius with just enough defense in this dissociation to allow him to accept that the monster comes from himself.

As Morbius, like Oedipus, finally recognizes the reality, he picks up on this language, crying that it's his "evil self." "Guilty, guilty! My evil self is at that door and I have no power to stop it."

As the monster breaks through Krell metal to get at them, he finally puts himself in its path, saying "I deny you. I give you up." As he is struck down, the beast disappears. Morbius tells Adams to turn some machinery that will set in motion the destruction of the planet.

This is the film's psychoanalytic explanation, that the destructive force of the planet is coming from the mind of Morbius, an enraged father protecting his daughter and keeping her close and under his protection. The monster from the id, human rage and jealousy, has been turned upon its fellow men and finally itself.

Like Oedipus, Morbius is aware of a terrible crime committed on his planet twenty years earlier, the death of his fellow colonists. Like Oedipus, Morbius, with much outside interpretation from Captain Adams, comes to realize that he was the murderer. But we have not exhausted Oedipus's crime. Yes, he discovered that he was his father's murderer, but that may have been his lesser crime. Oedipus also discovers that he has made love with his mother and that she bore his children. It is perhaps the act of incest that drives him to gouge his eyes, a brutal equivalent of castration.

One of the strangest and most important insights of Freud and of psychoanalysis is that our superego, our conscience is born in the cauldron of early childhood fantasy. It does not follow the pattern that it would take if constructed by a logical ethicist, leading to some very perplexing twists in which incest may be a more compelling crime than murder.

Morbius acknowledges no sexual crime. How could he in the relatively puritanical climate of film in 1956? Unlike Oedipus, he has not killed his father and certainly does not make love to his mother. But the analogy holds if we flip the generational picture and look at those relationships from the point of view of Morbius as a father, in rivalry with his future son-in-law for the love of his daughter.[5] That rivalry stands out in a brief dialogue between Alta and her father after the monster has attacked the camp, killing several men (including the first to kiss her, Lieutenant Farman).

Alta runs to her father screaming that she has had a terrible dream.

"There was blood and fire and thunder and something awful was moving in the middle of it. I could hear it roar and bellow."

---

[5] The contemporaneous play, *A View from the Bridge*, recently revived on Broadway, has similar dynamics, but the protagonist in Morbius's place is the girl's uncle who has taken on the role of father.

Morbius holds her in his arms and reassures her that a dream can't hurt her.

She says, "Not me. Not us. The thing I saw was trying to break into camp. It was gonna kill ... You'll take care of him for me, won't you father? You'll protect him."

He answers, "My darling, I'm completely helpless so long as he remains here so willfully."

Alta knows who it is the monster wants to kill, even if she has not yet identified the monster with her father, and he implicitly understands who she means. It is also evident at this point, with unspoken words, that she has chosen Captain Adams as her lover.

Sexuality plays a big part in this film. It is the scantily clad Alta, the only woman in the film, who provokes conflict amongst the men. It is her appearance that reinvigorates the plot. I pointed out that her entrance comes just after Morbius has described his sense that the monster is still present, lurking in his dreams and waiting to strike again. In fact, we later see that she is the catalyst for unleashing that monster as Morbius presumably recognizes the men's sexual attraction to his daughter.

Morbius appears to recognize that danger, initially warning Alta not to come to lunch with them and later warning her away from the ship. But he has no control over her as she thwarts him with her trick phrases, "But lunch is over; He didn't say how far away." This is cute, but it has to raise a question. If Morbius is so protective of his daughter as to unleash murderous rage, how is it that he is so lax in protecting her from masculine attention? We never see him angry or insistent with her.

It is not as if Morbius is incapable of righteous rage. When the captain and the doctor enter his study to find it empty, they begin to look at a set of hieroglyphs on his desk. Entering from an inside passage, Morbius admonishes them in a stentorian voice, "You'll find the household silver in the dining room and my daughter's jewelry on her dressing table." (For some reason that particular phrase has stuck in my mind over the years.) Later, he will rail at the doctor for trying to boost his intelligence through the Krell equipment. Why can't he control his daughter?

That is left to a surrogate. When Captain Adams finds his lieutenant, Farman "teaching" Alta how to kiss and hug, he sends him away and becomes infuriated. Alta is confused. She has never been spoken to this way, but she responds by trying to comply with his demand that she cover herself better, asking Robbie to make her a new dress that will cover everything.

Adams takes a parental tone with her, filling the gap left by her father. But we see through him, if not then, soon afterward. He sees her swimming and realizes she is nude. Turning his head away, he waits for her to come out and sees her in her new dress, which covers more, but is nevertheless quite sexy. Now, he kisses her and this time she responds in a way she didn't with Farman. She responds to the man who approaches her in a more parental way. He, in turn, reveals that behind his angry reproaches about her behavior with his lieutenant is his own sexual attraction to her.

Is the film giving us a more acceptable model for the thin line between parental protection and parental attraction? There is some evidence for this in Morbius's own anomalous reaction. Despite his stated concerns, he seems to be enjoying his daughter's flirtatiousness in the opening scenes. He wears an indulgent smile. Is his inability to control Alta an inability to exert a moral force with his daughter or evidence of his deep ambivalence about her raging sexuality? Why does an adolescent girl living only with her father and some pet animals wear only miniskirts and sleeveless dresses? Whose sexual pleasure is aroused?

We never see direct evidence of Morbius's sexual attraction to Alta, but the film presents us with an associative hint when Captain Adams appears to take on a parental role, scolding Alta and telling her to dress less provocatively, only to reveal that his remonstrance disguises and reveals his own sexual desire when we next see him kissing her.

Why does a father become so enraged at a man who covets his daughter? I'm reminded of a line from an old Ian and Sylvia song, "When he comes to call, her pa aint got no good word to say; that's cause he was the same in his younger days." It is not a leap to think that Morbius identifies with the men's attraction to his daughter. In fact, it is a more acceptable form of his sexual feelings towards her. This would explain his indulgence as she first titillates them, but it turns to rage when the sexuality becomes more overt.

It brings us back to Morbius's claim to being "a simple scholar with no ambition beyond a modest measure of seclusion." He is not merely alone working in his study. He is inhabiting the planet with his own beautiful adolescent daughter. We might wonder about his wife's death "of natural causes." We are quickly turned away from any questioning of her death. Her untimely death, described in passing, is as convenient to the plot as the death of Oedipus's father. Certainly her death allows us to imagine a planet on which a still virile looking Walter Pidgeon is living with a sexy, wide-eyed Ann Francis.

As the monster approaches them threateningly, the dynamics are brought as close to the surface as the censorship—Morbius's and the film's—will allow.

He tells Alta, "Say it's a lie. Shout! Let it hear you out there. Tell it you don't love this man."

She answers, "Not even if I could."

If Morbius identifies with the lascivious men, both in an understated pleasurable way at first, and in a more conflicted way when the kissing gets serious, and also projects his own sexual desires onto them, then his murderous rage, attributed so easily to the id alone takes on a new meaning, serving the superego as well. He attacks them as he would attack himself.

What's more, the focus on aggression and the selfish, envious evil self disguises the more deeply buried source of guilt, one which could not pass the censorship of 1956, the guilt over his incestuous fantasies about his daughter. Unlike Oedipus, Morbius plea bargains, accepting his punishment for the psychologically lesser crime.

As Adams tries to convince Morbius of his conflict, he, too, emphasizes the murderous rage, saying that he turns the monster on his own daughter because she has defied him. That is true, but we can see it is a half truth, allowing him to come to terms with his aggression while still disguising the more frightening sexual fantasy.

Even the famous monsters from the id can serve a defensive function. The ultimate act of self destruction as Morbius puts himself in front of his own raging beast and then as he destroys the planet and himself serves the needs of a ferocious superego and the need to cover up the sexual nature of his fantasies.

Apparently the original title for the film script was "*Deadly Planet.*" It was changed to "*Forbidden Planet*" because that sounded better. Or, perhaps someone had a sense of something forbidden "lurking somewhere close at hand, sly and irresistible and only waiting to be re-invoked ... ."

As the film ends, the planet explodes, and with it Morbius and the Krell machinery. Alta watches, conveniently and safely in the arms of Captain Adams, removed from the danger so terrible that even we the viewers can only glean it with our "subconscious minds."

The Artist (and A Star is Born)

THIS IS A MORE conventional Oedipal tale, told from the vantage point of the girl's Oedipus complex.

On the face of it, it is astounding that a silent film would win awards as best motion picture of the year; although, the anomaly may be a key to its success, as we may admire and enjoy something that is so different.

The film, *The Artist*, has a further burden. It centers around a silent film star, George Valentin, whose career plummets at the end of the silent era. It must elicit our sympathy for George, but he has many traits that are not sympathetic. At the outset, we see him as a self-indulgent narcissist, insensitive to the people around him. He particularly shows a careless negligence towards women. He struts on the stage after a debut of his newest film, showing off with his trained dog while the leading lady fumes, waiting for her chance to get on. He answers the rage on her face with coy smiles, completely ignoring her distress. A little later, he takes a similar attitude with his wife, playing with the dog and smiling cutely at her distress over a picture on the front page of the *Hollywood Reporter* of George being kissed on the cheek by a pretty young girl. He is full of himself, even stops to admire a larger-than-life portrait displaying him in top hat and tails as he walks down the steps of his lavish home.

This is carried over in his film persona, where he is a dashing hero, saving women and fighting for justice in Errol Flynn-type roles. He is the center of every scene, surrounded by supporting characters, including his leading ladies. If there is a rival for screen attention it may be his talented little dog, who is seen waking him and helping him escape from a foreign prison in his newest hit film.

George is an unlikely hero—stubborn, smug, entitled. With a slightly different presentation, we could easily imagine an audience gloating over his eventual downfall. But, we don't see him in this way. Our sympathy for George, and for the film, is rescued by his relationship with a young woman, Peppy Miller.

George meets Peppy outside the theater where his film has just opened. She is one of many admirers in the crowd as he comes out. Peppy drops her purse and leans over to pick it up. As she is getting up she touches his behind, creating some embarrassment on her part as she is suddenly outside the throng, standing facing him. At first he gives her a stern look, then smiles to show he was only playing, relieving the tension. They both smile and laugh for the crowd as he casually puts an arm around her. Finally she reaches over and kisses him on the cheek. A cameraman snaps the picture, which appears on the front page of the *Hollywood Reporter* with the caption, "Who's That Girl?"

The story evolves around a familiar theme. George gives Peppy her chance to be in movies. As her career soars, his plummets, so that Peppy becomes the glamorous star and George a shabby tramp. The theme is familiar because it is essentially the plot of *A Star is Born*, in which a legendary film actor, Norman Maine, supports the career of an unknown girl, Esther Blodgett, who achieves supreme success while his career disintegrates. There have been three versions of *A Star is Born*, but by far the best known is the 1950's version with James Mason as Norman and Judy Garland as Esther.

The films have subtle similarities in their openings, suggesting that the director of the *The Artist*, Michael Hazanavicius, was aware of the comparison. Each begins with a major Hollywood event that focuses on the established male star; in each, he meets by accident a young woman with no claim to fame; and, in each case the start of the relationship involves an impromptu dance. Norman stumbles on stage, drunk, while Esther is performing with a group, and she salvages the situation by improvising a dance with him. George meets Peppy after the debut of his film, and in the next scene they end up doing an improvised exchange of dance steps that appears to solidify their relationship.

Norman Maine is a less likeable character than George Valentin—a womanizer who seems to specialize in taking advantage of young women, a superstar who cavalierly and recklessly ignores the people around him—yet each is far more likeable when seen with and through the eyes of his young protégée. In *The Artist*, perhaps even more than in *A Star is Born*, it is the love story that captures our enthusiasm.

It is a love story that develops in playfulness. There is the initial accidental encounter outside the theater, marked by embarrassment but ending with a kiss on the cheek. In the following meeting, they don't see each other at first. Only their legs are visible to one another under some sort of canvas being held by stagehands. He spots her dancing and begins to mimic it and respond with his own improvised steps. She sees his legs moving and answers in kind. When the stagehands move on with their barrier, they have established a rapport and suddenly recognize one another from the day before. It is here that he intervenes with the director to get her a place in his next film.

We next see a series of takes from George's new film, in which he plays a spy meeting a contact at a party. In the first take, George glides across the room in which people are dancing. He bumps into Peppy and takes a turn with her on his way to his contact. But as we see successive takes, he becomes increasingly interested in Peppy, allowing the scene they are filming to disintegrate. The light humor gives the scene and the development of their relationship a touch of light innocence.

That innocence seems to fit the silent film mode that we are watching. It also lends itself to an underlying theme. As in *A Star is Born*, this is a story about an intergenerational romance, an older, well-established man and a young, unknown "innocent" woman. The playfulness resonates with the level of fantasy that the film evokes. That fantasy is brought to life in a scene that is as evocative as it is subtle.

Peppy sneaks into George's dressing room. Seeing his top hat and jacket on a coat stand, she begins to feel the texture of the jacket, then puts her arm in one sleeve so that she can put her hand through the sleeve and embrace herself, with the illusion that she is being held by him. She does it well and we are caught up in the illusion and the fantasy as he walks in and sees her. George approaches her and beckons her closer with his finger. We think he may kiss her, but instead he tells her, "If you want to be an actress, you need to have something the others don't," and he puts a tiny beauty mark above her lip with makeup pencil. They look at it together in the mirror, then stare into each others eyes seemingly about to kiss (the dog hides his head under his paws in apparent embarrassment or shame) when the chauffeur enters the room. That kiss will never be consummated.

For me, the telling moment, the "give-away" if you will, is Peppy playing with George's coat, putting her hand into the arm and embracing herself. It is endearing, as beautiful a characterization of daydreaming as I have seen in film. Without seeing the explicit daydream, we immediately sense it. We can empathize with this young person, only yesterday an outside admirer, as she indulges in a fantasy of love.

With little effort we can see that we are caught up in the imaginings of a child, the image reified and captured as we see Peppy play-acting like a little girl with George's jacket and top hat, a young girl in barely disguised love for the man of her dreams, the hero of her world, the older married man whom she dreams of marrying.

George is, after all, a married man. We have just seen him telling his chauffeur to buy some jewelry for his wife. That kiss that almost happens would be the start of an adulterous affair; but, in the world of fantasy at which we are engaged just beneath the surface, it would more importantly be experienced as incestuous, the realization of a girl's forbidden wish towards her father.

If we have any doubt, the film goes on to emphasize the generational difference as George falls from his pedestal and Peppy ascends. George is told by the director, "You and I belong to another era, George. The world is talking now. ... People want new faces, talking faces. ... I wish it wasn't like this, but the public wants fresh meat and the public is never wrong." George is confident that he can successfully make his own silent film, but as he is walking out, he sees a poster with the "new faces" and sees that Peppy is one of the featured "fresh meat." He runs into her as he is leaving. She writes down her name, clearly wants to meet him again, and refers to the young men following her around as "toys."

George attempts to finance his own silent movie, "Tears of Love," while Peppy is featured in a new film that will come out the same night. He is having dinner with his chauffeur at a restaurant the night before the openings, when Peppy comes in with a coterie of reporters. When asked why she is Hollywood's new sweetheart, she answers, not realizing that George is behind her,

"I don't know. Maybe because I talk and the audience can hear me." She goes on, "People are tired of old actors mugging at the camera to be understood."

No clearer statement could be made to show that they are symbolic of an older and a younger generation. After her picture has come out as a hit and his as a total failure, she comes by to tell him she saw his film and to apologize for what he overheard. She is accompanied by a young man who shakes George's hand telling him he was his father's favorite; but, it is clear that Peppy's interest is in George, who is polite, but holds back out of pride.

George's attachment to silence underlines his belonging to an older, surpassed generation. It was, of course, a reality that affected some silent film stars, but not others, and a film device that we can understand because of the dramatic change in culture. But the filmmakers make it a point of stubborn principle. We see it in the opening scene, in a "film within a film," George's newest hit movie. He is being tortured, tied to a chair, with headphones attached to his ears while his captors turn up the dial (presumably increasing the volume) trying to overcome his refusal to talk. He resists and ends up escaping, with the help of his little dog, saving his companion, a beautiful blonde, and riding off with her in a single prop plane evading gunshots, shouting "Free Georgia." The emphasis on silence is added as we see George walking onstage behind the screen in front of a large sign that says "Silence, no talking while film is in progress."

Later, in a tragi-comic dream sequence we see him as he is bombarded by noises that we hear with him, the phone ringing, the dog barking, people laughing, culminating in a feather falling to the ground with a loud boom as he wakens from his nightmare.

Silence is a vital part of George's identity and the identity of his generation, a gripping on to the world he has known in the face of change. We can look back smugly at George denying the significance of talking films, but any of us beyond the age of something have to embrace or resist the changes that mark us as belonging to an "older generation." Increasingly, we accept or reject and possibly mock the new forms of communication that abound and are taken up naturally and easily by younger people. Have none of us been caught short and left in our time by one or more of these new forms—texting, tweeting, all forms of social media? We are all too aware of generational differences in style and communication and few of us have not at some point dismissed it.

George's stubbornness and pride provide a needed element of the love story. A good love story requires an obstacle, a tension that keeps the lovers apart so that we are pulled towards the ultimate resolution. George loses his work, his fame, his marriage, money and possessions. At the same time, Peppy is achieving everything he has lost. She wants to help him, secretly buying all his possessions that he sells at auction to support himself. After George almost dies in a fire started when he attempts to burn his old films (saved by the heroics of his dog, who brings a policeman to drag him out), Peppy arranges for him to be brought to her opulent mansion. She has learned that in the fire he was clinging to one piece of film, the scene with her in the spy movie.

She comes to his bedside in the morning and helps feed him, reversing the generational nurturance. She brings him a script to read. (In *A Star is Born*, Esther gets the studio director to offer Norman a part, but he rejects it because he has only a supporting role.) George's pride and his unwillingness to act in a talking film cause him to reject it and to leave her home. As he is wandering in her mansion, he finds a room filled with all of his auctioned possessions, culminating in his finding the massive picture of himself in top hat and tails.

Finally, he is about to shoot himself, but Peppy drives to his rescue, arriving just in time to save him, reversing the *Perils of Pauline* theme. At the end of the film, she has found the solution. We see them doing an elaborate tap dance sequence together to the delight of the film director. Going back to their original bond in dancing, she finds a way for him to use his skills, skills that he brought from his era.

This is an Oedipal love story in which the tables are turned so that the admiring little girl achieves the status once held by her father, totally eclipsing her mother. (By this time, George's wife has long ago left him.) But it goes a step further, becoming an Oedipal rescue fantasy, not just a fantasy of a girl who becomes a star as her admiring father looks on, but a fantasy of a girl who looks to rescue the man she admired, the man who had pulled her from obscurity, given life to the new person she has become.

When I began to think about writing about *The Artist*, I tried looking up female rescue fantasies in PEP. I found virtually nothing. Perhaps I didn't search correctly, but I did try different approaches. Freud's original concept of the "rescue fantasy" had to do with a male fantasy of rescuing a fallen, immoral woman. Over time, the term became more commonly used to refer to analysts' fantasies of rescuing patients. Some of the literature refers to the maternal fantasy of the female analyst or therapist who indulges in a rescue fantasy directed at a patient. There are some references to a male fantasy of rescuing father which emphasize the unconscious aggressive component, but only two papers that directly addressed a girl's rescue fantasy of her father.

Fenichel (1949), using a case and general references from literature and myth of girls who rescued and protected fathers and father figures, traced the meaning to a fantasy of the girl being the phallus. It seems reasonable to assume that a girl's fantasy of rescuing her father contains some element of gratification at being or having the father's phallus. Certainly, we can see possible elements of that in *The Artist* with the reversal of fortune, which could stand for a fantasy of reversal of anatomy. It rings particularly true as helping to explain George's refusal to accept her help. He is portrayed as a phallic narcissist, his masculinity and self esteem all tied together. I think a much clearer case can be made for the role of the girl having or becoming the phallus in *A Star is Born*, but that's for another time.

I also found one recent paper by Cordelia Schmidt-Hellerau (2010) in which she speaks of female rescue fantasies directed towards the man based on a desexualized fantasy of being caretaker for the father rather than lover. In her abstract, she writes, "The Greek myth of Kore/Persephone captures a particular psychopathology of women who are torn between a deadened and often asexual husband (Hades) and an ongoing close relationship with a caretaking mother (Demeter). Psychoanalytic work often reveals that these women live in the shadow of their mothers' failed oedipal complex. Their identificatory preoccupation with maternal object preservation disrupted or distorted their oedipal development, and ever since continues to serve as a defense against sexual strivings." (p. 911)

I was thinking in terms of a much more common and not so pathological fantasy. We all know from observation that little girls often wish to take care of Daddy. It is a superficially desexualized fantasy that clearly defends against any incestuous underlying wishes.

The film maintains this defense. In the scene in the dressing room, early on, George first sublimates his attraction to Peppy, taking the appropriate role of mentor while provocatively putting an artificial birthmark above her upper lip. (The title of her hit movie that comes out when his flops makes reference to that "spot.") But as they stare at one another and appear to be incrementally moving forward to a kiss, we are saved from this adulterous and unconsciously incestuous moment by the shame and embarrassment of the dog and the intrusion of the chauffeur. Sometimes the superego takes strange form in films.

They never consummate that kiss. Peppy saves George and even feeds him, but in the end, their sexual embrace is sublimated in an elaborate and beautiful dance number. At the end of it, as they present themselves in front of the director, he smiles and vocally expresses his pleasure. When he asks them if they can do it again for another shot, George says his two spoken words, "With Pleasure!" We leave with a good feeling at the ultimate success of the love story and of the rescue fantasy. The asexuality, or should I say understated, sublimated or represented sexuality, seems suitable for the "innocent" era that the story represents.

George's pride is likely not the only barrier to the gratification of this love affair. We can now understand why the kiss was never consummated. At the point at which they are about to kiss, George is a married man. In the context of this film, that kiss would have been far too close to the realization of the incestuous fantasy. In *A Star is Born*, Norman is not married when he meets Esther, but he does eventually marry her, in effect consummating the relationship. Can it be that the violation of the incest taboo, the consummation of the little girl's Oedipal fantasy necessitated the tragic ending to that film? In any case, in *The Artist* the kiss never happens and the consummation of the fantasy is expressed in sublimated form, allowing for the un-conflicted, "innocent" happy ending.

Fenichel, O. (1949) The Symbolic Equation: Girl = Phallus. *The Psychoanalytic Quarterly* 18:303-324.
Schmidt-Hellerau, C. (2010) The Kore complex: on a woman's inheritance of her mother's failed Oedipus complex. *The Psychoanalytic Quarterly* 79:911-933.

4

Brothers

The Road to Perdition

WHEN A FILM HAS a narrator, we are often seeing the world through the subjective eyes of that narrator. Even analysts tend to forget when they are in a theater that what they are told refers to psychic reality which contains admixtures of the "real world" and fantasy. *The Road to Perdition* has a narrator, Michael Sullivan Jr., and I think it fair to examine the film as coming from his psychic reality.

Michael tells us a story that covers several weeks in his childhood. It begins with a picture of a happy childhood and a stable family, except for the fact that his father, Michael Sullivan Sr., is a top gunman for the local crime boss in a small 1930's mid-western town. Within that context, Michael appears to be part of a stable community. He lives with his father, mother and younger brother in a comfortable house. He rides his bike to school, has a snowball fight with his brother and reads a book about the Lone Ranger with a flashlight in his bed at night. His father works for John Rooney, who runs the town. Rooney treats Michael's father like an adopted son and plays with Michael and his brother in a grandfatherly way, giving them special attention and sneaking away for a few minutes from a funeral to play dice with the boys in the bathroom.

As we watch the story develop with an analytic eye, we begin to notice certain themes that repeat in different contexts, like a warning alarm of unconscious meanings. If we were sitting with a patient, we might find that we keep hearing about *brothers*. Fairly soon, we see different sets of brothers in different types of relationships. There is Michael Jr. and his brother, Peter, Michael's father and John Rooney's real son, Connor, and Finn McGovern, who is burying his brother.

The film gives us two venues for understanding Michael Jr.'s psychic reality. He shows us the surface of his psychic life in his very ordinary relationships with his parents and brother. We see hints of playful aggression in an opening scene in which he and his brother have a snowball fight. After his brother hits him with a snowball he falls to the snow as if shot to death, then throws a snowball from the ground hitting his brother squarely. It is normal, acceptable playful aggression between brothers. Any murderous impulses are well disguised and contained in the play.

These impulses are depicted in the adult world, the world of Michael Sullivan Sr., a world in which violent fantasies are acted out. It is not unusual for a film to present a single dynamic in two forms, side by side: as raw fantasy, suffused with open expression of drives and well beyond the experience of most people; and, in a more subtle depiction of the same dynamic much closer to our ordinary experience. In this case, the raw fantasy is presented in the murderous relationship between Michael Sullivan Sr. and Connor Rooney. The subtler expression is seen in Michael Jr.'s relationship with his younger brother, Peter. By implication, the more violent characters act out in adult form the hidden fantasies of the child.

Finn McGovern's brother has been murdered by John Rooney's men because of claimed theft from the gang. Finn is angry. With enough alcohol in him at the funeral, he begins by praising John Rooney, his and everyone's benefactor, but then begins to claim that his brother's killing was unjust. Before he crosses the line, Michael's father pulls him from Rooney's house, where the funeral takes place. In this brotherly relationship, any aggression between brothers is displaced. Finn did not murder his brother, in fact he defends him, but the brother has been murdered.

The violent fantasy will be played out directly in the relationship between the third set of brothers, Michael Sr. and Connor Rooney. It is apparent that Connor resents his father's relationship with Michael Sullivan. Connor is ugly, brooding and impulsive, childless and loveless. Michael has a family, the respect of the (criminal) community and the valued trust of John Rooney, who knows that Michael will know how to look out for his interests without being told. The contrast is striking when Rooney humiliates Connor at a business meeting over his uncontrolled violence, then walks off with his arm on Michael Sr.'s shoulder.

The violence begins in a displaced fashion, with the murder of Finn McGovern. Rooney sends Michael Sr. and Connor to talk to Finn, to make sure that he does not cause any trouble, but Connor kills Finn, forcing Michael to kill Finn's two gunmen. As they come out of the warehouse in which they have killed Finn and his men, they find Michael Jr. there, a witness to the murder.

It is important from our analytic standpoint that Michael Jr., our narrator, our "patient," is innocent of the violence he witnesses. He has been motivated by curiosity about his father. He is reading a book about the gun toting Lone Ranger, and has accidentally seen his father pulling a pistol from under his jacket as he prepares for dinner. His younger brother has asked him about their father's work, verbalizing Michael's own curiosity. His crime is curiosity and interest in his father. He sneaks into the box beneath the rear seat of his father's car and becomes a witness to murder. Michael Sr. reassures Connor that his son will not talk about what he has seen, and for the moment Connor appears to accept it.

But Connor has decided to kill the boy and the father. On the surface, he is protecting himself from a witness to his crime, but you don't have to be a psychoanalyst to sense that he is seeking fratricidal revenge against the adopted brother whom his father appears to favor.

Connor botches his revenge. Michael, clearly upset at what he has witnessed, gets into a fight in school, his one act of overt violence, and is kept after school. He is just coming home as Connor is leaving his house after killing Michael's mother and brother. It becomes apparent that he thought he'd killed Michael. Likewise, Connor had planned to arrange to have Michael Sr. killed by another man who owed him money, but Michael Sr. beats him to the gun and shoots him and his bodyguard.

If we line up the pairs of brothers, half of them are already murdered, the McGovern brothers and Peter Sullivan. Our "patient" narrator is overtly innocent, but his brother has been killed. Now, of course, Michael Sr. wants Connor dead for the murder of his wife and younger son. He refuses an offer by Rooney's accountant to accept money to leave for Ireland with his remaining son, shooting the accountant as a message. He takes Michael Jr. to Chicago where he approaches Capone's chief lieutenant, Frank Nitti, who tells him he has to protect Connor. In fact, Nitti arranges for a hired assassin to kill Sullivan at the behest of a shaken and very ambivalent Rooney.

Michael Sullivan and his older son set out on the road like the Lone Ranger and Tonto in an unlikely plot that has them robbing banks to steal Capone's money while Nitti's hired assassin chases them. This provides us with an overdetermined additional pair of brothers, not by birth or family, but by identity. For whatever reason, it is a common understanding in our culture to think of two men who share some common identity as metaphorical brothers. In this case I refer to the two killers facing off against one another, Michael Sullivan and the assassin, Maguire. In their first encounter, they face each other across tables in a country diner, holding a seemingly trivial conversation which somehow gives Sullivan warning. This is presented to us as pro against pro, gunslinger against gunslinger, the classic confrontation between two men with much in common.

As is common in such cinematic confrontations, they are different in their humanity. Sullivan is a family man who conveys a sense of decency and human concern that frankly seems incompatible with his profession. In fact, though I have known combat veterans who presented with this type of pattern, and I have treated men with psychopathic tendencies who could be caring as well, the Michael Sullivan we see in this film can be more reasonably understood as our narrator's idealized, wished for image of his father. Maguire, on the other hand, is more of a competent, outwardly refined version of Connor, with his schizoid, psychopathic character and complete absence of morality as we know it.

As such, he is a perfect vehicle, as is the psychopathic Connor, to express the film's theme of sibling aggression without arousing our guilt. The motives that arouse guilt are displaced onto the ugly characters, the ones with whom we can easily dis-identify. The characters, the brothers in this case, with whom we are made to identify, are either completely innocent of sibling murder or are presented as justified in killing a vile brother.

Outwardly, Michael Jr. appears to have a loving relationship with his brother. In the opening scene, we see them in a snowball fight which is clearly in good fun and in which Michael allows himself to be killed in mock play. We do not see them together a great deal before Peter is killed, but we do see them in their room together at night, with Peter asking Michael questions about their father. Peter also startles Michael by repeating something he had heard Connor say at the funeral, "It's all so fucking funny." With a little stretch, we could say that he has been subtly identified with Connor in the brotherly relationship.

But Michael Jr., our narrator, does give us hints about his inner world as patients often do through a dream, or in this case a hint of a dream. After Peter and his mother have been killed, Michael has one brief man to man talk with his father while they have a little respite in their journey, staying at a farmhouse with a childless couple while Michael Sr. recovers from a gunshot wound. Here, the younger Michael wakes up from a nightmare. We never learn what it is, but if we use the surrounding material as associations, we might guess at its latent content. In the scene preceding, the farmer's wife has been telling Michael Sr. how much his son admires him.

After telling his father that he has had a bad dream and turning down an offer to talk about it, Michael sits to talk to his father who is going over accounting books of Capone's gang, saying, "Math, huh," and telling his father that he hates math. His father tells him, "Me, too." After a short exchange about what Michael does like in school—bible stories—Michael says that Peter was good in math.

Father: "Was he?"

Michael: "Did you like Peter more than me?"

Father: "No. No, Michael. I loved you both the same."

Michael: "But you were different with me."

Father: "Was I? ... Well, maybe it was because Peter was just such a sweet boy, you know? And you were more like me and I didn't want you to be. I didn't mean to be different."

Michael says, "Good night," but stops to hug his father around the neck before returning to bed.

Michael's bad dream will always be hidden to us, but the surrounding associations concern his admiration of his father and his fear that his father favored his younger, sweeter, smarter younger brother. It is just a suggestion of sibling rivalry, just a hint of jealousy, but the film gives it greater meaning through its juxtaposition with the more open expressions of hostility in the other brotherly relationships between Sullivan and Connor and between Sullivan and the assassin, Maguire. In fact, in a further association, after Michael goes back to bed, his father comes across Finn McGovern's accounts, where he will find that Connor has been stealing from his father. It is in the juxtaposition of two such parallel relationships that a film often represents a realistic family dynamic and the fantasy that underlies it.

In this fantasy, the rivalry is for Father's affection. Rooney's wife, we are told, has died some years ago. Michael Sullivan's wife is present in the film, but is killed early. Most of the boy's interest is around his father, and it is he whom he asks about loving his brother more. This is a story about brothers and fathers in which the fathers are somewhat idealized action heroes in the mold of boys' fantasies. Even John Rooney is presented sympathetically, played by a charming Paul Newman. We never see him as purely cynical or as relishing the killing of one of his "sons." He refuses Nitti's suggestion that the younger Sullivan be killed, although we get the impression that Nitti gives the order anyway. He is always agonizing over having to choose one son over the other, and he begs Sullivan to leave, allowing him to spare them both. When Michael Sullivan shoots down his entire gang on a rainy night and faces him with his machine gun, Rooney tells him, "I'm glad it was you."

Similarly, Michael Sullivan is portrayed as a decent, caring father and man, belying the suggestions in the voiceover narration that he is considered a hardened criminal. This is the boy's view of his father.

In the end, Michael Jr. is able to foreswear violence while reaping the benefits of it. Having wiped out Connor and Rooney's entire establishment, Michael Sr. takes his son to his wife's sister's house in Perdition. The scene looks idyllic, with a beautiful house overlooking the waterfront and a friendly dog. However, the assassin is waiting for them there. He shoots Sullivan in the back while he watches his son play with the dog through the window. As he prepares to photograph his victim, his personal fetish, the boy comes up behind him with a pistol. Maguire approaches the boy to take the gun from him, sensing that he won't shoot, only to be shot from behind by the father. With Michael Sr.'s closing words, he expresses his great happiness that his son could not fire the gun. The father will presumably go to perdition (everlasting damnation), but the son is spared both everlasting damnation and the ravages of guilt. Afterward, we hear the boy say that he realized his father's wish was for him not to be a killer. He says he never carried a gun again. (It's not clear what role he played in WWII.) But in the film's underlying fantasy, he is the victor after all the bloodshed. Of all the film's brothers, Michael is now the only survivor.

He takes the dog and the car back to the farmhouse where the childless couple are more than glad to take him in. With no blood on his hands, he has achieved the goal of the rivalrous sibling. He has become an only child. What is more, in his closing soliloquy he appears to wipe out his memory of his mother and brother, establishing himself in his new life as the only boy of this happy couple with only memories of having had his father to himself.

"People always thought I grew up on a farm, and I guess, in a way, I did; but I lived a lifetime before that in those six weeks on the road in the winter of 1931."

The Prestige

I HAD SEEN THE film, *The Prestige*, at some point after it came out in DVD, but it had not made much of an impression on me until I walked in on a scene from it about a month after hearing of Jules Glenn's death and instantly realized, as if in one thought, that this was the theme of my next film essay and that it was connected to my memories of Jules.

Jules was a particularly beloved teacher and he had spoken with enthusiasm of his interest in the dynamics of twins. A search in PEP came up with four papers that Jules Glenn wrote on the subject of twinship between 1966 and 1986 as well as a book review of a translation of Otto Rank's essay on "The Double". The first was a clinical paper written in 1966, "Opposite-Sex Twins". He presented it as a rare clinical paper on the subject, dealing with the dynamics of non-identical twins. The succeeding papers approached the subject through the literary works of the Shaffer brothers, fraternal twins, and Thornton Wilder, whose twin brother died at birth.

In the second of his papers on the Shaffer brothers (Glenn, 1974b), Jules summarized some of the psychodynamics that had been identified in twins.

"Twins are generally brought up close to each other and develop extremely close relationships. The mother-child dyad is complicated by the fact that two children of similar appearance go through the developmental stages concurrently. The two infants coo to each other, watch and touch each other, play with each other, and later frequently develop a secret language together. As they grow older they engage in intimate, ambivalent games. They get to understand and react to the whims and moods of their siblings with much greater empathy and accuracy than is generally the case with brothers and sisters, often to the point that they become convinced that telepathic communication occurs. As Maenchen (1968) has so aptly put it, in some cases 'the twin symbiosis drains or replaces entirely the mother-child symbiosis' (p. 454). The intense affectionate ties between the twins are such that they love each other narcissistically as they consider themselves part of a complete person. They strive to be with the other in actuality or in fantasy, often through the presence of a substitute. They identify with and imitate each other. Sexual acting out of the libidinal attachment may indeed occur, leading to homosexual activity.

"But at the same time they are rivals. Their animosity originates genetically in the pre-oedipal rivalry for their mother. Each feels that the other has deprived him of his mother's love and supplies, as indeed he often has, for the mother of twins has much more trouble feeding and caring for her two children than do mothers with several children who are born years apart. One twin often has to wait while the other is fed or picked up; there is a real danger of the mother's doing an unsatisfactory job. At the same time each twin, even in childhood, finds in his sibling an unusual source of gratification. As I have pointed out (Glenn, 1966) this alternation of excessive frustration and excessive gratification can result in difficulty in separating self- and object-representations.

"Uncertainty about 'ego boundaries' leads to the twin's fantasy that he is half a person, that he has been deprived of half his body in the womb or after birth. Feeling deficient, twins may feel justified in trying to retrieve the missing part, even by stealing it back from the twin, or through displacement, from his substitutes. Or he may desire to steal from the mother, whom he pictures as the depriving figure. In either case the hostility may be intense and often has to be defended against. Destroying the twin is dangerous, since it involves harm to what is felt to be part of the self. In addition, the murderous impulses are contrary to the superego dictates. And, of course, the sibling is loved. One way of attempting to avoid hatred is to keep things equal; if each person shares equally there is no cause for rage. It is striking to see twins try to divide food or an inheritance exactly evenly, to an extent rarely seen in ordinary siblings. When things become unequal, murderous rage may follow. The painful antagonism may be avoided by the twins' complementing each other, each taking on traits and interests opposite to the other.

"The anxiety resulting from feeling incomplete, from being dependent upon, or sexually attracted to, an incestuous object whom one hates, leads a large number of twins to seek extreme independence of each other, thus masking the closeness. The desire to achieve identity as a non-twin, as a complete individual, can be intense." (pp. 373-374)

The film, *The Prestige*, is based upon Christopher Priest's novel of the same name. It tells a complicated story about a deadly rivalry between two young magicians, Alfred Borden and Robert Angier, in the late 19th century. As such, it bears a resemblance to the well-known Peter Shaffer play, *Sleuth* which Jules Glenn discusses at length. In *Sleuth*, two men engage in a cat and mouse game of trickery, each repeatedly turning the tables to outwit the other. "Milo tries to take Andrew's wife from him, and Andrew retaliates cruelly in the first act. Thereafter, Milo repeatedly strikes back, identifying with and imitating his opponent as he tries to make things equal, 'to even the score.'" (Glenn, 1974a, p. 291)

In *The Prestige*, Borden and Angier are two young magicians working together on an act in which Angier's wife is bound by them and dropped into a "locked" glass container filled with water. She drowns, presumably because Borden has used a different knot than was suggested to tie her hands. Angier blames him for her death and sets out to get his revenge, much as Andrew does in *Sleuth*, setting off a similar series of retaliations, each more violent than the last. Glenn discusses Sleuth in terms of the disguised twinship dynamics inherent in the ambivalent rivalry and sadomasochistic play between the two men.

Angier retaliates first by disguising himself and interfering with a trick that Borden is doing, "catching the bullet". The trick involves sleight of hand in which a person chosen from the audience shoots at the magician. The magician, in setting up the gun, palms the bullet so that nothing is projected, but Angier replaces the bullet and shoots off two of Borden's fingers. The theme of disguise and interference with the other's tricks continues, with escalating damage.

The plot centers around one magic trick in particular that Borden has perfected, "The Transported Man." He steps into a box and almost instantaneously appears coming out of another box at some distance from the first. Angier becomes obsessed with finding out how Borden performs his trick. He is told by the film's narrator, Cutter, the promoter/producer of Angier's magic show (called an "ingenieur" in the film) that the only way to do it is with a double. In fact, Cutter hires an actor to be Angier's double, but Borden manages to find the actor and undermine the show.

Angier has by this time taken a new lover, a woman who works in his act. He directs her to go to work for Borden in order to steal his secrets. He tells her to tell Borden that he'd sent her for that purpose but that she is really there to give Borden Angier's secrets, creating in her a double agent whose role and attachment becomes more complicated as the film proceeds.

In this, we can readily see the twinship dynamics that Glenn has outlined. We have these two men in a rivalry, with one trying to steal the other's tricks, in essence his identity. When Angier sends his girlfriend to Borden, they are essentially sharing and exchanging the same woman. In fact, she later comes back to Angier with Borden's secret notebook. Only later we find out that Borden has sent her deliberately with the notebook. We can easily recognize the themes of mutual identification, some blurring of self and object and a sharing of the same woman. Without much more, we could be thinking about twinship dynamics, but the plot thickens and darkens.

One of the well-known tenets of magic, and one which is talked about in the film, is the element of distraction. The magician attempts to draw the viewer to something irrelevant, keeping his mind and eye off the subterfuge. For our purposes, the focus on magic and magic tricks in this film is the distraction. The opening scene contains the key to our understanding the film's dynamics of twinship, but we do not see it at that point. What we see is a little girl watching a magic trick while Cutter (Michael Caine) narrates:

"Every magic trick consists of three parts, or acts. The first part is called the pledge. A deck of cards, a bird or a man. He shows you this object. Perhaps he invites you to inspect it to see that it is indeed real, unaltered, normal. But of course it probably isn't. The second act is called the turn. The magician takes the ordinary something and makes it do something extraordinary. Now you're looking for the secret, but you won't find it, because of course you're not really looking. You want to be fooled. But you wouldn't clap yet because making something disappear isn't enough. You have to bring it back. That's why every magic trick has a third act, the part we call the prestige."

We see a series of images while we are watching. In one set of images, we see a coherent scene in which Cutter performs a magic trick for the little girl, taking a small bird out of a cage (the "pledge"), making it disappear (the "turn"), and then reproducing it for her. Mixed in are images that we will later learn are part of the plot, an image of top hats, then images of Angier doing his act, "The New Transported Man" while Borden sneaks backstage where he sees Angier land in a locked box filled with water and watches him drowning. As Cutter concludes his narrative, we see that he is delivering it from the witness stand of a courtroom where Borden is on trial for Angier's murder.

We are drawn quickly to the conflict between Borden and Angier, a story that is told in flashback form from this trial scene. As the film develops, we learn that Angier draws Borden into a trap. Knowing that Borden will want to uncover the secret to his trick, he sets him up to be present to view Angier drowning so that he will be convicted of his murder. For those who have not seen the film, I will explain how he does this presently ("the prestige").

But we are distracted from the seemingly more mundane image, the magic trick performed for the little girl. In this trick in which a dove is made to disappear and then reappear, lies a key to understanding the twinship dynamics of the film. You see, we learn early in the film how this trick is done. The dove, the pledge, is placed in a collapsible cage. The magician places a cover over the cage, then collapses it, crushing the bird inside. He then produces another bird, identical looking to the first, creating the illusion that the bird has come back, when indeed it is his "twin" who has been spared in order to complete the trick. Here are the film's secrets: Two individuals posing as one; one dying that the other may survive.

The film accomplishes this trick through a combination of subterfuge and fantasy. It all hinges on the trick, "The Transported Man." Angier is obsessed with how Borden does the trick. After his attempt to perform it using an actor double is sabotaged by Borden, he becomes determined to find out. Cutter has told him that there is only one way to do it, with a double, but Angier refuses to believe that. He gets hold of Borden's diary through his former lover, Olivia, now Borden's mistress, but it is written in cipher and he needs the key. He forces Borden to give him the key by kidnapping someone very close to Borden.

To understand this, I must explain the evolution of Borden's household. (I think I said this was a complicated plot.) After parting from Cutter and Angier, Borden meets a woman, Sarah, whom he subsequently marries. In fact, he meets her when he is showing the disappearing bird trick to a little boy, her nephew, who sees through the illusion, crying bitterly about the bird that has been killed, seeing that the live one is a substitute. Soon after he and Sarah are settled together, Borden brings in a permanent houseguest, named Fallon, who he says is his *ingenieur* for his acts. Borden and Sarah have a child, the girl we see at the beginning of the film watching the disappearing bird trick. As the plot develops, Borden also takes on Olivia, Angier's former lover, as his own mistress.

Borden and Fallon are seemingly inseparable. It is Fallon who is kidnapped and buried alive by Angier in order to extort the key to the cipher. Borden gives him the cipher key, "Tesla", telling him that the key is the secret, then frantically digs out Fallon from his premature grave.

Throughout the film, we are given clues to Borden's secret, clues that reappear at the end when the truth is shown. The secret is not "Tesla"; that is another subterfuge. The secret is that Borden is a set of twins. Each takes turns disguised as Fallon, and each tries to fill the other in on what has transpired while he was Borden. Like her nephew, Sarah intuits the truth, but does not identify it. She continually tells Borden that at times when he says he loves her, he seems to mean it; at other times he does not. When Olivia comes on the scene, she calls Alfred Borden by a pet name, "Freddie". The twins have even gone to the trouble of amputating the ends of one twin's fingers to duplicate the amputation caused by Angier's bullet. They do it to support the act, The Transported Man, but it is clear that it comes natural to them to share a life, to meld into one person, Fallon being a silent, undemonstrative shell.

Borden has distracted Angier by telling him that the cipher key, "Tesla," is also the secret. Nikola Tesla is an historical figure, a Serbian born genius who invented the prototype for alternating current, was the first to demonstrate "wireless communication (radio)," but was an eccentric who eventually was perceived as being a "mad scientist" according to a Wikipedia article. Angier pursues him to Colorado, where he finds that Tesla has invented a machine that can reproduce any object placed in its electrical field, sending the double to a new spot at some distance. Angier buys the device to use in his Transported Man act. His plan is not merely to outdo Borden, but to trap him.

In fact, we see Borden and Fallon arguing about Angier's trick. One, seen as Borden, argues that he must find out what Angier is doing, the other warns him to leave Angier alone. Borden, in disguise, sneaks under the stage where he sees Angier fall into a glass box filled with water, identical to the one that Angier's wife, Julia, had drowned in at the beginning of the film. As Borden tries to save him, Angier drowns before his eyes. Cutter comes in on the scene, assuming that Borden has contrived to kill Angier.

Angier has allowed himself to drown, knowing that he will continue as the double, the truly identical twin, that will appear several yards away. One twin drowns that the other may survive alone. In fact, we discover that he has always had a double identity. Early in the film, he had told Julia that he used the name Angier because his family would not accept his being a magician. He is a wealthy aristocrat, Lord Caldlow. Angier dies, Borden is tried for his murder, and Lord Caldlow buys all of Angier's equipment.

As Lord Caldlow, he visits the now condemned Borden in prison. Recognizing him, Borden futilely cries out that the man he has been convicted of killing is alive. As a final act of retribution, Lord Caldlow "benevolently" takes in Borden's daughter, who will be orphaned with Borden's death. Borden's wife Sarah, no longer able to tolerate the incomprehensible fluctuations in her husband, provokes him to tell her the truth, does he love her. He says "not today" and she subsequently hangs herself, evidence of the breakdown of the dual identity.

But the final retribution, and the prestige, goes to Borden. Condemned to death, we see him telling Fallon, "You'll have to live for both of us now." He is hung, his last word, "abracadabra." As a "victorious" Angier starts to burn his machine and other artifacts in a hidden warehouse, the remaining Borden comes in, led there by Cutter, who now understands the truth. He shoots Angier, and as he watches him die, he explains that he and his twin had lived one life, but that he had loved Sarah and the twin who was hung, (Freddie), had loved Olivia. They had each taken turns being Fallon and each had been the one to go into the box and the one who came out to take the applause. As he walks off, the camera pans to show us what is being destroyed, a series of glass, water-filled cases containing the drowned versions of Angiers. The fratricidal rivalry is demonstrated in a "flashback" to Angier's first attempt to use Tesla's machine. He has a pistol by his side to use on himself in case the experiment does him some terrible damage. Instead, his double appears several yards away. Seeing him, Angier shoots him to death.

From that point on, Angier continues to kill himself by drowning, night after night, only to reappear as a new continuation of himself. In this fashion, each incarnation of Angier begins life by receiving the applause and ends it as "the man in the box." After his wife's death by drowning, Cutter had told Angier a story about a sailor he'd met who had nearly drowned, but had been revived. He said that the man told him that it was like going home. At the end of the film, he tells him that he had lied; that the man had said it was agony.

The film ends with the scene with which it had begun. Cutter shows the re-found dove to the girl, Borden's daughter. Then her father, Borden, enters and takes her in his arms. She has no need to see through the subterfuge, with the dove or the man. She is happy to be returned to her rightful father, who will now go on living a single identity.

At this point, the readers, particularly those who have seen the film, are ready to put all the pieces together, but I will nevertheless make the connections ("the prestige"). Glenn had described the twinship relationship as an ambivalent one. The twin is both a rival and a part of oneself. Thornton Wilder's twin, Theophilus, died in childbirth, and Glenn (1986) demonstrated that he was left with relief as well as guilt at having been the one to survive. In the Borden twins, we see the loss of self and object boundaries represented, as well as the intense attachment to the twin who is viewed as an extension of the self.

But the film more pointedly elucidates a murderous rivalry. For "Borden", the rivalry was subdued. We do see the breaking apart of the dual identity when Freddie tells Sarah that he does not love her "today," leading to her suicide. His death, however, is not caused by his twin, but by his other rival, Angier. Nevertheless, one twin dies and the other is left to live life for both.

With Angier, through the device of pure fantasy, we have the extreme of the identical twin, a fantasied double who shares not only the DNA, but also the memories and identity of the original. For him, there can be only one. He does not think to use his double to perform the trick. In fact, he uses his own death to destroy his rival. When we see Angier shoot his first double, we are made graphically aware of the fratricide.

There are a series of deaths in the film. Two women die, Julia by drowning, Sarah by hanging. Similarly, Angier dies by drowning and one of the Borden twins is hung. Repetition provides good dramatic effect, but it also should be a clue to unconscious content. To a psychoanalyst, the multiple images of people drowning in a box may bring up many associations, but one which will consistently appear, particularly in this context, is the image of the water filled womb. In his paper on opposite sex twins, Glenn talks about a patient's fantasies of being in the womb with the twin. I think it is fair to say, particularly for Angier, that we have a repeated image of one twin surviving while the other dies in the womb.

Arlow (1972) wrote about a fantasy that he witnessed in people who had been an only child, that a twin had been killed in the womb that he or she might survive alone, not unlike Thornton Wilder, whose twin was a stillbirth. Angier is both a twin and an only child, the wealthy Lord Caldlow, who appears to inhabit his estate in solitude except for servants.

In Jules Glenn's terms, *The Prestige* presents us with a graphic demonstration of the ambivalent dynamics of the twin. I suspect that he would want me to point out additionally that the deaths of the two women, Julia and Sarah, may represent the twin's ambivalence towards the mother, who must share her resources between the two loving rivals.

Ordinarily, I would stop at this point. My interest in film, unlike that of many others, is simply to use the film to demonstrate psychoanalytic principles, usually fantasies that are generally unconscious. However, that was not Jules's primary interest. He was more interested in the creative process and always started with the creative artist. His interest was in discovering more about the artist from the art. He wrote about Sleuth and other plays by the Shaffer brothers not to simply use the plays to demonstrate twinship dynamics, but to help us understand the motivation of the playwrights as well. Similarly, in his paper on Thornton Wilder, his starting point was Wilder's biography.

I am working backwards in this respect. However, out of respect for Jules, I did decide to do some investigation into the creative artists involved. I did not find detailed biographical information, but some was available on the Internet. I used a combination of IMDb (Internet Movie Database) and biographical web pages.

The film's director is Christopher Nolan. I found no evidence that he is a twin. However, he was a co-writer of the film. The principal writer was his younger brother, Jonathan Nolan. The film was written by brothers and directed by one of them. It is not a great stretch to suppose that two brothers, working in the same field, might be drawn to a story about fraternal rivalry and fratricide. IMDb lists as the film's "tagline" "A friendship that became a rivalry. A rivalry that turned deadly."

The film was based upon the novel by the British author, Christopher Priest. Again, I found no evidence from his biography that he is a twin. ... However, I did find on the IMDb website that he and his second wife are raising twin daughters. Coincidence? I don't actually know for a fact that they were born before the book was written, nor do I know if there were other twins in his family or his wife's. I also found that Priest has one other possible connection to twins. He has his own "evil twin". The expression is mine, but he essentially confirms the sentiment. From the IMDb website:

"Christopher Priest should not be confused with James Owsley, the American comic book writer who legally changed his name to Christopher James Priest (aka Christopher J. Priest, C. J. Priest, or simply Priest). Unfortunately, the two have been confused by consumers who buy works by one, expecting the works to have been created by the other. In a November 2004 interview, the 'real' Priest showed some anger about this confusion, saying he thought it 'a bit bleeding irritating to have my name pinched by another writer,' and made an open plea to DC Comics, Inc.: 'If Jim must use a pseudonym, why doesn't he pick a really silly one, like, say, Harlan Ellison?'"

Jules, I can only hope that you would have approved.

Arlow, J.A. (1972). The only child. *The Psychoanalytic Quarterly* 41:507-536.
Glenn, J. (1966) Opposite-sex twins. *Journal of the American Psychoanalytic Association* 14:736-759.
Glenn, J. (1972) *The Double: A Psychoanalytic Study by Otto Rank*. Translated and edited, with an introduction by Harry Tucker, Jr. Reviewed in Psychoanalytic Quarterly 41:433-435.
Glenn, J. (1974a) Twins in disguise-A psychoanalytic essay on *Sleuth* and *The Royal Hunt of the Sun*. *Psychoanalytic Quarterly* 43: 288-302.
Glenn, J. (1974 b) Twins in disguise II: Content, form and style in plays by Anthony and Peter Shaffer. *International Review of Psychoanalysis* 1:373-381.
Glenn, J. (1986) Twinship themes and fantasies in the work of Thornton Wilder. *Psychoanalytic Study of the Child* 41:627-651.

The Dark Knight

IN WRITING ABOUT THE film, *The Prestige*, focusing on the issue of twinship dynamics in memory of Jules Glenn, I pointed out that the director of *The Prestige*, Christopher Nolan, was not, to my knowledge, a twin, but did co-write the script for the film with his younger brother, Jonathan. The next film Nolan directed, also co-written with his brother, was *The Dark Knight*, making this film review a sequel.

It is not surprising that *The Dark Knight* was a huge box office success. It was a blockbuster about a well known comic book superhero, not to mention that one of the stars of the film, Heath Ledger, had died in his twenties with an overdose of prescription drugs shortly after shooting for the film was completed.

What was surprising was the film's critical acclaim. Manohla Dargis wrote in the *New York Times* (July 18, 2008), "Pitched at the divide between art and industry, poetry and entertainment, Christopher Nolan's follow-up to 'Batman Begins' goes darker and deeper than any Hollywood movie of its comic-book kind." According to another reviewer, Todd Gilchrist (IGN.com), the film functions "as a substantive and philosophical examination of why we need heroes, and then when we need them, what they mean."

The reviewers appear to be captivated by the dark quality of the story. This is not the simple story of a caped hero who saves the world. It is the story of a society so corrupt and corrupted that even the hero cannot escape its moral ambiguities. There is a turn early in the film that may catch us by surprise when we discover that a discussion of an arch criminal taking over the city refers to Batman, himself. The "Caped Crusader" is, after all, a vigilante who uses violent means to scare and eliminate criminals. Bruce Wayne (Batman's alter ego, for those of you who were born on the planet Krypton) is aware of this darker side of his alter ego. He finds hope in the new district attorney, Harvey Dent, whom he sees as a "White Knight" who may be able to accomplish through legal means what Batman does illegally.

The film is also quick to show us that the consequences of injecting the "caped crusader" into Gotham are not all good. The wealthy Bruce Wayne has put fear into the criminals of the city, but in doing so he has forced the organized criminal organizations to band together. In fact, the sudden presence of this superhero calls up his antithesis, a super anti-hero, the Joker.

Wearing clown's makeup, with a face that is marked by a grin literally cut into his face, the Joker has no identity. His goal is not personal gain or even power, but simply to wreak chaos on society and to force people who think themselves well meaning to face the dark side of their nature. He could have been created by Samuel Beckett—if Beckett had taken an even darker turn. He is more a modern terrorist than a criminal.

With devilish powers of manipulation, the Joker is able to drive the city into chaos, overpowering the criminals as well as the police. He brings out the violence in those who think of themselves as good by forcing them into choices in which they must sacrifice one life for another. By the film's end, he has transformed the seemingly incorruptible Harvey Dent into a crazed, vengeful killer.

The *NY Times* reviewer, Dargis is right that *The Dark Knight* was the sequential follow-up to *Batman Begins*, picking up where that film ended. But it is also a follow-up to *The Prestige*, its more immediate predecessor. The opening scenes could have been inspired by one of the themes in *The Prestige*.

In that film, a pair of 19th century magicians engage in internecine competition with each other, the competition revolving around a magic trick, "The Transported Man", that requires a double. We find out eventually that one of the magicians has a double, a twin, more accurately is a set of twins since they play their roles interchangeably. The other magician, an only child, creates a series of twins using a fantastical machine that can duplicate anything. Instead of creating a twin and sharing the act with him, he sets up his trick so that with each new act, his last incarnation of himself is killed, leaving his new double to go on until the next show, the survivor remaining an only child.

The opening scenes of *The Dark Knight* reproduce that theme of killing off doubles. The film begins with a well planned bank robbery conducted by a group of men wearing identical clown masks. They bear names loosely taken from the seven dwarfs. As each clown completes his task, one of the others kills him, under instructions from the mastermind of the robbery, reducing the number of shares into which the takings will be divided. At the end of the sequence, the last clown takes the loot, killing the last of his hired clowns and pulling off his own clown mask to reveal that he has a painted clown face. He is the "Joker". As in *The Prestige*, here in more symbolic form, we have a series of doubles who are killed off one by one, leaving the one unique and legitimate Joker.

As if to underline the point, in the next set of scenes, we see a group of faux Batmen attempting to stop a crime. When the real Batman appears, capturing criminals with more efficiency, he warns them to stop imitating him. He fears that he will inspire a rash of vigilantes. Unlike the Joker, Batman does not kill his doubles, but later the Joker kills one of them in a public demonstration, first getting him to acknowledge that he is not the real Batman. The real Joker and the real Batman each asserts his individuality, disowning and in the Joker's case, killing his doubles. In various subtle and sometimes unsubtle ways, the filmmakers create a world in which, similar to the world of *The Prestige*, the wish to share an identity is in conflict with the wish to be unique, an only child.

The issue of double identity is, of course, intrinsic to Batman, as it is to most "superheroes". He is, after all, two people, Batman and Bruce Wayne. Bruce Wayne is a leading citizen, a pillar of society. As Batman, he operates outside the law, both the law of the land and the laws of nature. He is able to do things that the entire police force cannot do. He has not only super powers, but also super rights and super responsibilities. But the film expands upon the theme. Like *The Prestige*, *The Dark Knight* is peppered with plotlines and images suggestive of the dynamics of twins.

What is most striking is the recurring images of doubles, characters who share traits, or even aspects of identity. In some instances, the resemblance is superficial, as with the bank robber clowns and the imitation Batmen. The Joker uses such a superficial doubling of identity early in the film, when, having failed to keep a promise to kill Harvey Dent because of the Batman's intervention, he keeps his promise by killing two men, one with the last name Harvey and the other Dent. Towards the end of the film, the Joker sets up a hostage situation in which he puts clown masks and unloaded weapons on the hostages, while disguising his gunmen as abducted doctors and nurses so that the police will confuse the hostages with the terrorists, killing the innocent victims. He also kills a Batman imitator, acting as if he has confused him with the real Batman, but eliciting a confession that he is not Batman, essentially mocking the similarity.

The film provides a more serious double for Batman in the district attorney, Harvey Dent. With the Joker threatening to continue to kill citizens until Batman reveals his true identity, Bruce Wayne decides that he must end the killing by revealing himself. As Batman, he tells Dent to hold a press conference at which Batman's identity will be revealed. Wayne attends the press conference, ready to reveal his identity as Batman, but Dent announces instead that he is Batman, making a sacrifice of himself while stealing Batman's identity.

This is reversed at the end of the film, when Batman partly takes on the identity of Harvey Dent. The Joker's violent manipulations have turned Dent into a psychotic killer bent on vengeance. With one side of his face deformed in a fire and the death of his fiancée imprinted in his mind, Dent goes on a killing spree against those involved in the conspiracy that resulted in her death and his disfigurement. His final act of revenge is aimed at Police Commissioner Gordon, because it was Gordon's hand picked men and women who were bought by the Joker to carry out this crime. Dent is about to kill Gordon's son to let him know what it is to lose a loved one, when Batman leaps at him, saving the boy but sending Dent to a deadly fall. Standing over Dent's body, Batman tells Gordon that the public needs for Dent to remain a hero. He offers to take the blame, himself, for Dent's crimes.

Gordon: "We bet it all on him. The Joker took the best of us and tore him down. People will lose all hope."

Batman: "They won't. They must never know what he did."
Gordon: "Five dead, two of them cops? You can't sweep that under."
Batman: "But the Joker cannot win. Gotham needs its true hero."
Gordon: "No!"
Batman: "You either die a hero or live long enough to see yourself become the villain. I can do those things, because I'm not a hero, not like Dent. I killed those people. That's what I can be."
Gordon: "No, no you can't! You're not!"
Batman: "I'm whatever Gotham needs me to be."

He is returning the favor of accepting the identity of the man who had accepted his identity earlier. In effect, they are behaving like twins, who, in Glenn's (1974) words, "identify with and imitate each other." (p. 373)

Bruce Wayne/Batman and Harvey Dent share many of the features of twins that Glenn has described. They share a similar role as hero and savior of Gotham. As such, they admire and respect one another. Wayne sees Dent as a possible legal successor to Batman, someone who could destroy the crime syndicate through legal means, possibly allowing him to put Batman into retirement. He refers to him at one point as Gotham's "White Knight" in pointed comparison to Batman, the "Dark Knight" of the film's title.

But perhaps their most important commonality is that they are in love with the same woman, Rachel Dawes, Bruce Wayne's childhood friend, who has promised that if he can ever be free of the role of Batman they will be together.

Each man clearly loves Rachel, but there is no way to truly share her. After being tricked by the Joker into saving Dent instead of Rachel, one of the film's several choices of this kind, Bruce Wayne says to his butler, Alfred, "She was going to wait for me. Dent doesn't know. He can never know." Alfred has a letter from Rachel that he was to give to Wayne: "... I need to be honest and clear. I'm going to marry Harvey Dent. I love him. I want to spend the rest of my life with him." She goes on to explain that she intends to keep her promise to be together with him if Gotham no longer needs Batman, "but as a friend." Alfred decides not to deliver the letter.

We could look at this as an Oedipal rivalry, but in the context of the film we may look to the dynamics of twins. In Glenn's (1974) words, "But at the same time they [twins] are rivals. Their animosity originates genetically in the pre-oedipal rivalry for their mother. Each feels that the other has deprived him of his mother's love and supplies, as indeed he often has, for the mother of twins has much more trouble feeding and caring for her two children than do mothers with several children who are born years apart." (pp. 373-374)

The Joker contrives to force Batman to choose between Dent and Rachel by telling him where they are each trapped with explosives set to go off in minutes. Batman goes to save Rachel, the woman, the depriving mother of Glenn's dynamics, sacrificing Dent, the twin; but, the Joker has reversed the locations so that Batman saves Dent, who is nevertheless disfigured in the ensuing fire while Rachel's location explodes. In effect, this punishes the rivalrous twin and the depriving mother of Glenn's dynamics.

Murderous rivalry brings us to Batman's other "twin", the Joker. Glenn emphasizes the struggle between twins in his analysis of Peter Shaffer's play and film, Sleuth. In Sleuth, two men play a series of nasty, nearly deadly tricks upon one another, ostensibly concerning their rivalry over a woman. I pointed out a very similar dynamic in *The Prestige* in which the two rival magicians keep increasing their violence towards one another.[1]

In *The Dark Knight*, it is as if Shaffer's characters or the two magicians from *The Prestige* were carrying on their private war with an entire city as their plaything, as we watch Batman and the Joker engage in their larger than life deadly game.

Going back to Jacob and Esau we know that twins are represented by contrast as well as by similarity. Batman and the Joker are at opposite poles, yet in ways more alike than like any of the other characters in the film. The others are mortals; Batman and the Joker function at

---

[1] In *The Prestige*, the violence between the magicians begins when one of them believes that his wife's death was caused by the other's recklessness, essentially over his depriving him of his woman.

a level far beyond that of humans. From the outset, they have in common that they are fantastical creations of the imagination, archetypes of good and evil, suddenly made to appear in a formerly stable society, with dramatic effects upon that society. They anticipate and manipulate the world of Gotham; the others are virtually helpless, pawns in their hands. It is as if they both come from the same place, or perhaps from two perfectly opposite places.

Much about their relationship is spelled out in their two extended face to face confrontations. In each case, one appears to be in charge, but the other controls the action.

The first is in the police station. The Joker has been captured and is being interrogated, first by Commissioner Gordon who is trying to find out where the Joker's men have taken Harvey Dent. He leaves the interrogation room to "get a cup of coffee" and Batman suddenly appears in the room, standing behind the Joker. Batman, playing the "bad cop", slams the Joker's head into the table and pounds his hand, only getting quips in response. Then the dialogue really begins.

Batman: "You wanted me. Here I am."

Joker: "I wanted to see what you'd do. And you didn't disappoint. (He laughs.) You let five people die. Then you let Dent take your place. Even to a guy like me, that's cold."

Batman: "Where's Dent?"

Joker: "Those mob fools want you gone so they can get back to the way things were. But I know the truth. There's no going back. You've changed things forever. Forever."

Batman: "Then why do you want to kill me?"

Joker: (Laughs) "I don't want to kill you. What would I do without you? Go back to rippin' off mob dealers? No, no, no. You, you complete me."

Batman: "You're garbage who kills for money."

Joker: "Don't talk like one of them. You're not, even if you'd like to be. To them you're just a freak like me. They need you right now. When they don't, they'll cast you out like a leper. See, their morals, their code—it's a bad joke, dropped at the first sign of trouble. They're only as good as the world allows them to be. I'll show you. When the chips are down, these, these civilized people, they'll eat each other. See, I'm not a monster. I'm just ahead of the curve."

At this point Batman grabs the Joker and holding him up, demands that he tell him where Dent is. There's an exchange about rules and breaking rules, and then the Joker plays his trump card.

Joker: "There's only minutes left. You're gonna have to play my little game if you want to save one of them."

Batman: "Them?"

Joker: "For a while I thought you really were Dent, the way you threw yourself after her."

At this point, Batman appears to be losing control of his rage, pulling a chair out of it's bolts and placing it against the doorknob to keep out any interference, then manhandling and beating the Joker, who doesn't stop talking.

Joker: "Look at you go ... does Harvey know about you and his little girl?"

Batman smashes him against the wall, yelling, "Where are they?"

Joker: "Killing is making a choice."

Batman punches him and repeats his demand.

Joker: "A choice between one life or the other, your friend or his blushing bride-to-be."

Batman hits him again and the Joker laughs wildly.

Joker: "You have nothing. Nothing to threaten me with. Nothing to do with all your strength. Don't worry! I'm going to tell you where they are. Both of them, and that's the point—you'll have to choose."

Early in the film, the Joker has told someone how he got the scars on his face, saying that his father, brutalizing his mother, looked at him, saying "Why so serious?" and cut the corners of his mouth to give him a permanent grin. He later gives other explanations for his face, suggesting that there is no one real truth to his life. But in this scene we see something akin to domestic violence, and what is most striking is that the Joker is in control and enjoys it, as he taunts the abusive Batman, "You have nothing. Nothing to threaten me with. Nothing to do with all your strength." This is pure sadomasochism, and it emphasizes the pleasure of the controlling masochist, the victim turned sadist.

The words are also very revealing in another way, as well. The Joker tells Batman, "You're not one of them. You're a freak like me." He is emphasizing a point that reverberates through the film, that they are related by their similarities, brothers in their fantastic abilities and freakish devotion to their beliefs. He also connects them in another way. Batman is incorruptible, always seeking good and justice, and the Joker is chaotic, always seeking to undermine what Batman hopes to build. It is in this context that the Joker tells Batman, "You complete me." He sees himself and Batman as parts of a whole, incomplete without each other.

We see more about this in their next and final face to face confrontation. This time, it is the Joker who appears to be in control. In a re-enactment of what he did earlier with Rachel and Dent, he has rigged two ferries with explosives, one filled with convicts and the other with ordinary citizens attempting to flee the city. Each boat has a detonator switch with which the other boat can be blown up. The Joker has told them that if one boat blows up the other, they will be spared, but if both are still intact, he'll blow them up at midnight. This is part of the Joker's promise to show Batman how civilized people behave when the chips are down. (His other proof is his corruption of Dent.)

The Joker has set up the two outwardly identical ferries, one of which must be blown up so that the other can survive, like twins fighting for survival. One of the ferries holds convicts, the dark side, while the other holds ordinary citizens, the innocents; but, the parable reveals that they are not so different. There is selfishness and murderous impulse in the "innocents" and noble intentions in the convicts, one of whom throws the detonator into the water.

Batman finds the Joker in an abandoned building overlooking the harbor, gets through his men with the help of a SWAT team, but is attacked by a pack of Rottweiler's guarding the Joker. As he throws off the last of the dogs, the Joker stabs him and manages to get him down under a heavy window frame, hanging over the edge of the building. As midnight strikes, the Joker is surprised and disappointed that neither ferry has been blown up.

Batman: "What were you trying to prove? That deep down, we're all as ugly as you? You're alone."

Joker: (He shows Batman the remote to blow up the two ferries.) "Ya gotta do everything yourself. I always have—and it's not always easy. You know how I got these scars?"

Batman: "No. But I know how you got these."

Batman unleashes blades that cut into the Joker and throw him back. Having seen the remote, Batman kicks the Joker over the edge of the building, grabbing the remote. As the Joker falls, he is cackling, seeming to enjoy the ride, but Batman shoots a grapple hook and pulls him back up, hanging upside down.

Joker: "You. You just couldn't let me go, could you? This is what happens when an unstoppable force meets an immovable object. You truly are incorruptible, aren't you? (The Joker is laughing as the Batman secures him upside down.) You won't kill me out of some misplaced sense of self-righteousness, and I won't kill you because you're just too much fun. I think you and I are destined to do this forever."

Batman: "You'll be in a padded cell forever."

Joker: "Maybe we can share one. They'll be doubling up, the rate this city's inhabitants are losing their minds."

Once again, we see the intense sadomasochism, the Joker seemingly enjoying his own pain, telling Batman that he won't kill him because he's *too much fun*. Once again, the Joker expresses the wish for them to remain forever playing with each other in this way. I'll go back to another of Glenn's (1974) descriptions of the dynamics of twins. I have italicized the features that seem to particularly apply to Batman and the Joker.

"Twins are generally brought up close to each other and develop extremely close relationships. The mother-child dyad is complicated by the fact that two children of similar appearance go through the developmental stages concurrently. The two infants coo to each other, watch and touch each other, play with each other, and later frequently develop a secret language together. *As they grow older they engage in intimate, ambivalent games. They get to understand and react to the whims and moods of their siblings with much greater empathy and accuracy than is generally the case with brothers and sisters*, often to the point that they become convinced that telepathic communication occurs. As Maenchen (1968) has so aptly put it, in some cases 'the twin symbiosis drains or replaces entirely the mother-child symbiosis' (p. 454). The intense affectionate ties between the twins are such that they love each other narcissistically *as they consider themselves part of a complete person. They strive to be with the other in actuality or in fantasy*, often through the presence of a substitute. They identify with and imitate each other. *Sexual acting out of the libidinal attachment may indeed occur, leading to homosexual activity.*" (p. 373)

It can be argued that the only sexuality in this film is the homosexual sadomasochistic violence between Batman and the Joker. In the Joker's words, the fantasy is that they will be together forever in sadomasochistic play, well above and removed from the society of mere mortals. And then, we get the sealing image.

"We're going to do this forever."

"You'll be in a padded cell forever."

"Maybe we can share it. They'll be *doubling* up ... ."

For a moment, we can imagine Batman and the Joker locked together in a padded cell, like two brothers together in the womb.

The Joker has come out of nowhere. When he is imprisoned, it is reported that his fingerprints match nothing in the files. It is as if he arrived in Gotham with no past. To my mind, there is the clear suggestion that the Joker arose in *response* to Batman. The Joker is his antithesis, and in that sense the missing twin that makes him whole.

I suspect that this is actually the filmmakers' intention, that as a pure, incorruptible hero, Batman is not a whole person. The evil and chaotic violence must be somewhere. The film displaces it to Batman's doubles, Harvey Dent and the Joker, essentially engaging in "splitting". It is as if the film is pulling in two directions, trying to set up an all good and an all bad twin, Batman and the Joker, but continually finding that that dichotomy does not work.

The film's ending conflates these diverging impulses. Batman takes upon himself the responsibility for Dent's crimes so that he will be hunted by the police as a murderer; but, at the same time, we, the viewers see him as the good twin, the innocent.

The Nolan brothers have once again given us a dark tale with the underlying form of twins, or brothers, who share between them good and evil, heroism and villainy, with just a touch of ambiguity about where the innocence really resides. These are lessons learned, perhaps, in the making of *The Prestige*, or perhaps in their own relationship as brothers.

Dargis, Manohla "Showdown in Gotham Town". *New York Times*, July 18, 2008.
Gilchrist, Todd "Review of 'The Dark Knight'". IGN.Com, June 30, 2008.
Glenn, J. (1974) Twins in disguise II: Content, form and style in plays by Anthony and Peter Shaffer. *International Review of Psychoanalysis* 1:373-381.

5

Selves

A Beautiful Mind

THERE IS A FUNDAMENTAL paradox which we each must bear alone.

We experience the world through our personal consciousness in a manner that puts us perpetually at the center; yet, we know that we are not at the center. It is only in the quiet of our minds that the contradiction can be resolved. For those who are creative, all of us, more or less, there are quiet moments when we enjoy the solitude— alone with beautiful music, a work of art, a daydream, swinging on a hammock, reading a book, losing ourselves in an idea or other creative work, enjoying the pleasure of ourselves. The creators of the film, *A Beautiful Mind*, have captured that human quality in John Nash. This is a man who can immerse himself in the patterns of mathematics. They have found a link between the solitariness of genius and psychosis and a need that we all share, quietly.

These private moments are particularly treasured when we find ourselves in a harsh environment, when the world around us is not so beautiful as the inner world, when "The truth is that I don't like people much and they don't much like me." We are introduced to Nash as he meets his fellow aspiring mathematicians around a punchbowl in a Princeton courtyard. The others seem to know each other, while Nash is a stranger to them. A confident young man named Martin Hanson joins the group. After greeting the others, he turns to Nash, who is standing by the punchbowl, and says,

"I'll take another."

"Excuse me?"

"A thousand pardons. I simply assumed you were the waiter. ... An honest mistake."

"Well, Martin Hanson. It is Martin, isn't it?"

"Well, yes, John it is."

"I imagine you're getting quite used to miscalculations. I've read your preprints, both of them, one on Nazi scientists and the other on non-linear equations, and I am supremely confident that there is not a single seminal or innovative idea in either one of them. Enjoy your punch." (Nash walks off.)

"Gentleman meet John Nash, that mysterious West Virginia genius, the other winner of the distinguished Carnegie scholarship."

Through Nash, we experience the pleasure of genius, strength and physical beauty along with qualities that we experience at our most uncomfortable moments, the social ineptness and defensive sarcasm of the outsider, an inability to relate to those around us, a facility for saying the wrong thing, particularly to those we most want to please and attract.

A pretty girl at a Princeton bar is drawn to Nash's good looks, but he doesn't know what to say. She suggests he buy her a drink and gets his reply.

"I don't exactly know what I'm required to say in order for you to have intercourse with me, but could we assume that I've said all that. Essentially we're talking about fluid exchange, all right, so could we just go to the sex?"

"Oh, that was sweet." She slaps him. "Have a nice night, asshole."

One price of too much self-indulgence is loneliness. We see Nash staring out his window at the students in the courtyard. At our loneliest, we hope to have one friend, a "secret sharer," who can appreciate the splendid isolation. Small children sometimes have imaginary friends, using their minds to create what the world does not provide. Others find a kindred soul. Nash has his roommate, Charles Herman, a brash English major with a British accent to boot, to whom he can unburden himself in a rooftop discussion over a whiskey flask.

"My first grade teacher told me that I was born with two helpings of brain and only half a helping of heart."

"Wow, she sounds lovely."

"The truth is that I don't like people much and they don't much like me. "

"But why, with all your obvious wit and charm. Seriously John, mathematics is never going to lead you to a higher truth. And you know why? Because it's boring."

"You know half these schoolboys are already published. I can't waste time with these classes, these books, memorizing the weaker substance of LESSER MORTALS. I need to work through to the governing dynamics, find a truly original idea. That's the only way that I'll ever distinguish myself, that's the only way that I'll ..."

"Matter!"

Charles is in tune with Nash's needs and his pain, but others are not. Hanson goads him, asking him what he'll do if he never makes his original discovery. While Nash works on his bargaining equilibrium, he is irked by Hanson's successes.

Those of us who, like Nash, depend upon the pleasure of ourselves become prisoners to the need to have the world appreciate our qualities. The more we come to depend upon our personal skills and achievements to establish our place, the more vulnerable we are to failure. Again, I speak of all of us, at times. We can feel the ache when we see the young graduate student, Nash, supplicating with a professor, who tells him, "The faculty is completing mid-year reviews. We're deciding which placement applications to support."

Nash mumbles rapidly about his first and second choices, but the professor interrupts him.

"Your fellows have attended classes. They've written papers and published."

"Oh, I'm still searching sir."

"Your original idea."

"Governing dynamics, sir."

"It's very clever, John, but I'm afraid it's just not nearly good enough."

The professor enters the faculty dining hall, with Nash in pursuit. Nash beseeches him about projects he has been working on, still speaking very rapidly, interspersing a request for a meeting with Einstein. Once again the professor interrupts him to point out what is going on in the dining hall.

A white haired man is seated at a table in the forefront while colleagues come to his table and one by one lay their fountain pens in front of him. The professor tells us,

"It's the pens, reserved for a member of the department that makes the achievement of a lifetime. Now what do you see John?"

"Greatness."

"Well, try seeing accomplishment."

"Is there a difference?"

"John, you haven't focused. I'm sorry, but up to this point your record doesn't warrant any placement at all. Good day."

Nash looks on as the great man continues to receive congratulatory handshakes. The camera pans away from him as he stares as if to make us feel small with him and distant from the group he is watching. As the scene fades out, it fades into mathematical formulas scrawled on Nash's window. We see a sad and frustrated John Nash bang his head against that window. His roommate Charles tries first to console him, then joins him in venting his anger and frustration by pushing his desk out of the window.

You don't have to be a mathematician to feel the ache of ambition. I doubt that there is a member of the audience who has not at some point experienced the frustration of one's failures alongside the dreams of accomplishment and recognition.

But through Nash, we can gratify that fantasy. Sitting in a college bar with his half mocking colleagues, Nash consolidates the idea for his "bargaining theory." A group of pretty girls enter the bar and all the young men have their eyes on the beautiful blonde in the middle. Nash, who has never had any success with women, uses his mind to develop a strategy that will make them all winners. Interestingly it involves the very cooperation and taming of individual ambition that Nash lacks.

"Adam Smith needs revision. If we all go for the blonde, we block each other, not a single one of us is going to get her. So then we go for her friends, but they will give us the cold shoulder because no one likes to be second choice. What if no one goes for the blonde? We don't get in each other's way and we don't insult the other girls. Soon we'll win, that 's the only way we all get laid. Adam Smith said the best result comes from everyone in the group doing what's best for himself. Right? That's what he said. Incomplete, incomplete, because the best result would come from everyone in the group doing what's best for himself and the group."

His mathematical solution to the problem of "governing dynamics" for cooperative bargaining is hailed as brilliant by his professors and wins him a coveted position with the defense contractor, Wheeler Labs, and a beer toast from his rivals, especially Hanson. For the moment, we can share his elation. But such a fire needs constant stoking.

His office in Wheeler Lab at MIT is small and hot. Nash has only been called to visit the Pentagon twice in years. The job includes teaching graduate students whom he knows will never understand mathematics as he does. Even being featured with others on the cover of Fortune Magazine is not enough. He sees his duties as a grind that keeps him from his true love, relieved only by secret victories. He later tells Charles that at first he thought his work was trivial until something came up.

Nash is introduced into the pentagon as "the analyst from Wheeler Lab." He looks confident now as a group of military men speak to him.

"We've been intercepting radio transmissions from Moscow. The computer can't detect a pattern, but I'm sure it's code."

"Why is that, General?"

"Ever just know something, Dr. Nash?"

"Constantly."

Nash looks up at a screen with seemingly random numbers and appears to be calculating, reading patterns in the chaos. We see different sets of numbers lighting up, completing some form of pattern.

"I need a map."

He tells them, "These are latitudes and longitudes" across the U.S. Map.

As Nash walks out he sees a mysterious man in civilian dress looking on. His visit to the Pentagon is followed up by a secret visit from the mysterious observer, Colonel Parcher. Like Charles, he appreciates Nash's abilities and can draw him out on his loneliness, although in a less friendly way.

"So, John, no family, no close friends, why is that?"

"I like to think it's because I'm a lone wolf, but mainly it's because people don't like me."

"Well there are certain endeavors where your lack of personal connections would be considered an advantage. ... You see John, what distinguishes you is that you are, quite simply, the best natural code breaker that I have ever seen."

Parcher recruits Nash for a top secret project to track the movements of Soviet agents through their hidden messages in newspapers and periodicals. Nash becomes deeply involved in deciphering messages—we see him frantically, obsessively, marking items from newspapers and magazines, the evidence of his efforts pasted on the walls of his office. He is drawn even further into a secret inner world.

But nature provides a counterweight to these solitary pleasures; Freud called it "object love." A beautiful young woman, Alicia, is drawn to Nash's raw beauty of body and mind. She ignores his social awkwardness.

"I'm wondering, professor Nash if I can ask you to dinner. You do eat?"

He answers awkwardly, but agrees. She manages him in social situations, and unlike the other women is not put off by his odd speech. As they sit by a river bank on a summer day, Nash tells her,

"I find you attractive. Your aggressive moves towards me indicate that you feel the same way, but still ritual requires that we continue with a number of platonic activities before we have sex. I'm proceeding with those activities, but in point of actual fact all I really want to do is have intercourse with you as soon as possible."

He expects a slap, but gets a passionate kiss.

The solitary Nash needs help deciding what to do about Alicia when Charles arrives for a visit, his orphaned niece, Marcy, in tow. Charles responds with enthusiasm and wisdom upon hearing of the relationship. "God that's wonderful!" Nash tells him things are going well enough and he's thinking of asking her to marry him, but he can't be sure. Charles tells him, "Nothing's ever for sure, that's the only sure thing I know."

Alicia is at her persevering best when John makes his awkward attempt at a proposal.

"Alicia, does our relationship warrant a long term committal? I need some kind of proof, some kind of verifiable data."

"I'm sorry, give me a moment to redefine my girlish notions of romance." She asks him how he knows the size of the universe is infinite without proof.

"I don't. I just believe it."

"It's the same with love, I guess."

And so the battle lines are drawn between the lure of narcissistic perfection and the pleasures of loving and relating. It is because we all have these competing urges that we, the audience are lured by Nash's struggle. It is because we can all at some level empathize with his ambitions that we can readily accept his psychosis.

The film makers have been clever. The film deliberately does not follow the usual conventions for depicting psychosis. We do not see jangling images intruding upon John Nash's sanity, nor whispering voices or discordant music plaguing the mind of the character and the audience. Instead, we merely enter into a man's life as he experiences it with no conventional cues about what is real and what is madness. We experience Nash's delusions as part of his reality. If we can be fooled by the delusional material, accepting it as reality in the context of the film, then we can easily empathize with John Nash believing the same.

The psychosis is an extension of Nash's inner world. The secret work for Parcher takes on a cloak and dagger quality as Nash leaves packets at a secret drop. He and Parcher are chased in a car by two foreign agents in a scene out of James Bond. Nash becomes afraid for his life. His wife becomes alarmed at his growing paranoia. By this time, the viewer, knowing in advance the theme of the film, is suspicious that we are entering the area of psychosis, but not sure just where it began or what it entailed. The answer is a surprise.

We see Nash going to give a lecture at a mathematics convention. His friend Charles arrives to attend, saying that he was in town and thought he'd hear his friend speak. Nash is upset and becomes more upset when he sees strange men entering the lecture hall. He obviously thinks they are agents bent on attacking him. He begins to run. By this point, we suspect that they may be part of his delusional system, but when they catch up with him, we discover that they are flesh and blood. They are led by a man who introduces himself as a psychiatrist. Eventually, they are forced to subdue and medicate Nash with his friend, Charles, looking on worriedly from the crowd.

I don't know what each viewer's reaction to this scene is, but the ambiguity, the fact that we cannot be certain if the men chasing Nash are real or imagined, demonstrates the film's success in getting the audience to share in Nash's confusion of reality and delusion. A moment later, we realize that our sharing of the delusion has gone further. The men chasing Nash at the lecture were real, but Charles was not! Charles is not a secret sharer, but an imaginary friend. Charles and Colonel Parcher are both part of Nash's delusional world. Even Alicia, who has never actually met Charles, cannot believe that Nash did not have a roommate at Princeton.

The delusions are particularly believable because they have been part of the needed resolution to the narcissistic wound. Having been made to feel his wounded narcissism earlier, we can easily identify with Nash's satisfaction at being recognized by Parcher as the world's greatest genius at seeing patterns. In an earlier scene, we have seen

Selves

Nash demonstrating this ability by playing a game with Alicia in which she named any shape and he would find it in the stars. In retrospect, that scene is a caution, reminding us that the ability to find patterns does not necessarily mean that the patterns are anything but random. Similarly, we feel the loss of the always helpful and much needed Charles. Charles appeared to represent a better side to Nash, more in tune with the real world and people, someone we might well have counted on to help him cope with his mental illness.

From this point on, the lines are clearer for us. We are no longer inside Nash's delusional world. Nevertheless, we remain sympathetic to his narcissistic needs. When Nash complains that the thorazine he is being given interferes with his ability to do his work, I, for one, was sympathetic to the dilemma. It is not surprising that faced with the loss of his work and his position, he is drawn back to the gratifying delusions.

The filmmakers keep us focused on the underlying conflict that is closest to our own, the struggle between narcissistic ambition and object love. Nash's preoccupation with his delusions becomes a danger to his wife and baby. It comes to a head in the dramatic form that comes naturally to film as the externalized inner world fights for its life. Nash has left the baby in the bath with the running water about to drown him. He tells Alicia that Charles was watching the baby. As Alicia tries to call the hospital, we see Parcher approaching her with a gun. Nash rushes at him, knocking down a frightened Alicia with the baby. As she runs out, Nash's thoughts become confused, with Parcher and Charles telling him to do away with Alicia.

Nash is forced to make a choice, but his solution is a compromise. He uses his "beautiful mind" to solve the dilemma of distinguishing reality from fantasy, providing himself with the narcissistic pleasure of solving a problem while choosing object love.

"She never gets old. Marcy (Charles's niece) can't be real. She never gets old."

He has figured out a means to reality testing, much as he had solved mathematical puzzles that defied other men. He is warned that without medication the fantasies may take over, but he decides to fight the illness, with Alicia's help. Their love for each other will pull him from his narcissism. He tells her to leave for her safety, but she returns. Facing him, she says,

"You want to know what's real? This." (She touches her hand to his face.) "This." (She brings his hand to her face.) "This." (She brings his hand to her breast.) "This is real. Maybe the part that knows the waking from the dream, maybe it isn't here." (She touches her hand to his head.) "Maybe it's here." (She touches her hand to his heart.) Finally, she enlists his narcissism as an ally. "I need to know that something extraordinary is possible." He nods agreement and they embrace, sealing the compact.

Nash returns to Princeton, where he is taken back with open arms by his old rival, Hanson. He is still haunted by his hallucinations, but he can share his experience with Alicia. He tells Charles that he has been a good friend, but he will no longer talk with him. We see him gradually return to a semblance of the academic life moving from campus oddity to involvement with students, and, eventually, teaching.

Finally, the narcissistic wound we experienced with Nash early in the film is healed in symbolic and dramatic fashion. He receives a visit from a man he does not know and asks one of his students to verify that she is seeing him—he is real. They walk towards the faculty dining hall, but Nash is not sure he is welcome. The visitor lets Nash know that his bargaining theory has become a staple of modern economics and has even been used in fields that Nash had never dreamed of. They sit in the dining room for tea, and the visitor explains that Nash has been selected to receive the Nobel Prize for his work. As they sit, other men get up from their tables one by one and in a re-creation of the ceremony we witnessed earlier with Nash as a small, distant, envious observer, they leave their fountain pens lined up in front of him, completing the gratification and healing the wound.

Nash's Nobel acceptance speech is again a gratifying compromise, declaring the victory of object love over narcissism while solidifying narcissistic gratification. Looking at Alicia in the audience, he says,

"I have always believed in numbers, in the equations and logics that lead to reason. But after a lifetime of such pursuits, I ask, what truly is logic? Who decides reason? My quest has taken me from the physical, metaphysical, the delusional and back, and I have made the most important discovery of my career, the most important discovery of my life. It is only in the mysterious equations of love that any logic or reasons can be found. I'm only here tonight because of you. You are the reason I am. You are all my reasons. Thank you."

What began as a quest for perfection has ended as a love story.

Up in the Air

WHEN I WROTE ABOUT the film, *A Beautiful Mind*, my focus was on the conflict between narcissism and object love. In the end, object love won the day, but both narcissism and object love were gratified as Nash devoted his Nobel acceptance speech to his love for his wife.

That film is one of a number that juxtapose narcissism and object love. The most common pattern in this hidden genre has to do with a central character with special talents who ultimately finds value in loving another person. Examples include *Mr. Holland's Opus*, *Finding Forrester*, and *Good Will Hunting*. We might also include *Schindler's List* and *As Good as it Gets*, which obviously share other themes.

In each of these examples, we, the viewers, can enjoy the pleasure of identifying with someone who has special talents that set him apart.

Narcissism has been looked at in various ways in the psychoanalytic literature, the most prominent coming from Self Psychology, which points to a separate line of development, but also stresses a defensive function in those traumatized early in life by disconnects with primary objects. Rothstein (1980) has written about a defensive fantasy, which he has called "The narcissistic pursuit of perfection," the title of his book on this subject. Without taking sides in the debate about mechanism, we can agree that these films allow the viewer to vicariously indulge in a fantasy of superiority and narcissistic perfection through the genius of their characters, real or fictional, such as John Nash or Will Hunting. In each of these films, that fantasy of perfection is juxtaposed with a sense of pain and a difficulty loving.

Which brings us to the most recent film in this series, *Up in the Air*. The central protagonist, Ryan Bingham, is not presented to us as a genius in the obvious way. Nevertheless, he may appeal to our desire for narcissistic perfection in a different way. Played to perfection (pun intended) by George Clooney, Ryan is both literally and figuratively above it all. Most comfortable above the clouds, he conveys a sense of cool, self possessed unflappability that in a bygone day we attributed to someone like Carey Grant, his demeanor and his suit seemingly never rumpled even when he is outwardly distressed. Like the characters in the other films in this series, he has removed himself from humanity and human caring. In fact, he is portrayed as an extreme caricature, a poster boy for emotional isolation.

I first saw this film at a time when I was particularly aware of the issue of narcissism and object love, having recently suffered the loss of the object of a great portion of my love. That loss had made me acutely aware of how important loving an object—not in the abstract, but as a vital part of my daily existence—was to my equilibrium. I had found myself turning at times to narcissistic satisfactions to help fill the void, and I was intently aware of the difference.

The film, from a novel by Walter Kirn, is based upon two strange premises. The first is a highly unusual, perhaps improbable job. We first see Ryan Bingham facing distressed, angry, worried people who are being told they are being fired from their jobs. His job is firing people, or as he describes it in response to one man's question, "Who the fuck are you?"—"I don't work here. I work for another company that lends me out to pussies like Steve's boss who don't have the balls to sack their own employees."

It was incredibly timely, as we faced high unemployment, many out of jobs or fearful of losing their jobs. We can easily empathize with the distress and rage as people hurl their abuse at Ryan Bingham, the hired messenger. He, in turn, looks perfectly cool and well dressed, a handsome, dapper George Clooney somehow maintaining calm in the face of the storm that confronts him. He makes no attempt to sugar coat it for us, the audience, points out his own lies and deceptions without apology, even suggests some sympathy with his victims and disgust for their employers. What comes through is that he is above it all.

Which brings us to the second premise, Ryan's predilection for spending time in commercial airliners. Ryan tells the aforementioned Steve that "we'll be in touch with you soon," then tells us that he'll never see Steve again. We see him quickly and efficiently getting ready to travel out, handling his belongings with James Bond-like precision. He examines one small leather carrying case as if he were a jeweler looking at the workings of a fine watch before deftly folding it and placing it in his suitcase. Making his way quickly into an airport, he tells us, "To know me is to fly with me. This is where I live." We see him move quickly and effortlessly through the airport security checkpoint as we viewers remember our own clumsy and frustrated efforts in an identical setting.

In the film's first few minutes we are confronted with two major modern-day bugaboos, tragic job loss and annoying airport stress. And through it all, we hear Clooney's relaxed voice and see him handsome and unruffled. That is this film's version of the narcissistic pursuit of perfection being used to deftly defend against trauma.

As we see Ryan sitting comfortably in a plane, the film gives us a little odd joke that we might cast aside as airplane humor, but which actually is the first of a series of subliminal messages. The stewardess comes through the aisle and asks him, "Do you want the cancer?" He is at first confused, but she then explains, "Do you want the can, sir?" Bingham laughs, saying, "No, I'm fine." But like a parapraxis, this slightly amusing but unnecessary encounter provides us with an entrée into the film's conflicts.

Just beneath the surface of this cool unflappability lies a world of danger. Throughout the film, we will hear little sound bites that remind us of the presence of calamity and trauma. Some of them come from Ryan amidst his pleasant, but cynical patter. While giving a critique on how to manage airport security, he reminds us of our mortality: "Old people are worse. Their bodies are littered with hidden metal and they never seem to appreciate how little time they have left on Earth."

A little later, he is describing his philosophy of his job: "We are here to make limbo tolerable, to ferry wounded souls across the river of dread until the point where hope is dimly visible—and then to stop the boat, shove them in the water and make them swim."

Throughout the film, we hear the plaintive wails of those being fired, but some provide us off screen images of common suffering: "And I guess without benefits, I'll be able to hold my daughter as she, you know, suffers from her asthma that I won't be able to afford the medication for."

Or, intimations of mortality dropped into a battle of the sexes debate: "Men get such hard-ons from putting their names on things. It's like you guys don't grow up, you need to pee on everything. Fear of mortality. It's like, 'Yeah, you're gonna die one day.'"

Ryan again, responding to a question about marriage saving us from dying alone: "Starting when I was 12, we moved each one of my grandparents into a nursing facility. My parents went the same way. Make no mistake, we all die alone. Now, those cult members in San Diego with the Kool-Aid and the sneakers, they didn't die alone. I'm just saying there are options."

While maintaining the light airy touch that it's title implies, the film is peppered with subliminal reminders of the dark corners of illness, trauma and, most often, mortality that must be kept in the periphery, in this case through narcissistic fantasy.

Bingham's other occupation is as a motivational speaker. He motivates people to cut loose from the material objects, and, later, the object relationships, that give them solace.

"Imagine for a second you're carrying a back-pack." He has the audience imagine filling it with all the belongings they have grown attached to and upon which they depend. "Feel the weight as that adds up." By the time the car and home are stuffed in, they are incapacitated. Now they are urged to set it all on fire. "Let everything burn and imagine waking up tomorrow with nothing. It's kind of exhilarating, isn't it?" We could almost imagine that he really believes the people being fired are entering a world of freedom.

The cracks in the armor appear early. Three things happen in rapid succession. (Actually it seems everything in this film happens in rapid succession. That is part of its charm.) He meets a woman, finds out about important changes in his work setup and has a demand put on him by his family.

The woman, Alex, seems by far the most benign of the three. She is a playmate, a kindred spirit who travels the country, is knowledgeable about travel and appears to have no ties. In a cute scene, we see them comparing their assorted plastic like two children playing "go fish." After love making, they sit at their back to back laptops in their underwear figuring out where in their itineraries they can set up another rendezvous. They speak in a rapid patter of cities, hotels, itineraries and airport initials and enjoy text sex from hotel rooms in different cities. She tells him to think of her as himself with a vagina. She is most impressed by his American Airlines Concierge Key card, likening his number of miles to penis size, telling him she finds the card "pretty fucking sexy."

The family ties look like a blip on the screen. Ryan takes a call from the older of his two sisters who pulls him into a family responsibility. His younger sister is to be married in two weeks and she asks Ryan to do something for the wedding couple. She wants him to carry a large poster with their images so that he can take photos of them at some of the sites he visits.

The most immediate threat to his narcissistic bliss comes from the job. He is called back to the home office in Omaha for a meeting of the entire company at which his boss, a sarcastic, sadistic SOB, presents "a young woman from Cornell," Natalie Keener, who has convinced him that they should do their business through computers so that the company does not have to pay its employees to travel all over the country to fire people. They can do it right from the home office. The young woman and her ideas bring in still another bugaboo for many of us, the anti-humanist, efficient and scientific (evidence based?) bearer of bright new ideas to cut through the waste of what we've been doing all our lives. As Ryan expresses our group frustration, "I don't think a My Space page makes you qualified to re-wire an entire company," he even makes a plea to his boss for the humanistic side of the dirty work he does. "What we do here is brutal, and it does leave people devastated, but there's a dignity to the way I do it."

The boss forces him to take Natalie with him on the road to "show her the ropes," as an alternative to just being taken off the road and put in front of a computer monitor. His blissful privacy has been disrupted. As if to add symbolic emphasis, he receives the enlarged photograph of his sister and her fiancé and finds it doesn't fit into his neat packing arrangement, forcing him to travel with the top of the picture sticking out of his bag. The illusion of perfection has been broken. As to the woman, that seems to be going well, but he does express fear about letting her into his life. To her "I am the woman that you don't have to worry about," he responds, "Sounds like a trap." For a while, the film moves along in standard comedy style as Ryan and Natalie odd-couple across the country, with tepidly clever dueling dialogue interspersed with more firings and angry hurt people. We see Ryan at his best with a middle aged man who fears his kids won't respect him, convincing the man to follow his dreams to be a chef. We see them taking pictures for his sister, and Ryan even gets to show us he has an interest in the history of air flight when he tells Natalie about the historic importance of the St. Louis airport.

The darker realities come through in the snippets of dialogue described above, in the angry and plaintive cries of those being fired, and, more directly in one encounter when Natalie does her first firing and confronts a woman who calmly tells her, "There's this beautiful bridge by my house. I'm gonna go jump off it." As if highlighting the film's ethos of pushing back such concerns, Ryan tells Natalie, "I wouldn't worry about it."

But the heart of the story is not about the economy and firings or remodeled jobs. It has to do with the conflict between narcissistic isolation and loving relationships. With Natalie looking on, Ryan's motivational lecture moves on to filling the backpack with people. He starts with casual acquaintances, cousins, aunts, siblings, parents "and finally your husband, your wife, your boyfriend, your girlfriend. ... Make no mistake, your relationships are the heaviest components in your life. You feel the weight of those straps cutting into your shoulders, all those negotiations and arguments and secrets and compromises ... ." His closing line lays down the gauntlet.

"Some animals were meant to carry each other, to live symbiotically for a lifetime, star-crossed lovers, monogamous swans. We are not those animals. The slower we move, the faster we die. We are not swans. We're sharks."

The rest of the film focuses on this credo. We see Natalie receiving a text message, and then she begins to cross examine him about his not wanting to get married and have a family. He deftly pushes aside her arguments, pointing out that most relationships end badly and generally everyone dies alone. The throw-out line about the Kool-Aid being an option suddenly pushes her to awkward tears and loud wails of pain as she announces that her boyfriend, Brian, has broken up with her with a text message, "I THINK IT'S TIME WE C OTHER PEOPLE."

Just at this point, Alex meets up with them. Over drinks, Ryan and Alex attempt to help Natalie through her grief. The hidden beauty of this scene is that as they soothe and spar with Natalie—sitting beside each other facing her, sometimes answering in unison—they become a couple. There is even a soft illusion of a family dynamic as the older couple tries to guide the youngster through a growth promoting crisis. This dynamic continues as the three of them crash a corporate disco party in which Natalie cuts loose and picks up a guy while Ryan and Alex play the happy couple, dancing while they try to keep an eye on Natalie and sitting off the end of a boat, feet dangling in the water, talking softly and smiling at one another. She knows about his "backpack" talk and he tells her just before kissing her, "Recently, I've been thinking that I needed to empty the back-pack before I know what to put back in it."

It's Natalie who puts into words what we have been made to feel. "You have set up a way of life that basically makes it impossible for you to have any human connection. And now this woman comes along and somehow runs the gauntlet of your ridiculous life choice and comes out on the other end smiling just so you can call her 'casual'?" She pushes Ryan to offer more of a relationship to Alex, and although he initially protests, circumstances converge upon him and us as we find ourselves moving in a familiar and pleasant romantic direction.

As the time approaches for Ryan to go to his sister's wedding in Wisconsin, he finds Alex and asks her to be his date for the weekend. "Look, I'm not the wedding type, right? But for the first time in my life, I don't want to be that guy alone in a bar. I want a dance partner. I want a 'plus one.' And if you can stomach it, I'd like it to be you." The next moment we are looking at his and her (blue and red) rolling suitcases moving through the airport together.

Now, we are really set up as we watch her accompany him deftly amidst his family and through his childhood memories, breaking into the high school to look at his pictures as a basketball star. We cannot help noticing that they make a beautiful and thoroughly charming couple. It would appear that in classic genre form, object love has won the day.

When his sister's groom gets cold feet, Ryan is called upon, with great irony, to defend marriage. Jim's fears go back to the film's underlying intonations of death.

"Well, last night I was kind of laying in bed and I couldn't get to sleep, so I started thinking about the wedding and the ceremony, and about our buying a house and moving in together, and having a kid and then having another kid. And then Christmas and Thanksgiving and spring break and going to football games. And then, all of a sudden, they're graduating, they're getting jobs, and they're getting married, and, you know, I'm a grandparent. And then I'm retired. I'm losing my hair. I'm getting fat. And then the next thing you know, I'm dead. I'm just like … I can't stop from thinking, "What's the point?" I mean what is the point?"

Ryan focuses the point, "Look, Jim, I'm not gonna lie to you. Marriage can be a pain in the ass. And you're kind of right. This all is just stuff that leads to your eventual demise. And we're all on running clocks, and they can't be slowed down or paused, and, you know, we all end up in the same place. There is no point." But then he argues for relating, "If you think about it. Your favorite memories, the most important moments in your life, were you alone? … Life's better with company. Everybody needs a co-pilot."

Anyone who has ever seen a romantic comedy is ready for what follows. Ryan abandons his backpack speech, leaving a confused auditorium full of people. He grabs a plane to Chicago and appears at Alex's doorstep, ready with his line, "I was in the neighborhood."

But as it turns out, this is not a romantic comedy. Object love does win out, but not via romance comedy. We feel the impact through tragedy. As we look on with Ryan as Alex answers the door, we see her looking upset and hear children's voices in the background and a man's voice asking, "Hey, honey. Who's at the door?" To which Alex answers, "It's just somebody who's lost."

Alex has been living a double life and she later, by cell phone, reproaches Ryan for threatening her security.

"That's my family. That's my real life."

"I thought I was a part of your real life."

"I thought we signed up for the same thing."

"Try and help me understand exactly what it is that you signed up for."

"I thought our relationship was perfectly clear. I mean, you are an escape. You're a break from our normal lives. You're a parenthesis."

"I'm a parenthesis?"

In a rough draft on identification in different literary forms, Jacob Arlow (2010) writes of tragedy that in it we share in the conflicts of the central character in such a way that we are deeply affected in an enduring way that transcends the end of the performance. Cornered by threats to his narcissistic construct that has provided him with safety, and lured by the romantic possibilities and above all the enchantment of meeting a kindred soul with whom he can share his world, Ryan has indeed fallen into a trap. Now he feels the full weight of the backpack, the pain of loss that he has avoided throughout the story. And with him, we can feel that ache of loneliness at love lost.

The film adds irony as Ryan achieves his goal of 10 million miles in the air as he is returning, forlorn, from Chicago. He meets the chief pilot, who hands him his award, but it is a hollow moment. Narcissistic perfection has crumbled beside the enormous loss it was designed to offer protection from.

We are never told what losses, what traumata Ryan was warding off. We don't need to be told, we can substitute whatever losses we have suffered that turn us to narcissistic pursuits for compensation and protection.

Ryan does become more human through his painful epiphany. He donates thousands of his flier miles to his sister and her groom. He writes a winning letter of recommendation for Natalie who gives up her own narcissistic quest in Omaha, perhaps after learning that the first woman she fired did indeed jump off a bridge.

In true tragic fashion, painful reality breaks through the facades we use to ward it off and Natalie, at least, moves on, back to San Francisco where she originally intended to work before being lured to Omaha by her now former boyfriend.

At the end, we see some of the people who were reacting earlier to being fired. Now their statements reinforce the value of relating, of object love:

"I would say without my friends and my family I wouldn't have made it."

"It would have been a lot tougher if I had to make it on my own."

"When I wake up in the morning and look over and see my wife, that gives me the sense of purpose."

"It's not all about the money. Money can keep you warm. It pays your heating bills, you know. It can buy you a blanket. But it's not as ... Doesn't keep you as warm as when my husband holds me."

"My kids are my purpose, my family."

By contrast, we see Ryan entering an airport, looking up at a massive arrival/departure screen and in a voice-over saying,

"Tonight most people will be welcomed home by jumping dogs and squealing kids. Their spouses will ask about their day, and tonight they'll sleep. The stars will wheel forth from their daytime hiding places. And one of those lights, slightly brighter than the rest, will be my wingtip passing over."

I wrote earlier that I first saw *Up in the Air* while attempting to emerge from my own grief after a personal loss. You might think that this ending would have left me depressed, in lasting identification with Ryan in his tragic failure, to use Arlow's concept. On the contrary, I left the theater with a good feeling. First of all, I was acutely aware that I was not like Ryan Bingham. I had loved and knew I would love again.

But even in my identification with Ryan, I was left with a sense of hope. I was less affected by his failure to find love than by his having become aware that he was capable of loving. Yes, perhaps he is now feeling he will not find another Alex, but to be frank, someone who looks and talks like George Clooney should be able to find someone to love.

Arlow, J. A. (2010) Shifting identifications in literary forms. *PANY Bulletin* 48:3.
Rothstein, A. (1980). *The Narcissistic Pursuit of Perfection*. New York: International Universities Press.

About Schmidt

> "A life is not important, except in the impact it has on other lives."
> JACKIE ROBINSON

WHAT HAPPENS WHEN A life loses its importance to other lives? Films have prominently focused on narcissistic issues in such films as *Mr. Holland's Opus* or *It's a Wonderful Life*, among others, in which the main protagonist must modify grandiose ambitions of youth in exchange for recognition from the people touched by his life. *About Schmidt* tackles a much riskier form of narcissistic issue; what happens when someone with narcissistic object ties loses those wan, but vitally important connections.

At the same time, the film has the potential to touch those of us who are not as one-sidedly narcissistically motivated as Warren Schmidt. Although different theoretical schools argue about its origins, there is no school of analysis that does not consider object relations at the center of it's theory. Even loners, the Silas Marners of the world, are at least unconsciously preoccupied with their earliest attachments. *About Schmidt* allows us to think about the importance of our object relations by demonstrating what happens when they are lost. If Jackie Robinson was right, then our lives lose all importance when we no longer have any impact on others.

At Warren Schmidt's retirement party, his best friend tells him, "What means something, what really means something, Warren, is the knowledge that you devoted your life to something meaningful, to being productive and working for a fine company, hell, one of the top-rated insurance carriers in the nation, to raising a fine family, to building a fine home, to being respected by your community, to having wonderful lasting friendships." This speech will prove negatively prophetic as we see Schmidt lose his meaningful relationships with his job, his daughter, his best friend and his wife. At retirement age, he finds that he is irrelevant, a complete outsider to the world around him. It is as if he were viewing a preview of his death, the ultimate complete removal of object ties. Ironically, each loss that Schmidt endures erodes his narcissistic shell, pushing him towards object relatedness.

We are introduced to Schmidt as he is preparing to leave his office for the last time. The sign on his building tells us that he works for "Woodmen" insurance, and, indeed, he looks like a "wood man." He is expressionless, waiting stiffly for the clock to strike five so that he can leave. We are left to wonder if he is waiting out the time because he is reluctant to leave or because he is committed to routine. Whether or not the former is also true, we can't help feeling that routine and obsessional rituals have been the clockwork of his life. In retrospect, we will look back to it to see that as with many people, the compulsivity of routine has helped disguise the vacancies in his life. At his retirement party that follows, he sits woodenly by his wife, looking expressionless and perhaps bored, stepping out at one point to get a drink at the bar.

Schmidt is given the usual assurances about his value. He is told by his young successor that he is welcome to come back to the office to provide advice, reassurances that belie the fact that he is no longer of use. He returns to the job with an innocence apparent to the viewer. The younger man does not know what to do with him, finally finding a way to get him out of the office. As he is leaving, Schmidt sees that his files have been thrown in the trash. The symbolism is not subtle. Although we may inwardly laugh at Schmidt's naiveté, it is likely that most viewers' associations will turn to the potential meaninglessness of our life's work after we retire, and perhaps at a more distant level to the time when we will be gone and forgotten.

Outwardly, Schmidt appears cool to his fate. He lies to his wife about the office visit, telling her that they needed him to fix some problems, showing us his wounded pride. But his feelings, particularly his "narcissistic rage," come out only in his "analysis".

Early in the film, Schmidt is watching TV when he sees an advertisement for a charity that supports children in developing countries. He calls the number and agrees to sponsor a child in Africa. When he receives the child's name and picture, he is encouraged to correspond. It is through this correspondence that he maintains the object tie that appears to maintain him as all others are lost. For most of the film, the boy, Ndugu, functions as a silent analyst, an epistolary transference object. The boy's unresponsiveness proves to be technically perfect for Schmidt's needs. It is only in his letters to the boy, Ndugu, that Warren Schmidt can openly express himself.

Schmidt's correspondence with Ndugu demonstrates to the viewer just how narcissistic and schizoid he is. He writes to the boy as if he were writing to a middle class American his own age. He appears to have no realistic view of his correspondent, using him as what Self Psychologists would probably call a "mirror transference." The content also demonstrates his narcissism and his narcissistic rage, which he has outwardly controlled under his expressionless mask. After a few polite words, inappropriate to a 6 year old African boy, but fairly neutral, he suddenly ventilates:

"Dear Ndugu,

My name is Warren R. Schmidt and I'm your new foster father. I live in Omaha, Nebraska. My older brother, Harry, lives in Roanoke, Virginia with is wife, Estelle. Harry lost a leg two years ago to Diabetes. I am 66 years old, recently retired as assistant vice president and actuary at Woodmen of the World Insurance Company *and God damn it if they didn't replace me with some kid! All right, so maybe he's got a little theory under his belt and can plug a few numbers into a computer. But, I can tell right off that he doesn't know a damn thing about genuine real world risk assessment or managing a department, for that matter, the cocky bastard.*" (erases "cocky bastard")

Schmidt resumes some control, but quickly expresses his feelings about how he has changed: "Anyway, 66 must sound pretty old to a young fellow like yourself. It sounds pretty old to me, too, *because when I look in the mirror and see the wrinkles around my eyes and the sagging skin around my neck and the hair in my ears, the veins on my ankles I can't believe it's really me.*"

He gives a history of his narcissistic ambitions: "When I was a kid, I used to think that I was special, that somehow destiny had tapped me to be a great man, not like Henry Ford or Walt Disney or somebody like that but, you know, somebody semi-important. I got a degree in business and statistics and was planning to start my own business someday, build it up into a big corporation, watch it go public, you know, maybe make Fortune 500. I was gonna be one of those guys you read about. But, somehow it just didn't work out that way. You gotta remember I had a topnotch job at Woodmen, a family to support. I couldn't exactly put their security at risk. Helen, that's my wife, she wouldn't have allowed it."

He is just hinting that his wife has thwarted his ambitions: "But what about my family, you might ask, what about my wife and daughter? Don't they give me all the pride and satisfaction I might want? Helen and I have been married 42 years. Lately, every night, I find myself asking the same question, 'Who is this old woman who lives in my house? Why is it that every little thing she does irritates me? Like the way she gets the keys out of her purse long before we reach the car and how she throws our money away on her ridiculous little collections. And tossing out perfectly good food just because the expiration date is past. And her obsession, her obsession with trying new restaurants. And the way she cuts me off when I try to speak. And I hate the way she sits and the way she smells. For years now, she has insisted that I sit when I urinate. My promise to lift the seat and wipe the rim and put the seat back down wasn't good enough for her. No."

He is more positive about his daughter, but the disappointments still come through: "Then there's Jeannie. She's our only. I'll bet she'd like you. She gets a big kick out of different languages and cultures and so forth. She used to get by pretty good in German. She'll always be my little girl. She lives out in Denver, so we don't get to see her much anymore. Oh, sure we stay in touch by phone every couple of weeks and she comes out for the holidays sometimes, but not as often as we'd like. She has a position of some responsibility out there with a high tech computer outfit so it's very hard for her to break away. Recently, she got engaged, so I, I suppose we'll be seeing even less of her now. The fellow's name is Randall Hertzel. He's got a sales job of some sort. Maybe Jeannie is a little past her prime, but I still think she could have done a heck of a lot better. I mean this guy's just not up to snuff if you ask me, not for my little girl. I'll close now and get this in the mail. Here I am rambling on and on and you probably want to get on down, cash that check and get something to eat. So best of luck in all your endeavors.

Yours very truly, Warren Schmidt."

As we see from this first letter, Schmidt is disappointed and angry with his life and the people close to him, but even these slender threads are to be broken. Schmidt is settling into his retirement, a seemingly reluctant participant in his very active wife's plans—she has convinced him to buy a mobile home—when his life is changed even more dramatically. He goes out to mail some letters and returns to find his wife dead on the floor, the vacuum cleaner she had been operating whirring on without her. Now, he is truly alone, left without his guide and buffer.

"Dear Ndugu,

I hope you're sitting down. I've got some bad news. Since I last wrote to you, my wife, Helen, your foster mother, passed away very suddenly from a blood clot in her brain."

He attempts to cover over his difficulties without Helen, telling Ndugu that he is managing well, while we see him languishing in an unkempt house, piling frozen dinners in his mobile home. Finally we see him in Helen's room dealing with his grief by putting on her cold cream and going through the clothes in her closet. Here he is more open in his letter.

"It occurred to me that in my last letter I might have misspoken and used some negative language in reference to my late wife. But you have to understand that I was under a lot of pressure following my retirement. I'm not going to lie to you Ndugu. It's been a rough few weeks and I've been pretty, you know, broken up from time to time. I miss her. I miss Helen. I guess I just didn't know how lucky I was to have a wife like Helen until she was gone. Remember that, young man. You've got to appreciate what you have while you still have it."

The loss has moved him a little beyond his narcissistic isolation. As the letter has proceeded, he was able to move from bravado and concern about covering his weakness to an acknowledgement of his need for another person.

At this point, his relationship with his wife takes another bad turn. While going through her things, he discovers a shoe box filled with love letters to her from Schmidt's best friend, Ray. His rage pulls him out of his grief and lethargy. He throws the letters at Ray, defies Helen by standing to urinate and takes off in the mobile home to try to spend some time with his daughter in Denver before her wedding. We see now that he began the film in a state of lethargy and unconscious dependence. His wife's death uncovered his intense neediness. Her betrayal now somewhat frees him to become more active. Unfortunately, when he calls his daughter from the road, she tells him not to come so soon, reminding him of his loneliness.

Schmidt does not reveal these narcissistic wounds in his next letter, but he describes an attempt to heal the wound. "I've decided to visit some places I haven't been to in a long tine. So much has happened in my life that I can't seem to remember whole sections of my life that are just ... gone. So you might say I've been trying to clear a few cobwebs from my memory. My first stop was none other than Holdrege, Nebraska. I thought it would be enlightening to visit the house where I was born 67 years ago next April. We moved away from Holdrege when I was not much older than you, and I've often wondered what our old house would be like today. Funny, I never forgot the address—12 Locust Avenue."

Even this tangible tie is removed. There is a tire store where his house used to be. Nevertheless, the now object hungry Schmidt reminisces, telling the salesman in the store where his bedroom used to be. In the background we hear children singing "Ring Around A Rosy" and we hear Warren's mother calling his name and telling him she loves him as he wanders through a playground.

Just as Schmidt continually attempts to disguise his feelings, the film, itself maintains a sardonic humor—we see him getting parking tickets while he tells Ndugu about his wonderful sight seeing trip and while he is buying Hummel figures in a store—that covers over his search for maternal love. "Helen loved Hummels." The parody continues when Schmidt meets a younger couple who invite him for dinner in their mobile home. They are caricatures of overly friendly neighbors who laugh raucously at every joke, but when the wife, alone with Schmidt, tells him that she senses his inner anger, fear and loneliness we sense derivatives of the underlying emotions. Schmidt tells her she has understood him better than his wife ever did and puts his head on her shoulder. Almost instantly, the film's defenses are raised as Schmidt attempts to kiss her leading to a farcical escape from her angry response.

Nevertheless, the film takes another serious turn, if momentarily. Schmidt calls Ray's answering machine to try to make amends, perhaps in response to his own attempt at adultery. That night, he parks at a wooded spot by some water. He lights candle on top of the mobile home and sits the Hummel figures around him while he tries to make peace with Helen. For once, he expresses his feelings directly, rather than through a letter.

"Helen? What did you really think of me? Deep in your heart. Was I really the man you wanted to be with? Was I? Or were you disappointed and too nice to show it? I forgive you for Ray. I forgive you. That was a long time ago. And I know I wasn't always the King of Kings. I let you down. I'm sorry, Helen. Can you forgive me? Can you forgive me?" He sees what looks like a streak of light in the sky, like a shooting star, but too quick even for that. He takes it as a sign.

"And so, Ndugu, I must say it's been a very rewarding trip. And this morning, I awoke from my night in the wilderness completely transformed. I'm like a new man. For the first time in years, I feel clear. I know what I want, I know what I've got to do, and nothing's going to stop me ever again. Meanwhile, along with the usual check, I'm enclosing a little something extra to spend as you please. Yours very truly, Warren Schmidt."

Schmidt's new determination is to convince his daughter not to marry Randall. We are not told explicitly how this connects with his coming to terms with his own marriage, but we might infer that he does not want her to settle for a lifetime with a man she will not really love. Randall is a caricature, a poster boy for failure who has a wall of plaques documenting his "honorable mentions" and has pulled his family members into a pyramid scheme. Schmidt is equally horrified by the dysfunctional extended family that has embraced his daughter. The film again turns to its defenses, presenting this extended section as farce. Schmidt corners his daughter for a moment to first beg and then insist that Jeannie not go through with the marriage, embellishing his plea with a tale of a bizarre dream in which space alien Randalls kidnap Jeannie. He ends up paying for his past sins of narcissism as she tells him, "All of a sudden you're taking an interest in what I do? You have an opinion about my life now?" Schmidt is forced to accept, finally making a gracious speech at the wedding.

"Dear Ndugu, you'll be glad to know that Jeannie's wedding came off without a hitch. Right now she and Randall are on their way to sunny Orlando—on my nickel, of course. As for me, I'm headed back to Omaha. I'm driving straight through this time, and I've made only one stop—the impressive new arch over the interstate at Carney, Nebraska—an arch that commemorates the courage and determination of the pioneers who crossed the state on their way west. You've really got to see it to believe it. And it kind of got me thinking."

His perspective has changed, now. In fact, he has momentarily given up any conscious or unconscious grandiosity: "Looking at all that history and reflecting on the achievements of people long ago kind of put things into perspective. My trip to Denver, for instance, is so insignificant compared to the journeys that others have taken, the bravery that they've shown, the hardships they've endured. I know we're all pretty small in the big scheme of things, and I suppose the most you can hope for is to make some kind of difference."

But it has left him conscious of his underlying depression: "But what kind of difference have I made? What in the world is better because of me? When I was out in Denver, I tried to do the right thing, tried to convinced Jeannie she was making a mistake, but I failed, Now she's married to that nincompoop, and there's nothing I can do about it. I am weak ... and I am a failure. There's just no getting around it."

He describes an existential loneliness, facing the end of his life, that may be common to all of us: "Relatively soon I will die, maybe in 20 years, maybe tomorrow. It doesn't matter. Once I am dead, and everyone who knew me dies, too, it will be as though I never even existed. What difference has my life made to anyone? None that I can think of. None at all. Hope things are fine with you. Yours truly, Warren Schmidt."

Despite the film's attempts to distract with parody and farce, we are brought, with Schmidt, back to the inner need behind the narcissistic defenses, the need to find meaning in relationships with others, to be "important" through object love. At this point, the film brings in its *deus ex machina* as Schmidt receives his first and only response to his letters.

"Dear Mr. Warren Schmidt, my name is Sister Nadine Gautier of the order of the sisters of the sacred heart. I work in a small village near the town of Mbeya in Tanzania. One of the children I care for is little Ndugu Umbu, the boy you sponsor. Ndugu is a very intelligent boy and very loving. Recently, he needed medical attention for an infection of the eye, but he's better now. He loves to eat melon, and he loves to paint. Ndugu and I want you to know that he receives all of your letters He hopes that you are happy in your life and healthy. He thinks of you every day, and he wants very much your happiness. Ndugu is only 6 years old and cannot read or write, but he has made for you a painting. He hopes that you will like his painting. Yours sincerely, Sister Nadine Gautier."

Schmidt opens the drawing, which shows two crudely drawn figures, one larger than the other, holding hands. He quietly breaks into tears and then we see a hint of a smile on his face. The drawing depicts Schmidt and Ndugu. He has been of importance, made contact with a child. In the world of imagination, the drawing depicts a parent and child, a loving union between mother and son, perhaps, that the film has only vaguely hinted at as the wish underlying Schmidt's unhappiness. We have not been told the source of his unhappiness, his penury, his need to sardonically hold people at bay, his failure to relate. If this were a real analysis, it would be just beginning

6

Outsiders

King Kong

WHEN THE NEW BLOCKBUSTER remake of *King Kong* came to theaters a few years ago, I thought I would take a closer look at the original film. Most of the monster pictures of the past are relatively forgotten, but somehow *Kong* has held its place in our imagination. I remember reading many years ago that it out-rated nearly all other old films on New York City television. How many of us associate to Kong when we think of the Empire State Building? Without Kong, Fay Wray would be known only to movie trivia buffs. In fact, a few years later, the "blockbuster" has faded into the lists of films we can scroll through on television while the clumsy, grainy original still holds an iconic spot in many of our minds. What I found when I examined the classic *Kong* was that that is not an accident.

Over the years, there have been a number of interpretations of the story. The film, itself portrays it as a modern day "Beauty and the Beast," opening with a quote across the screen, attributed to an Arabian proverb. "And lo, the beast looked upon the face of beauty. And it stayed its hand from killing. And from that day, it was as dead." The allusion is repeated several times in the film by Carl Denham, an adventurous filmmaker who sets the action of the film in motion, culminating in the final line, "It was beauty killed the beast." Like all of the interpretations, it rings true. This is clearly a story of a powerful, proud beast who comes to a mighty fall (from a great height) because of his obsession with a beautiful woman.

Browsing the websites about Kong, I learned that there was a sociopolitical interpretation in the film theory literature that the abduction of Kong from his home island, where he reigned, bringing him in chains to New York, was a representation of slavery. Kong represents white peoples' fears of African Americans, brought here by duress from a different culture, imagined to be primitive and violent. Kong's pursuit of Ann Darrow fits the cultural myth of the oversexed primitive man pursuing the chaste blonde beauty. At one point, the native chief wants to trade six of his women for "the woman of gold" and Denham comments, "Blondes are scarce around here." In effect, this is a fantasy that displaces lust and violence to the stranger. From this viewpoint, Kong is a 40 year precursor of *Sweet Sweetback* and the "Blacksploitation" films.

Then there is the commonly held view—I don't know to whom to attribute it—that Kong is a metaphor for our struggle with increased industrialization and technology. In this view, Kong is a sympathetic figure, torn from the natural world in which he was a monarch and ultimately brought down by modern technology in the form of airplanes and machine guns. He dies in the modern jungle of New York City, a tragic hero who encapsulates our frustration with an ever changing, more complicated, man-made world that pulls us out of nature.

Mark Rubenstein in a beautifully written paper in *American Imago* (1977), sees Kong as a totem animal, symbolic of the primal father as depicted by Freud in "Totem and Taboo". Kong is worshipped by the natives on Skull Island, who dance in ritual gorilla costumes and sacrifice a woman from the tribe to be his bride. The people on Skull Island and the people on Manhattan Island represent the primal horde that eventually kills this powerful father. With Kong's death, we experience complicit guilt in his murder.

What is immediately striking is that every one of these interpretations is very plausible. This film is evocative of multiple interpretations on multiple levels. This should not surprise us, since the film has had enduring appeal for over seventy years.

I have seen the film a few times over the years, and have the impression that it affected me differently each time. I don't have a distinct memory of seeing it for the first time, but my recollection is that I was quite young and that I was very frightened of Kong. As a small child, I recall being relieved when the planes finally shot him down. I was terrified that this powerful monster could destroy the world I knew. This is our reaction to most monster films. I don't think many people are cheering for a giant T Rex rampaging through the city, eating people haphazardly, but Kong, in a humanoid form, does evoke our sympathy, a sympathy I was able to experience more as I matured.

The film begins with a promise of the primitive and exotic. Before we see anything, we read the Arabian proverb, already suggestive of unknown mysteries and different cultures, followed by the pounding of a large metallic gong that brings the title to the screen. As the story opens, we are quickly told about an adventurous and reckless filmmaker, Carl Denham, who is secretive about his cargo as his ship sits on a New York dock. We quickly learn that this will be a voyage to an unexplored island inhabited by primitive natives and foreboding denizens. Clearly, a sense of adventure, curiosity and danger is evoked.

The second theme that is introduced is the vulnerability of women and the need to protect them from danger. The first self-proclaimed protector is a theatrical agent who refuses to provide Denham with an actress to join the voyage as a star for his next film. Denham wants a woman to add a love interest to his wildlife adventures, but the agent tells him that he would not put a woman into such danger, "the only woman on a ship with the toughest mugs I ever looked at."

Denham argues, "Why, there are dozens of girls in this town tonight in more danger than they'd ever see with me."

The ship's mate, Jack Driscoll, counters, "Sure, but they know that kind of danger."

In the comment about "this town" and the allusion to the crew, we are reminded that the primary danger to a woman comes not from wild animals that will kill them, but from wild, lustful men. This is reinforced in the next scene, when Denham, desperate to find a woman to take with him by the morning (before the authorities find out they have explosives on board), wanders into the poorer areas of the city in search of his star. He rescues Ann Darrow, close to starvation and accused of theft by a fruit peddler. After giving her a meal, which she eats with gusto, he proposes to take her for an adventure. "It's money, and adventure, and fame. It's the thrill of a lifetime. And a long sea-voyage that starts at six tomorrow morning." Seeing that she is scared about what he wants her for, he reassures her that "this is strictly business. I'm no chaser." He is not one of those unconscionable lustful men who prey on poor girls. (No, he is a filmmaker who would expose her to any danger to foster his creativity and his ambition.)

Then there is Jack, the first mate, who tells Ann that it is bad to have a woman on a ship. He is uncomfortable, with a movie cowboy innocence, trying to explain that a woman is a distraction on a long voyage. He even accidentally slaps her, displaying inadvertently (unconsciously) that men can be rough with women.

So that even before we reach Skull Island, we have been titillated with a promise of unknown excitement, while also reminded that we must control our sexual desires. Ann is an object of desire that must be protected, ostensibly from the desire of others, but clearly also from our own passion. As the ship approaches the supposed coordinates of the uncharted island, it moves in a thick fog, increasing our sense of foreboding, as well as curiosity and a desire to see. Finally, the fog lifts and we see the island at a distance and hear the beating of drums.

Sexuality and aggression, bound tightly in conflict to this point, is displaced to the island natives. As the boarding party begins to hear native chanting, Jack Driscoll, the mate, distances himself from them, saying that they are "Up to some of their heathen tricks." The natives, with their relative nudity and gyrations as they engage in a ritual dance evoke in us a sense of relatively unrestrained sexuality and aggression. They are less protective of women. A young woman is tied down in a kneeling posture with a flower wreath on her head. We learn that she has been chosen to be the bride of Kong. Unlike the civilized Denham, these people do not need to disguise or disown their willingness to sacrifice the woman for their own needs, in this case to placate the God-like Kong and, as Rubinstein points out in his paper, to ask for his protection. Like Sendak's "Wild Things", the island's natives represent the repressed impulses of the "civilized" characters and audience. Through them we get a somewhat frightening sense of what would happen if we did not control the id. In fact, they, too, desire Ann, the "woman of gold", wishing to trade six of their women for her so that she can be presented to Kong.[1]

Even the natives displace the full expression of their drives. The native chief does not want Ann for himself, but for the deified Kong. Even before we have seen him, Kong has become the ultimate expression of unbridled sexuality and aggression. As an object of fear and worship, Kong has the exaggerated power of a father imbued with all the brimming sexuality and aggression of a child.

The encounter with the natives seems to gently lift some of Jack Driscoll's repression. Back on ship, Jack is able to express his love for Ann, after a coy shipboard flirtation, and to propose marriage to her. We might think that he is responding to the rivalry brought up by the chief's desire to acquire Ann to be the bride of Kong. That rivalry heats up immediately. After Jack makes his proposal and kisses Ann, a party of natives sneaks aboard the ship and abducts Ann.

Jack's approach to Ann is gentle and respectful. He is somewhat diffident, even as he kisses her. He behaves the way a man should behave in a 1933 film. His rival, Kong, is a true "monster from the id." He is huge and his face is ferocious, with sharp teeth and a face

---

[1] For those interested in the slavery theme, here is another bit of evidence, in this case with the woman being looked at as a belonging who can be bartered and used.

caught in perpetual grimace. With one huge paw he grabs the screaming Ann and pulls her free of the ropes with which the natives have tethered her between two poles. This is the sexualized assault that we have been warned about since the start of the film.

What impresses us most about Kong is his size. In fact, the entire interior of the island is designed to make us feel small. The rescue party from the ship, led by Denham and Jack Driscoll, looks Lilliputian as it enters the jungle of Skull Island. Even the trees are huge. Before they ever see Kong, the sailors are attacked by a series of massive dinosaurs. (One of the remarkable features of *King Kong* is that "Jurassic Park" is the second billing. The animator for Kong developed his technique working on the silent film, *The Lost World,* a few years before and simply used the same flexible manikins for this film.)

As we identify with the human characters, we are awed and frightened at feeling so small. That experience itself returns us to a sense of childhood, of having to navigate in a world in which we are seemingly the smallest objects. We see the men overthrown from a raft, knocked off a tree and eaten by a dinosaur, shaken off a huge log by Kong, who grabs it with one paw. A scene in which men are killed by giant spiders was edited from the film and never seen as part of it to my knowledge. Size is always the key element in this particular *genre* of monster film. It reduces grown men and women to the helplessness of childhood and beyond. In this film, there is an added element that reinforces a sense of reversal.

The filmmakers gave the giant gorilla traits that we would associate with monkeys. He displays a primitive curiosity. It also gives him a child-like quality. Kong is continually prodding and sniffing with a look of wonderment as if he is still learning his world. At one point, he reaches down over a cliff edge to try to get to Jack Driscoll who has survived attacks in which most of his fellow rescuers had perished. Jack pulls out a knife and stabs the finger reaching for him. Kong pulls back his paw and then examines it as if curious and baffled as well as hurt.

Most infant-like is Kong's tendency to examine objects by putting them into his mouth. At various times we see him grab a terrified man and put him into his mouth. He invariably spits him back out. Unlike other cinematic predatory monsters, Kong is not eating his victims, he is using a very typical infantile method of exploration. This quality is part of what makes Kong so evocative for us. He is like a giant, powerful toddler on the loose, every young parent's worst nightmare.

Kong's infantile nature also allows him to give innocent expression to sexual desire. Jack Driscoll kisses Ann as he proposes to her aboard the ship, but Kong moves the act forward by peeling off pieces of her dress as if they were flower petals, looking at each piece with a bewildered curiosity as if discovering for the first time that the clothing is not part of the woman. The censors apparently feared that the audience's focus would be on the partially stripped young woman rather than the petals of the dress, keeping this scene out of the film for at least two decades.

It is not only his childlike behavior that enlists our sympathy for Kong. It is also the fact that in the world of Skull Island, he is the only one who can protect the helpless Ann Darrow. As he carries her through the jungle that he knows so well and she not at all, he is like a parent or nanny carrying a helpless child. Whenever he is distracted and must put her down, she seems to get into trouble.

At one point, he leaves her sitting on a tree limb high above the ground while he goes to check on his tiny pursuers. A Tyrannosaurus happens along and is blindly wandering towards Ann's perch. Kong hears Ann's screams, diverting him from his pursuit of Jack Driscoll, and returns to protect his new possession from this threat. In a later scene, after again leaving her alone on a ledge outside his mountain cave, Kong must rescue Ann from a pterodactyl that is attempting to fly off with her. In each case, we naturally hope that Kong will win the battle, implicitly accepting him in his role as her protector.

Kong looks infantile as he prods the limp head of the vanquished T. Rex, as if to make sure it is dead, but also with what seems a childlike curiosity about the mechanism. Moments later, he is protective (parental?) as he frees Ann from beneath a fallen tree trunk and gently scoops her up. We have a reversal of roles as the infantile Kong protects the adult Ann Darrow; but, the roles are also conflated in each of them. Kong is primitive, but capable and protective, while the mature Ann is naïve and helpless in this strange environment.

As Kong rescues Ann from the dinosaur and carries her to the safety of his mountain cave, Jack Driscoll is in pursuit, intent on saving her from Kong. These two rescuers present us not only with a rivalry for possession of the woman, but two objects for identification. Although we are rooting for Jack to save Ann and bring her back to the world she knows, we must also root for Kong to save her from the monsters of Skull Island, a feat beyond Jack's capability.

Not only do we have multiple identifications, but also shifting roles for the characters in the Oedipal drama. Jack and Kong are rivals for Ann, but the role of father and son, if we think of it as an Oedipal rivalry, is ambiguous. The tiny Jack Driscoll is very much like the boy, Jack, in "Jack and the Beanstalk", attempting to steal from the powerful giant who has killed and represents his father. But he is also in the role of the Oedipal father, the rightful and accepted possessor of Ann's affection, who has had her taken from him by the child-like Kong.

The "Jack and the Beanstalk" association may have been intended. Jack Driscoll attempts to escape with Ann from Kong's lair by climbing with her down a vine. Kong finds them and tries to pull them back up only to have them fall into a providentially placed lagoon below them.

I believe that much of the appeal of this film comes from the multiple shifting identifications it affords us. As we follow the rapid paced adventure and gape at the sheer enormity of its creatures, we rapidly and preconsciously identify with Jack, Kong and Ann. As we do, we can simultaneously experience the power of the Oedipal father, the envy and revenge of the child and the terrified excitement of the mother, being coveted and fought over, possessed and rescued. Through Kong and the primitively portrayed natives of the island, we can experience sexual and aggressive passions, while through Jack Driscoll, we gratify such desires in more muted form while gratifying our ego ideal.

All of this comes to its culmination back in New York. Like the giant in the fairy tale, Kong chases after Jack and his stolen bride only to be knocked out by a gas bomb thrown by Denham and brought in chains to captivity where he is displayed on the stage of a theater, shackled in a position much like the one Ann was in when he took her. Ann and her fiancé, Jack are brought up to the stage, and when photographers start shooting off flashbulbs, Kong becomes enraged, thinking that they're hurting Ann, according to Denham.

The rest is history. The enraged Kong tears through New York City, mindless of human life as he looks for Ann. In a scene which was censored out for many years, he pulls another woman out of her apartment and seeing she is not Ann, drops her to her death. He has the single-mindedness of a bonded infant. Finally, in what is perhaps the least probable event in the film, he finds Ann in the middle of Manhattan. As he carries her to the highest spot on the island, the newly built Empire State Building (a huge object of our world), we have to be struck by the gentleness with which he treats her in contrast to his indifference to the destruction he creates to every other person and object. He places her down gently on a ledge atop the skyscraper to face the airplanes. Once again, Jack climbs the mountain, this time from the inside, to bring her to safety In a recapitulation of the scene with the pterodactyl, Kong swipes down one of the planes, but they are too numerous and finally shoot him down. We can see his pain as he sways atop the building, holding his wounded chest.

When Kong falls to the ground, someone says that the airplanes got him. Denham corrects them that "it was beauty killed the beast," a phrase that at this point has added meaning for us. It represents for each of us both the moral lesson, learned in our identification with Kong, that left unfettered our passions will end in our destruction, and the pleasure of Oedipal victory in our identification with the more mature and sublimated Jack. As for our identification with Ann Darrow, she has enjoyed the intense sadomasochistic passion of being loved by a supremely powerful and unbridled hairy ape as well as the more sublimated pleasure of a more conventional marriage to the smaller, but still brave Jack Driscoll.

Rubinstein, Mark (1977) King Kong: A myth for moderns. *American Imago* 34:1-11.

Moving Pictures: Films Through a Psychoanalytic Lens

The Lives of Others

THE "PRIMAL SCENE" IS a phrase coined by Freud (1918) to highlight the effects upon a child and the adult that follows of witnessing parental intercourse. Since it has a great deal to do with watching, it should be no surprise that it lends itself to film in general and in this case, no surprise that it particularly lends itself to a film that has to do with state surveillance.

I have not yet met anyone who saw *The Lives of Others* who didn't speak highly of it. It allows us a frightening view of a totalitarian state (East Germany, circa 1984) that rivals anything in Orwell's imagination. Big Brother is watching and we watch along with him. It also gives us a story of miraculous transformation as a hardened Stasi agent, an "idealist" who lives for the state, becomes a rebel and a closet romantic.

It is a film that can be looked at from many perspectives, but I will focus on one, looking at the film through the prism of the dynamics of the primal scene. I'll use as my text on the primal scene, Arlow's paper, "The Revenge Motive in the Primal Scene" (1980). Arlow's premise, in a nutshell, is that many if not most people experience and organize primal scene memories and fantasies (having to do with witnessing parental intercourse) as an envious onlooker, left out of the parental couple. This leads to fantasies of revenge and reversal, in which the subject projects herself into the primal scene, removing one of the partners or forcing someone else to view her in some version of a reconstruction of the primal scene. He points out that people who have experienced the primal scene in childhood often find ways to expose their own children to the primal scene or its equivalent, in effect reversing their position, making themselves one of the lovers who is observed. He also points to fantasies of revenge against one or both of the partners witnessed in the primal scene and to a frequent confusion of memory and distortions of perception in those affected by primal scene exposure. Arlow used the film *Blowup* as an example of these dynamics, most eloquently the loss of trust in memory suffered by someone affected by witnessing parental intercourse or its equivalent. All of these dynamics come strongly into play in an examination of *The Lives of Others*.

A skeptic might argue that *The Lives of Others* because of its subject matter, state surveillance, is inevitably going to be about voyeurism and that our ideas about the primal scene are merely tacked on to something that has nothing to do with it. We can turn that argument on its head and ask how such material could not evoke unconscious reactions to the primal scene. But I will go one step further. The filmmakers use the dynamics of the primal scene, presumably without conscious awareness of those dynamics, to exact upon the agents of the East German government (GDR) exactly the forms of revenge that Arlow's patients exact in fantasy upon their parents.

The film tells us that the representatives of the repressive government envy the freer, more fulfilling lives of the people they dominate and constantly observe. Like the primal scene child, these totalitarian agents are forced to watch others live and love. In the film, the people being observed are artists, accustomed to self expression and passion, accentuating our sense of the gap between them and their masters. Ironically, the powerful government officials appear to resent the greater freedom of their subjects.

Colonel Grubitz, a leading figure in the Secret Police, the Stasi, demonstrates this envy in describing methods for dealing with different types of creative artists. For one group, typified by one of the film's central characters, the recommended approach is temporary detention.

"Complete isolation and no set release date. ... Know what the best part is? Most type 4's we've processed in this way never write anything again. Or paint anything, or whatever artists do."

He wishes to destroy the creativity that he cannot emulate. In another scene, Grubitz teases and verbally tortures a young man who is trying to tell a little joke about Erik Honniker, the head of the East German government.

A second representative of the regime, Bruno Hempf, the Minister for Culture, is in direct sexual competition with a younger, handsomer, more talented playwright, Georg Dreyman. After sitting through Dreyman's play, the Minister, Hempf, sits at a party enviously watching Dreyman dancing with his lover and the play's leading lady, Christa Maria Sieland. Like Arlow's patients, Hempf contrives to interrupt this primal scene derivative, going to the microphone to make a speech in order to stop their dance. He goes to them afterwards and attempts to dance with Christa Maria himself, but she politely rebuffs him.

Hempf intrudes upon the couple more directly than this. We soon learn that he has been having a secret affair with Christa Maria, coercing her with his influence over her career. He has encouraged Grubitz to begin a surveillance of Dreyman, hoping to catch him in subversive activity so that he can remove him completely from Christa Maria.

The filmmakers are showing us that this was a government that, out of envy, tried to drain the life and love out of its citizens. One of those citizens describes the helplessness and hopelessness of the primal scene observer, forbidden to be part of the action. He is an older, supposedly brilliant director, Jerska, who has been blacklisted. He tells Georg Dreyman, "What is a director if he can't direct? He's a projectionist without a film, a miller without corn. He is nothing. Nothing at all." It will drive Jerska to suicide.

But the center of the story, and the focus of the primal scene dynamics, revolves around the Stasi agent, Gerd Wiesler, who conducts the surveillance of the lovers. We first see him, in the film's opening scene, as a participant in a muted primal scene. He conducts a brutal interrogation of a man who knew someone who defected to the west. The young man is brought into a bare interrogation room where he is forced to sit on his hands as he answers questions from his cold, dispassionate interrogator. We soon see that this interrogation is the centerpiece of a class given by the interrogator for young, aspiring Stasi agents who listen to taped excerpts of the interrogation. When one student remarks that not allowing the man being interrogated to sleep is inhuman, Wiesler, the instructor/interrogator pointedly makes a mark in the student's file, we assume a black mark against him.

Wiesler is the consummate voyeur. He is a man presented to us as having no personal relationships, a wardrobe designed to be unnoticed, a box-like apartment that lacks the personal touches of a motel room and a face and voice that show no expression or feeling. He is "designed" not to attract attention. He has no life or personality of his own. Seemingly his only function is to observe the lives of others. Yet, somehow he is drawn into the action of the people he is observing as the story unfolds.

Wiesler's primal scene experience begins even before his official surveillance. He is taken to see one of Dreyman's plays by his superior, Colonel Grubitz, who describes Dreyman as "the only non-subversive writer we have." Wiesler is skeptical, saying that Dreyman is someone who should be watched. They sit in a box in a corner above the theater with opera glasses, looking down on and commenting not only on the play and the playwright, but even on the theater goers below, particularly Bruno Hempf and his entourage. After the play, when Grubitz goes down to the orchestra section to talk with Hempf, Wiesler stares down at them from his box and at Dreyman and Christa Maria, his leading lady, as they embrace.

We can use the reaction of one prominent viewer, the *New Yorker* (2007) film critic, Anthony Lane, who wonders why Wiesler is immediately suspicious of Dreyman. Lane looks for an explanation in Wiesler's envy as a lonely observer.

"What is it that alerts him? The curtain call, brimming with a warmth that he, as a Stasi operative, will never feel? The kiss that Christa Maria exchanges with Dreyman? Or, most wounding of all, their happiness?"

Immediately, we find ourselves in the midst of Arlow's dynamics.

As Wiesler and his technicians set up the intricate wiring in Dreyman's apartment needed to conduct the surveillance, we are reminded of another aspect of the primal scene, the prohibition against watching and remembering what was seen. Pseudo-stupidity has been associated with primal scene experiences. Dreyman's neighbor across the hall, a middle aged woman, watches them working through the peephole in her door. When the work is finished, Wiesler, somehow knowing that she is watching, goes straight to her door and threatens her that if she speaks of what they have done, her daughter will lose her position at the university. The woman, of course, agrees to ignore what she has seen.

The film's central primal scene dynamics are built around Wiesler's surveillance of Dreyman and Christa Maria. Even before the apartment has been wired, we see Wiesler personally observing his subjects from the street. He looks up at a window to see Dreyman and Christa Maria kissing. He notes it in his book. He spies Christa Maria coming out of a car and notes down the license plate, to learn later it is Hempf's car. At first, Wiesler is an impassive, seemingly disinterested observer. He writes in his first report, for instance, "presumably have intercourse." By contrast the man who takes the other shift, a coarse, lower level agent, is openly pleased to listen to the love making. "These artists! They're always at it!"

We see the first sign of emotion when Wiesler sees Hempf about to let off Christa Maria from their tryst. We, the viewers, have been witness to this tryst, a nasty looking scene in which the old, burly Hempf forces himself on a seemingly disgusted Christa Maria. This, too, is a variant of the primal scene, noted for us as we see Hempf's driver peeking into the rear view mirror. The contrast is striking between this sordid sexual encounter, with the overweight, older Hempf pulling off his pants to reveal a particularly unattractive view of his buttocks, and the affectionate intimacy that we see between the attractive Georg Dreyman and Christa Maria. Despite his power, Hempf remains the outsider, trying to intrude into the primal scene, but achieving only a furtive sexual encounter in the back of a car.

Wiesler, of course, has not witnessed this primal scene. Perhaps he has imagined it. However, the film viewer has been set up to feel disgust and anger at this sordid scene, putting us in sympathy with any anger or disgust that Wiesler is possibly feeling. What we see is that when he sees Hempf's official car pulling up in front of Dreyman's building, Wiesler suddenly leaves his position of pure observer and leaps into the action. Saying, "Time for some bitter truths," he repeatedly activates the buzzer to Dreyman's apartment, so that Dreyman is forced to go down to the street door to see who is there. There is no one at the door, but Dreyman sees Christa Maria coming out of Hempf's car.

This is a turning of the tables that Arlow describes, a revenge in the form of having one of the lovers forced to be in the position of the outsider, watching the primal scene. In this context, Wiesler's comment, "Time for some bitter truths" would appear to express his envy and anger as he revenges himself on Dreyman in particular and the lovers together, very likely in the hope of interrupting their relationship. It does not happen. When Dreyman begins to approach Christa Maria who is lying in bed, she asks him to "just hold me." We leave them with Georg embracing her.

At this point, we get a clue into Wiesler's reactions. He is awakened from his listening, presumably to the lovers sleeping embraced, at the end of his shift. We see him heading to his home, where he arranges for a visit from a prostitute, a quick, impersonal bit of sex with Wiesler sitting on a recliner, his shirt still on as the somewhat overweight woman has sex with him. It is more reminiscent of Hempf's sordid sex with Christa Maria than with the lovers in bed. As if to emphasize the loneliness and primal scene envy of the Stasi, the prostitute lets him know that she visits a "a bunch of you guys" in his building. When it is over, he holds her and pushes his face between her breasts. As she pulls away, he asks her "stay awhile", but she tells him she has another customer in half an hour.

The viewer is obviously struck by the contrast with the affectionate embrace of Georg and Christa Maria. But from our view through the dynamics of the primal scene, we see something else as well. The seemingly impassive Wiesler, having shown some emotion by trying to interrupt the lovers and break them apart is now expressing his envy by trying to engage in love making of his own, only to find that his plea to be held, to have the prostitute stay longer, is coldly rebuffed.

Arlow stresses the wish of the primal scene witness to enter into the action. Wiesler appears to be attempting to do it through identification with the lovers. In fact, in the next scene, we see him enter the apartment. He kneels beside the bed where the lovers have embraced and made love, then goes a step further, stealing Dreyman's book of Brecht poetry. As Dreyman comments on its being missing, we see Wiesler in rapt attention in his apartment reading a love poem with hints of longing for the breast:

"One day in blue moon September,
silent under a plum tree,
I held her, my silent pale love,
In my arms like a fair and lovely dream.
Above us in the summer skies
Was a cloud that caught my eye.
It was white and so high up.
And when I looked up,
It was no longer there."

The identifications continue. Wiesler listens as Dreyman hears that his friend and mentor, Jerska, has hung himself. Dreyman goes to the piano and plays a sonata that Jerska had given him as a birthday present, entitled "Sonata for a Good Man". Christa Maria stands behind him as he plays, but we also see Wiesler listening. His eyes have a far off look. There is the barest expression on his face that conveys rapt attention. When Dreyman says, "Can anyone who has heard this music, I mean truly heard it, really be a bad person?" we may feel that these words are meant for Wiesler, mesmerized by the music and fully drawn into his fantasies of being merged with the lovers.

Wiesler begins to behave, uncharacteristically, like a good man. He meets a little boy in his elevator as he heads home. The boy asks if he is really with the Stasi and reveals that his father has told him that the Stasi are bad men who put people in prison. Wiesler is about to ask the boy his father's name, but stops himself, implicitly protecting them. Through his identification with the lovers of the primal scene, Wiesler has undergone a fundamental change.

All of this prepares us for the larger step that comes next. It is the night of Christa Maria's assignation with Hempf. Hempf is more determined than ever to catch Dreyman and tear the lovers apart. Grubitz is eager to accomplish this for his own ambition. But Wiesler is now secretly identified with the lovers as he listens to Dreyman ask Christa Maria not to leave. He tells her that he knows where she is going and asks her not to go (reminiscent of Wiesler's plea to the prostitute to "stay".)

Dreyman tells Christa Maria, "You don't need him. I know about your medication, too, and how little faith you have in your talent. Have faith in me at least, Christa Maria. You are a great artist. I know that. And your audience knows it, too. You don't need him."

She answers back that she does need him, that she needs the whole system, as does he. She tells him that he is in bed with them as well, that for all their talent, they can easily be destroyed as Jerska was destroyed.

Wiesler listens to this dramatic verbal version of the primal scene with such intensity that his relief, who startles him with his entrance, assumes that Georg and Christa Maria have been "banging."

Totally absorbed, Wiesler enters a nearby bar. He has begun his second double vodka when Christa Maria enters the same bar a few minutes later for a cognac. He cannot resist once again entering the action, this time more directly. He approaches her, and in a subtle dialogue, he reinforces what Dreyman has told her. He tells her that he is her audience, and that she is a great artist. He urges her to be true to herself. She, in turn, tells him that he is a good man. We later learn that she returned to Dreyman without visiting Hempf.

This is a turn on Arlow's dynamics that demonstrates the plasticity of human defenses. Envy has found gratification not in revenge, but in identification and altruism. The outcast observer can find his way into the primal scene by identifying with the lovers. Instead of gratifying his envy by breaking them apart, he becomes a powerful agent to hold them together, much like Cyrano de Bergerac, using the defense that Anna Freud (1936) referred to as "a form of altruism" by which the subject can achieve his libidinal goals vicariously.

Wiesler increasingly becomes their protector, writing false reports as Dreyman becomes involved in truly subversive activity in response to Jerska's suicide, writing and publishing an article on suicide in East Germany. With these false reports, Wiesler is not only protecting the lovers, but also fulfilling the role of a primal scene "victim" who learns to deny what he has seen.

But the film will give the primal scene witness his revenge, nonetheless. It is accomplished though a dramatic, tragic turn of events worthy of the operatic stage. It centers around a hidden typewriter. The Stasi is eager to uncover the author of the subversive article, now published in *Der Spiegel*. Grubitz suspects Dreyman, but Wiesler's reports say nothing about the article or its publication. The Stasi has information about the typeface used for the manuscript, but cannot identify the owner. It was written on a typewriter smuggled in for the purpose and hidden by Dreyman under a board between two rooms in his apartment. It appears that he will be safe from discovery unless betrayed.

Angry that Christa Maria has snubbed him by remaining loyal to Dreyman, the other Oedipal loser, Hempf, takes his revenge by revealing to Grubitz that she has been getting drugs (probably tranquilizers) illegally from a dental office.

Faced with arrest and the loss of her acting career, Christa Maria decides to cooperate with Grubitz when asked about the suicide article. At first she reveals the plot, but does not tell them about the typewriter. Grubitz brings Wiesler in to interrogate her. He successfully gets from her the location of the typewriter, using his position as "her admiring audience" while threatening the loss of her career. But in his final betrayal of his bosses and the state, he then removes the typewriter before the Stasi arrive.

Arlow stressed in his paper that one common feature of the primal scene dynamics, at least for men, has to do with the boy's betrayal by the mother, the love of his life. I have seen a similar dynamic in films with significant primal scene dynamics, including *L.A. Confidential* and *The Crying Game*. Here, the woman is once again portrayed as the weak link, the betrayer not only of the witness, but also of her lover. She is made to pay for her betrayal, fulfilling a revenge fantasy related to the primal scene.

Dreyman had been warned by his friends not to trust Christa Maria. We are not told why. Perhaps they know of her flirtation with the minister, perhaps they sense a weakness in her character, perhaps it betrays a mistrust of women on their part. Dreyman does not believe she has betrayed him because when the Stasi first came to his home, they did not find the typewriter. He knew that she knew its location.

Now, Grubitz returns and quickly finds the spot where the typewriter should be hidden. In a moment of disillusionment, Dreyman looks directly at Christa Maria. Guilty and ashamed, she impulsively runs out into the street in front of an oncoming truck. The first to reach her is Wiesler, who tries to tell her that it wasn't necessary because he had hidden the typewriter. She dies before Dreyman gets to her, asking her forgiveness for suspecting her.

The critic, Lane, wrote, "I was already reaching for my coat. So why press onward? … Against all odds though, the best is yet to come."

I have referred to this tragic scene, guilt and suicide as operatic. In this case, the opera aint over until the primal scene victim is gratified. If the film had stopped here, Dreyman would have gone on feeling guilty over his distrust that sent Christa Maria to her death. He now believes that she saved him. Of Wiesler, he knows nothing.

Wiesler is demoted by Grubitz, who knows that Wiesler has betrayed him, but cannot prove it. He exiles him to opening letters in a Stasi basement. Wiesler has failed in his attempt to keep the lovers together, failed in his altruism and also has been relegated to a meaningless position. Neither he nor the viewer is in a position to enjoy the full gratification of primal scene revenge.

But the film has one last twist. We move forward past the reunion of Germany. In a chance meeting with Hempf, Dreyman learns that indeed he was under surveillance. He goes back to his apartment and finds the hidden wires. Baffled, he seeks out his Stasi records and discovers the entire transcript. He sees the false, protective reports filled out by Wiesler, identified only as HGW XX17.

Dreyman seeks out the identity of HGW XX17, now a letter carrier walking the streets with his usual anonymity, but decides not to violate Wiesler's privacy by approaching him. He thanks him in another way.

Dreyman knows now that Christa Maria did, indeed, betray him and that it was Wiesler who saved him. In the film's final scene, Dreyman recognizes Wiesler as the "good man" to whom he plays his music, allowing him to take Christa Maria's place in the primal scene.

Wiesler is drawn into a bookstore by a large advertisement for Dreyman's new novel, "Sonata for a Good Man." Leafing through the pages, he sees, "Dedicated to HGW XX17, in gratitude." When the cashier asks if he'd like it gift wrapped, he answers, simply,

"No, it's for me."

This is the ultimate revenge and the ultimate gratification for the primal scene observer.

Arlow, J.A. (1980) The Revenge Fantasy in the Primal Scene. *Journal of the American Psychoanalytic Association* 28: 497-736

Freud, A. (1936) *The Ego and the Mechanisms of Defense.* (Revised edition, 1966) New York: International Universities Press.

Freud, S. (1918). From the History of an Infantile Neurosis. *The Standard Edition of the Complete Psychological Works of Sigmund Freud,* 17:1-124.

Lane, A. (2007) The Current Cinema: Guilty Parties: The Lives of Others. *New Yorker*, February 12, 2007.

Capote, To Kill a Mockingbird, Breakfast at Tiffany's

SOMETIMES AS ANALYSTS AND analytic therapists, we find ourselves pulling together diverse pieces of what we hear from a patient to create a cohesive narrative. I have used considerable poetic license in patching together a composite psychoanalytic biopic of one boy and his wayward mother from three films, works of fiction that were created separately over decades.

Capote, based on Gerald Clarke's biography, tells the story of Truman Capote's writing of *In Cold Blood*. It covers the period from 1959, when Truman Capote becomes interested in writing an article for the *New Yorker* on the murder of an entire family in a farmhouse in Kansas, to 1965, when the killers are executed by hanging. The film unobtrusively gives us the pieces to put together the character and pathological narcissism of the central character.[2] Two other well known films intersect with this one to help us understand the childhood antecedents.

The Outsider

The film presents us with a seeming contradiction. We first see Truman Capote at a late night party in Manhattan. The scene is in stark contrast to the preceding one in which an adolescent girl enters a quiet farmhouse on a Kansas morning to find her best friend murdered in her bed. Holding a drink, Capote is the center of a circle of admirers and friends who are delighted by his repartee, his stories, his exaggerated gestures and his famous friends.

"I had lunch with Jimmy Baldwin the other day."

Someone asks, "How is he?"

"He's a lovely man. And he told me the plot of his new book and he tells me he just wants to make sure it's not one of those problem novels. I said, Jimmy, your novel's about a Negro homosexual who's in love with a Jew. Wouldn't you call that a problem?"

His story brings laughter. Even such a snatch sets the viewer up as

---

[2] I believe that a film based on a biography should still be treated to a greater or lesser extent as fiction. The observations and speculations here should be understood as based on the characterization of Capote in the film, with an indefinite relationship to the historical life of Truman Capote.

an admiring, perhaps envious outsider looking into a special world. The contradiction is that it is Capote who is the outsider.

That comes out when Capote arrives in Kansas. His odd and effeminate mannerisms, his high pitched voice and sensitive demeanor appear false and out of place in the prairie. He initially acts as if he is still in New York, telling an investigator in the office of the Kansas Bureau of Investigation, "Bergdorf's." When the man clearly doesn't know what he's talking about, he adds, "The scarf, it's from Bergdorf's." He also makes the mistake of telling Alvin Hughes, the lead investigator, that he doesn't care if they find the killers or not, that he just wants to see how the town reacts. Hughes tells him, "I care." Mirroring the investigator's confusion about Bergdorf's, Capote invites an explanation. "I care a great deal if we catch who did this as do a lot of folks around here." As the investigators are leaving, one of them points to his hat, "Sears and Roebuck."

He looks even more incongruous, even perverse, trying to approach the best friend of the murdered girl outside the high school, prompting his research assistant, Nelle to ask him to let her do this part of the research. We learn about Capote's subjective insight into his role with two comments he makes, the first on the phone to his lover, Jack:

"I saw the bodies today. ... I looked inside the coffins."

"That's horrifying."

"It comforts me, something so horrifying it's a relief. Normal life falls away, but then I was never much for normal life. Yeah, people here won't talk to me. They want someone like you, like Nelle. Me they hate."

The contradiction is explained for us as we watch Capote ingratiate himself with the townspeople. He changes his clothes to fit in better, shedding the Bergdorf's scarf and the bright colors for a conservative dark suit. He uses his literary fame to get inside the chief investigator's home. His wife is a "reader," a fan of Capote's novella, *Breakfast at Tiffany's*. He also brings an autographed book to the sheriff's wife in order to get a close look at one of the killers after they've been arrested.

More importantly, he applies his acute perceptiveness about people to win them over. He and Nelle do get to talk with Laura, the girl who discovered her friend's body. They ask her about Danny, the dead girl's boyfriend. She says, "Danny is pretty shattered. Nothing terrible has ever happened to him before" and tells them how people in town have been talking about Danny. Here, Capote uses his personal sense of difference to reach Laura empathically. He touches on a part of himself, the sense of being a stranger that resonates with many adolescents.

"Oh it's the hardest when someone has a notion about you and it's impossible to convince them otherwise. Ever since I was a child people always have thought they have me pegged because of the way I am, the way I talk, and they're always wrong."

Capote, as he is shown in the film, is an odd man who sees himself as an outsider—someone who "was never much for normal life"—who uses his perceptiveness to empathize with others so that he can fit in. It would be wrong to call him a chameleon because he certainly does not blend in to his surroundings; but he adapts by finding out how to shine in his new environment.

We should probably not be surprised that he craves the attention and adulation he creates. Despite repeated protestations in the film that he does not lie, we see that he will create boastful lies to garner attention and admiration, even bribing a porter on a train to praise him in front of his old friend and research assistant, Nelle. He is later quietly resentful when Nelle becomes the center of attention, saying to himself, "I don't see what all the fuss is about."

THE KILLER

Perry Smith, the killer that Capote draws close to in order to get his story for *In Cold Blood*, is also an outsider. It makes him an easy target for Capote's empathic seduction. Capote's first words on seeing Perry kept alone in a small kitchen cell in the sheriff's office are probably meant to be empathic with his victimized state: "They put you in the woman's cell." Perry's mother was an alcoholic who could not raise her children. He grew up in an orphanage. It is when he has learned that that Capote tells him, "We're not so different as you might think," and tells him about his own traumatic childhood with his "Mama."

Perry's eventual description of the murders reinforces the theme of the outsider. We might see Perry as affectionately envious of the members of this loving family. He nestles their heads on pillows before killing them, protects the girl from his partner. That envy also turns to murderous rage as he describes why he killed the father to begin the mass slaughter.

"He was looking at me. Just looking at me. Looking at my eyes. Like he expects me to kill him—expects me to be the kind of person who would kill him. I was thinking —this nice man, he's scared of me. I was ashamed. I mean, I thought he was a kind man, a good … a gentleman. I thought so right up to the moment I cut his throat. I didn't realize what I'd did till I heard the sound."

The dialogue is enigmatic, but it suggests that Perry killed the father when he realized that the man saw him as an outsider, a threat, someone who did not belong in his world and his family. He felt ashamed of his role, murdering in a somewhat dissociated rage. It is this sense of exclusion that seems to bind Perry and Truman together. As we shall see, neither had a father, although Truman eventually had a stepfather whose name he took for his own.

Capote is using his similar experience to get what he wants from Perry, but in this case, the identification appears to go deeper. Nelle asks Truman if he has fallen in love with Perry. He answers,

"I don't know how to answer that. … It's as if Perry and I started life in the same house. One day he stood up and walked out the back door while I walked out the front. With some different choices, he's the man I might have become."

To learn about the inside of that metaphorical house, we are aided by outside sources.

Childhood

On his way to Kansas, Capote sits in his train compartment with his research assistant and lifelong friend, Nelle, when a porter comes in with his bags and tells him how honored he is to meet such a wonderful author, talking about how his last book was even better than the first and capping it with, "Just when you thought it couldn't get any better."

Nelle sees through the ploy. "Truman, you're pathetic. You paid him to say that."

He is surprised that she has seen through him so easily, but we soon learn that they have grown up together, in Alabama, where Truman stayed with his aunts. Fortunately, we have fictionalized "home movies" of their life in Alabama.

The train porter lets us know that Nelle is actually Nelle Harper Lee. We later see her celebrating the sale of her novel, *To Kill a Mockingbird*, to a publisher and still later see a party celebrating the opening of the film made from that novel. (An unhappy Capote, bemoaning interminable delays in the publication of his own book, mumbles drunkenly, "I don't see what all the fuss is about.").

Early in the film, *To Kill a Mockingbird*, six year old Scout and her older brother, Jem, meet a funny looking boy, who introduces himself.

"I'm Charles Baker Harris. I can read. You got anything needs reading, I can do it." Jem thinks he's 4 1/2 because of his size, and is surprised to learn he is "going on seven." The boy, whose nickname is Dill, answers, "I'm little, but I'm old."

Dill comes from Meridien, Mississippi, but is visiting his aunt. He is boastful, and more than willing to embellish if not outright lie. He has told them his mother is a photographer's assistant who "entered my picture in the 'Beautiful Child' contest and won five dollars on me. She give the money to me and I went to the picture show 20 times with it." When Scout asks about his father, he first says he doesn't have a father, later backtracks when Scout says if his father's not dead, he must have a father. He tells Scout's family's housekeeper,

"My Daddy owns the L&N Railroad. He's gonna let me run the engine all the way to New Orleans." No wonder that Nelle/Scout years later sees so easily through his ploy with the train porter.

Early in life, Truman/Dill[3] has learned how to cover over his weaknesses, turning them into strengths. His oddness forces him to use his imagination and perceptiveness to make others want to enter into his world.

Dill is a continuously curious fellow who keeps urging Scout and her brother into trouble. He is particularly curious about the mysterious Boo Radley. Jem tries to scare him with stories about Boo, who stalks at night. Dill appears frightened, but even more curious, egging Jem on to go into the Radley's yard to try to sneak a peak at Boo.

Dill is drawn with sadomasochistic excitement to this violent man. His aunt tells him that Boo stabbed his own father in the leg one day, then went back to what he was doing, cutting newspaper. Boo was held in the courthouse basement for some time after that. Dill is eager to see that jail where Boo was held.

"My aunt says it's bat-infested, and he nearly died from the mildew. Come on! I betcha they got chains and instruments of torture down there."

It presages his fascination with Perry Smith. We are left to speculate about the interest of a boy who is ashamed that he has no father, an abandoned son, in a man who has stabbed his father unprovoked and another who brutally murdered the father of a family. But, we learn that Capote's sadomasochism and his interest in imprisonment also has origins in his relationship with his mother. In *Capote*, he tells Perry,

"I was abandoned repeatedly as a child. My mama'd drag me along to some new town so she could take up with another man she'd met. Night after night she'd lock me in the hotel room. Mama'd turn the latch and tell the staff not to let me out no matter what. I was terrified—I'd

---

[3] According to extra commentary on a DVD, the screenwriter of *To Kill a Mockingbird*, Horton Foote, was told by Harper Lee that Dill was Truman Capote.

scream my head off—till finally I'd collapse on the carpet next to the door and fall asleep. After years of this she just left me with relatives in Alabama."

Whether we take this as an accurate description or another dramatic embellishment, it gives us a window into Truman's inner world.

Neither *Capote* nor *To Kill a Mockingbird* shows us Dill's life with his mother. To get a glimpse of "Mama," I think we have to turn to yet another film. Holly Golightly, the central character in *Breakfast at Tiffany's*, is a delightful character, more endearing perhaps for Audrey Hepburn's characterization. She is portrayed as a "drifter" (from the accompanying song, "Moon River") who uses men and allows them to use her. She calls them "rats and super rats," but takes $50 to go to the powder room and $100 per week from mob boss, Sally Tomato, to carry coded messages in the form of weather reports to his lawyer while she looks for a rich man to marry her.

Holly appears to have only one attachment, to her brother, Fred, who shared a wild, sad childhood with her, stealing for food. We are told that she married Doc Golightly at 14, but abruptly abandoned him and his children to explore the world. She has changed her name from Lula Mae to Holly. For most of the film, she toys with her neighbor, Paul Varjak, while pursuing rich men. She calls him Fred, seemingly denying his identity to make him her brother.

Like Capote, Paul is a writer. We see him falling in love with Holly, wanting to help her, wanting to possess her. He is hurt by her continual rejection of him. We can easily imagine some of Capote, himself, in Holly as well, this narcissistic woman who lives off the adulation of others.

We come upon Holly as a young woman, not yet a mother, at least in the literal sense. But the film does give us a reminder of the child whose "… mama'd drag me along to some new town so she could take up with another man she'd met."

When Paul walks into Holly's apartment on his arrival in New York, he almost steps on a cat. The cat screeches.

Paul says, "I'm sorry. Is he all right?"

Holly says, "Sure, sure, he's O.K. Aren't you Cat? Poor old Cat. Poor slob. Poor slob without a name. I don't have the right to give him one. We don't belong to each other. We just took up by the river one day."

We will see Cat under foot again at a crowded noisy party in Holly's apartment. We see him jumping on intoxicated party goers or leaping up to shelves, trying to get out of the way of the crowd.

Cat has two moments that might get us into the head of that little boy, left locked in a hotel room, moving from town to town with such a mother. When Holly receives a telegram telling her that her beloved brother has been killed in a jeep accident, she goes into a frenzy, smashing things in her apartment. Almost out of notice, we see her tearing a cover off a nightstand that Cat had jumped onto, throwing him violently up against a door, screeching. We can easily imagine the child, Truman/Dill getting lost in the rage of such a narcissistic woman. At that moment, Cat does not exist for her.

Because he is a cat, we do not think of him as we would a child. Cats are tougher. But the film completes the equation at the end. Holly's plans to marry a rich Brazilian have fallen through. Paul picks her up in a cab with Cat and her other belongings, thinking he'll take her with him, but she wants to go to Brazil anyway (jumping bail) to look for rich men. He tells her he's in love with her. She says he wants to put her in a cage, that she and Cat are a couple of "no name slobs" who "don't even belong to each other." Stopping the cab, Holly pushes Cat into the street in the rain to fend for himself in an alley with garbage cans.

At this point, Cat becomes an abandoned child. In the film's tearful, happy ending, a disgusted Paul gets out of the cab a few blocks later to leave Holly. He tells her that she's afraid to accept a world in which people do care about each other. Holly follows him, and finds him looking for Cat. "Where's Cat?" she asks. For a few poignant moments, it appears they will not find him. Holly's distress tells us that she has learned to care. Cat shows up to the vibrant tones of "Moon River." In the final scene, Paul and Holly embrace and kiss with Cat held between them. Holly kisses Paul and pets Cat. They are an intact, loving family. It is a scene that the boy, Capote, could only dream of. His reality, beneath the flamboyance, was as a nameless cat in his Mama's world.

The Enactment

Although we never see Truman's Mama directly in any of the films, we have one more shadow of her presence in Capote's relationship with Perry. Perry Smith presents a particular dilemma for Capote. He attempts to use Perry for his purposes. Perry uses Capote as well to get legal help and support. But Capote cannot successfully maintain his detachment.

He describes his ambivalence to Nelle,

"Jack thinks I'm using Perry, but he also thinks I fell in love with him when I was in Kansas. Now, how both of those things can be true is beyond me."

Whether his ambivalence towards Perry is truly "beyond" Capote's awareness or not, it leads to an enactment of their mutual pathological mother/son relationships.

When Capote goes to the prison where Perry and his co-defendant, Richard, are being held, he learns that Perry is refusing all food. Capote buys cans of baby food and begins to spoon it to Perry, telling him, "It's OK. It's Truman, it's a friend." He nurses him back to life, visits him regularly. Perry shows him a picture of his mother, tells him about the orphanage, talks of "me and Linda" (his sister).

But Truman's lover, Jack, importunes him to return. Capote comes to a decision. He arrives at the prison with a stack of books for Perry and seems to be ready to leave the books outside the sleeping Perry's cell when Perry is startled awake.

Capote doesn't enter the cell. He tells Perry,

"I have to fly back East."

Perry asks "When?"

Truman answers, "An hour. I miss you already. Write me every five minutes."

Perry cries out, "Capote! Capote!" as Truman turns and walks out of the cell block.

Time passes. Capote works on his book. Nelle visits him and Jack in Spain, carrying a plaintive letter from Perry.

"Dear Friend Truman, where are you?" He gives a definition of "death by hanging" from a medical dictionary and adds "not too comforting as we lost our appeal. Missing you—alone and desirous of your presence. Your amigo, Perry."

Truman defensively tells Jack and Nelle,

"I write him all the time. I've been so focused on the book, lately."

With Perry, Truman has recreated the trauma of both their childhoods, abandoning him abruptly to a small cell, walking out on him to chase after a man. The enactment pushes Capote into the role of a cruel abandoning mother.

We never see directly how Truman's mother interacted with him. In Holly Golightly, we see perhaps an idealized version of her, a character who, with her faults, is universally loved. Now, we see Capote as a colder Holly using his guile and empathy to extract from Perry the story that he needs. He lies to Perry about the title of his book, denying that he has christened it, "In Cold Blood." He lies to him about Perry's sister, telling him that she missed him and sent him pictures out of love, when, in fact, she described him to Capote as a pure psychopath and gave him the pictures to get rid of them.

Capote finally uses Perry's desperate need for the attachment to the man who suckled him when he was near death and whom he hopes will save him from the hangman. He lets Perry know that the one thing he wants from him, the only thing that will get his full attention, is the story of that night. In its characteristic style, the film does not spell out for us why Perry tells him about the murders, but it appears that at this point it is his last means of holding Truman close.

Unfortunately for him, with the story told, Capote no longer needs him for his project. The enactment takes a still more gruesome turn as Capote finishes his book and must wait for the final chapter, the execution of Perry Smith and his accomplice. Now Capote avoids Perry with more intensity, avoiding his pleas to help with another lawyer, knowing that each delay of the execution, every appeal, delays the completion of his masterpiece. He drinks more heavily, even drinking by mixing liquor into the jars of baby food that he had used to feed Perry, spooning it out of the jar. He drunkenly complains to Nelle that he is being tortured by the delays. Now, the enactment is not just of an abandoning mother, but of a mother who wishes her son's death.

When the last appeal has failed and the date of execution has been set, Perry begs Capote to visit him. Capote drinks heavily and hides under his covers, clearly terrified. It is Nelle who prods and shames Capote into visiting Perry and Richard on the night of their execution, after he had tried to ignore Perry's desperate telegrams. At Perry's request, Capote agrees to be present at the execution. With him, we see Perry hung.

Truman is deeply shaken, trying to rationalize his guilt. He tells Nelle, "It was a terrible experience and I will never get over it. There wasn't anything I could have done to save them."

Nelle, still the truth telling Scout, answers, "Maybe not. But the fact is, you didn't want to."

We are told as the film comes to an end that Capote's epigraph for his last (unfinished) book was, "More tears are shed over answered prayers than unanswered ones," a testimony to the grief and guilt that comes from angry wishes. In the final scene, a somber Capote leafs through Perry's journal, stopping to look at his childhood picture with his sister and his drawing of Capote. In the film's epitaph, we are told that *In Cold Blood* made Truman Capote the most famous writer in America, but that he never finished another book and died in 1984 of "complications due to alcoholism."

7

Transferences

Slumdog Millionaire

SLUMDOG MILLIONAIRE IS A wonderful example of life imitating art; or, perhaps of life riding on the heels of art. The film, taken from the novel *Q and A*[1], is a rags to riches tale of a poor orphan from the slums who wins the grand prize on the Indian version of "Who Wants to be a Millionaire." It has had its own rags to riches story. An independent film made with a view to DVD distribution wins worldwide awards, culminating in the Oscar for best film of 2008.

Perhaps as analysts we should not be surprised that this film about an underdog which is itself a successful underdog should have in its fabric a childhood Oedipal fantasy, the ultimate underdog drama.

The film's underdog hero is Jamal Malik, a 20 year old orphan from the Bombay/Mumbai slums who has successfully answered the first eight questions on the "Who Wants to be a Millionaire" TV show and

---

[1] The script writer made significant changes to the plot. According to the IMDb website, the book did not contain the love story, which is central to the film.

is one question away from winning the show's top prize, 20 million rupees.

As we enter, a skeptical police officer is trying to elicit a confession from Jamal that he has cheated. Torture having failed, he methodically takes Jamal through each question from the show to see how an uneducated "slumdog" could have the answers. But Jamal responds to the questions more like a good subject on the couch than a quiz show contestant, each one evoking associative memories from his childhood.

Through this series of flashbacks, we follow Jamal's life from early childhood up to his police interrogation. It is a picaresque adventure in which Jamal and his older brother, Salim, survive against all odds in a hostile world. That in itself is inspiring, but we are drawn into their story in large part by the interweaving of compelling Oedipal dynamics.

This brings us to our own first question. How do these dynamics play out for two brothers who have no father?

The boys' father not only is not present, he is never mentioned in the film. For our purposes, he never existed. We may look for substitute male figures, but on the surface, we find none. As small children, the boys live with their mother, who is their sole caretaker. They have a schoolteacher, but he mocks them, scolds them and hits them with a book in his cameo appearance. There are policemen who chase them, ignore them when they are racing from an angry mob, and torture Jamal as a young man to try to find out how he got the quiz show answers. One man who appears to be kind and nurturing proves to be the cruelest of all. In fact, the men who happen into their lives range from distant to hostile.

In these circumstances, the brothers deal very differently with maintaining a paternal image. The older brother, Salim, is feisty, returning hostility with hostility. In an early scene, when the boys are being chased through the slums of Bombay by an angry burly policeman, they turn for a moment and Salim goads the policeman with an obscene gesture, miming masturbation. Later, he attracts the attention of a powerful gang leader, Maman, by attempting to fight a man three times his size. It would appear at first that Salim has no internalized paternal image, but as the story develops, we shall find that he models himself after the most powerful and hostile of these men, emulating and working for gangsters, but always with intense ambivalence.

Jamal's internalized paternal image is presented even more subtly. Outwardly, he does not appear to attach himself to any man, but we get a glimpse of his internal idealization.

The first question that he must answer on the quiz show is, "Who was the star in the 1973 hit film *Zanjeer*?" Jamal's associations take him to an airport near their home where the boys found open air to play. He is sitting in an outhouse, his brother waiting outside. A man desperate to get in offers Salim money, but Jamal provocatively refuses to leave, frustrating the man and the brother. At this point there is much noise about the arrival of a helicopter with the movie star, Amitabh Bachchan.[2] Salim gets his revenge on Jamal by locking him in the outhouse while he runs off to see the movie star.

Undaunted, the star struck Jamal pulls out a picture of Amitabh and holding it over his head to keep it clean, he dives down into the fecal waste to make his escape. Covered in excrement, he runs through a parting crowd to present the photograph to Amitabh for his autograph. Amitabh fulfills his role by calmly signing the autograph brought him by the excrement covered boy.

From snatches of film images recalled by Jamal, we see Amitabh Bachchan fighting evil adversaries with aplomb equal to his handling of the unusual autograph. This little scene, seemingly intended to advance the story, gives us insight into Jamal's internal world. Faced with the absence of a father in a male world that is universally hostile, Jamal has found a hero, an idealization that he can carry with him with unusual tenacity.

The contrast between the boys and the tension between them is emphasized in the subsequent scene in which Salim recoups his lost money (from the outhouse) and gets his revenge by stealing and

---

[2] Amitabh Bachchan is an Indian film star, known for many dramatic roles including his role in the potboiler, *Zanjeer*. Source: IMDb website

selling Jamal's precious autograph while their mother is washing Jamal. In a scene reminiscent of the film *Cinema Paradiso*, Salim offers the autograph to the projectionist at the movie theater, who gives him two coins for it. Those who have seen *Cinema Paradiso* may be struck by the contrast with that film in which there was a loving relationship between the male projectionist and the fatherless boy. Here, the relationship is mercenary.

The young boys do have a mother. In the glimpses we get of her, she is kind and protective. In the first flashback, we see them literally running into her protective arms when the fat policeman is chasing them. She tells the policeman, "I'll take care of these two," leaving him frustrated and cursing. We next see her washing Jamal after his dive into the excrement, talking to him about his autograph.

But her role is a brief one. In her last appearance, she is washing clothes in a canal while the boys play nearby with a ball. It is a momentarily pleasant scene that gives us an image of the last memory of innocence. Suddenly a mob races through the streets attacking Moslems. Jamal's mother screams at the boys to run. As she faces them she is struck from behind with a bat. With the boys looking on, she falls face first into the water, obviously dead. Jamal's immediate response to the Quiz question that evokes this memory is, "I wake up every day wishing I didn't know the answer to that question."

Without maternal protection, male hostility becomes more intense, reaching, in fantasy, the level of castration. Accompanied now by a little girl, Latika, also abandoned in the riots, they meet Maman. He heads a gang that takes in children, seemingly for humanitarian purposes, but actually to use them as beggars and prostitutes. If Maman is a father figure, cloaked perhaps in a maternal disguise, he demonstrates the intensity of Oedipal rivalry, literally mutilating a boy, Arvind, by burning out his eyes to make him a more effective beggar.

It is during their time with Maman and his gang that Salim's role in the film's fantasy becomes better defined. There is a mutual attraction between Maman and Salim. Maman is intrigued by the potential in the feisty rebellious boy and adopts him as a child taskmaster over

Transferences

the other children. Salim, now traumatized by his mother's violent death, is drawn to the position of power, developing a partial, although ambivalent identification with the powerful gangster.

In doing so, Salim's role as a transitional figure becomes more prominent. He is neither child nor adult. The other children rebel against his tyranny by putting hot peppers near his genitals when he is sleeping. They laugh at his humiliation and pain, this mock attack on his genitals preparing us for the more serious attack in which Maman takes out a boy's eyes.

Nevertheless, faced with his own advancement and his loyalty to Maman versus his loyalty to his brother, Salim saves Jamal from the mutilation, splashing ether into the face of one of the men so that they can make their escape with Latika trailing them. They get away, jumping onto a freight train, but Latika is left behind, losing her grasp of Salim's hand as the train pulls out.

I will momentarily defer a fuller discussion of Latika's role. She had attached to the boys when they were running and hiding from the mob after their mother's death. Salim wants no part of her, but when Salim is pretending to try to sleep, Jamal welcomes her to join them under cover from a rain storm. Salim sees her as drawing trouble to them, but Jamal sees her as "the third musketeer." The boys, having read Dumas's book in their classroom, have already fancied themselves Athos and Porthos; but, in Oedipal tales, three is a destabilizing number.

Without Latika's female presence, the boys enter a period with little tension between them. The two musketeers thrive as petty thieves on the trains, then duping and stealing from tourists at the Taj Majal. There is a lightness to most of these scenes.

But Jamal pulls Salim back to Bombay, now Mumbai, to look for Latika. When they find her, their ambivalent relationship intensifies in a raw Oedipal drama in which Salim takes over the paternal role. He is now a well developed adolescent, while Jamal is smaller and still boyish. Jamal has been obsessed with finding Latika, but Salim only becomes interested in her when he peeks through a curtain and sees that she is "sexy."

Jamal in his innocence thinks that they will simply find Latika and take her with them, but when they are confronted by Maman and his men, they need his older brother to protect them. Salim draws a gun and ultimately shoots Maman at point blank range. It stuns both Latika and Jamal, but she recovers more quickly, the innocent Jamal having to be practically dragged from the scene.

The children escape to a seemingly abandoned hotel, where they play out the Oedipal drama. Salim is now a man who has killed. He gets drunk and leaves to enlist in the service of another gangster, Javed. Latika, still painted for dancing and enticing men, is also no longer innocent. She is touched by Jamal's finding her, but when he avoids looking at her as she comes out of the shower, she tells him in a tone that is kind, but perhaps patronizing, "You're a sweet boy, Jamal." It is clear that he is still a boy, glorying in being reunited with his childhood girlfriend, but not prepared for Oedipal rivalry.

When Salim returns, he throws Jamal out of the room so that he can have Latika to himself, telling Jamal that he is the elder now. When Jamal resists, Salim points the revolver at his face, telling him that the man with the Colt .45 has the power. There is a moment when it appears that he will shoot Jamal as he has shot Maman, but Latika intervenes, telling Jamal to leave. She is more mature than Jamal, more accepting of the realities of power and sex. She is willing to be with Salim to save Jamal from a possibly deadly confrontation. The three children have played out the Oedipal drama, with a betrayed and devastated Jamal forced to leave Latika to Salim, forced out of the conjugal bedroom

As Jamal's memories approach the present, we discover that he has lost track of his brother and Latika, but he has not lost his anger or his intense need to be reunited with Latika. He finally is able to find Salim, punching him when they meet and asking about Latika. Salim's response is, "Still?" and tells him to forget about her, "She's gone." But we soon see that she is not gone. She is living with the gangster, Javed, Salim's boss.

Using his street smarts to talk his way into Javed's home, we have a partial reprise of the Oedipal theme as the two young people talk furtively in Javed's kitchen while ostensibly trying to make lunch for the ornery older man. My association was to "Jack and the Beanstalk." As in the earlier scene, Latika pushes Jamal out for his own safety.

But this sets them up for Salim's final betrayal of his brother. Jamal has told Latika that he will wait for her every afternoon at the train station. He waits for her patiently until, to his own surprise, he sees her there below him. He calls frantically to her and finally she looks up at him, a smile on her face, a scene we have glimpsed at the beginning of the film and at other points along the way, until now without understanding. This moment of joy turns sour as Jamal sees his brother leading a gang of thugs who are racing to retrieve Latika. Jamal is left helplessly standing outside the car she has been dragged into and hears her scream his name as one of the thugs cuts her face. That betrayal prepares him and us for the next to last question in "Who Wants to be a Millionaire."

The question is about cricket. "For 10,000,000 rupees: Which cricketer has scored the most first-class centuries in history? (A) Sachin Tendulkar, (B) Ricky Ponting, (C) Michael Slater, or (D) Jack Hobbs."

During a commercial break, Jamal finds himself alone in the rest room with Prem, the host of the show. Throughout the film, Prem has been playfully condescending towards Jamal. Now, he tells him that they have much in common. "Guy from the slums becomes a millionaire overnight. Do you know who's the only other person who's done that? Me." In a sense, they are brothers. Jamal tells him that he doesn't know the answer to the question. Prem says, "Maybe it's written." When Jamal goes to the sink, he sees that Prem has marked the letter "B" on the foggy bathroom mirror.

But Jamal has been prepared for this by his interactions with his real brother. Salim has betrayed him by selling the autograph and by throwing him out of the bedroom with Latika. He has left her behind when they escaped from Maman jumping the freight train and now he has again taken her from Jamal at the train station. Jamal senses that Prem, "the only other person who's done that," will play the rival rather than the supportive older brother. He uses a 50/50 lifeline to eliminate two of the choices and then deliberately does not choose "B," the answer that Prem has fed him, giving the correct answer, "D. Jack Hobbes."

Now all the pieces fall into place. We discover why he is being interrogated by the police. Prem has fed him an answer and seeing he did not take the bait is convinced that Jamal is cheating. Or, alternatively, Prem is determined to eliminate a rival one way or the other. Jamal explains that he went on the show because when he was in Javed's kitchen, he saw Latika watching the show. Having lost track of her again, he hoped that she would see him on the show and contact him. This explains why he has kept on even when in danger of losing all the money he has won. The money is not the goal.

But there is one thing that has not been explained, leading to another question that we may ask. Why is Jamal so obsessed with Latika? Salim questions it over and over. Latika tells him that she did not expect him to remember her. We know from his experience with Amitabh's autograph that Jamal can be persistent when chasing an ideal. But why Latika?

It is here that we must look to the transforming power of trauma and the power of transference. We never learn what has happened to Jamal's father, but we see that he is intensely loyal to the image of the man who has taken that role in fantasy. We do see how he loses his mother. It is traumatic to a degree that anyone watching the film can feel it intensely, yet it is a matter of a moment. As the film moves on, we flash back to it once, again in passing.

Another image takes its place, the image of Latika smiling at him at the train station. It is an image that combines hope and loss, a happy moment that has come to stand for another trauma, having Latika taken from him.

In fact, Latika is taken from him three times, at the railroad yard when they jump the freight train escaping from Maman, at the hotel room, when Salim forces him out at gun point and at the train station, when Salim retrieves her. We have an additional image that comes after the 8th question when we see a desperate Jamal returning to Javed's house only to find that everyone is gone. That is what motivates him to go on the show.

We have a recurring trauma, each time the loss of a girl/woman that Jamal loves. The film reinforces our awareness with recurring images of the young Latika being left in the train yard and the older Latika smiling at him at the station. In each case, she looks at us, at Jamal, just as his mother looked just before her death. Outside the train station, a helpless Jamal stands outside the car, watching as one of the thugs cuts Latika across the side of her face, recreating an image of the original trauma. It is this recurring trauma and the transference associated with it that drives the engine of the film.

Why do I use the term transference? Transference refers to the transfer of powerful emotions and attitudes from someone in the past to someone in the present. In analysis it develops through an ongoing relationship, but in this film, the transference is direct and immediate.

When Jamal's mother is killed, he and his brother race from the rioters, seeing further atrocities as they go. On the way, they pass a small, frightened girl, who eventually chases after them. Salim wants no part of her, perhaps his own transference reaction, but Jamal wants her to be part of their family, to be the third musketeer, to help replace the loss of his mother.

During the extended sequence in which the boys live off tourists at the Taj Majal, they sneak in one night during an outdoor opera, finding an opportunity to grab purses from under the stands. But Jamal becomes intrigued by the scene below where Orpheus sings and cries his heart out over the dead Eurydice. It is this reminder of his mother's death that pushes him on his quest. But the images that accompany this scene are not of Jamal's mother. We see the young Latika standing in the freight yard as Jamal and Salim move away on the train. We see her again running in the freight yard, trying to catch up to them. We see the older Latika anxiously looking around for him at the train station, and then we see her smiling up at him, the train racing past her in the background. It is no coincidence that in the next memory, the boys have returned to Mumbai because Jamal feels compelled to re-find Latika.

Jamal cannot forget Latika because he needs her to repair the traumatic loss. With each loss of her, the intensity becomes even greater to overcome the trauma, to undo the loss, to create a traumatic memory that carries a hope of reunion. It is this maternal transference that adds intensity and poignancy to the Oedipal drama in the hotel room.

The love story is driven by this fantasy of replacement, as perhaps every love story is to some extent. We intuitively understand Jamal's need to re-find Latika. He cannot re-find his mother because she is dead, and if she were not dead, she would be his mother and not his friend and lover. But through the power of transference, Jamal can accomplish what Orpheus could not.

All of which prepares us for the final question, the one that will bring Jamal the show's top prize, 20 million rupees. The question has to do with completing the Oedipal triangle.

"Question 9: For 20,000,000 rupees: In Alexander Dumas' book *The Three Musketeers*, two of the musketeers are called Athos and Porthos. What is the name of the third Musketeer? (A) Aramis, (B) Cardinal Richelieu, (C) D'Artagnan, or (D) Planchet."

This does not sound like a 20 million rupee question. But at this point in a film, if it has succeeded, such bits of reality are a minor annoyance. We disregard the discrepancy because we are driven at this point in the film by fantasy. The question, of course, fits our needs perfectly. Jamal has been persevering on the show because he is looking for the third musketeer. He knows the name of the third musketeer, but "Latika" is not one of the answers.

And Latika is not the only transference figure. Throughout the story, there has been a powerful male figure who is not totally a murderous rival, such as Maman or Javed and not so much an idealized fantasy figure who will come to the rescue, such as Amitabh, but some of both. In the film's denouement, that transference figure, Salim, plays his part to gratify the Oedipal fantasy.

Along with Jamal, the audience has been gradually drawn to view Salim as a transference figure. Yes, he has betrayed his brother repeatedly, keeping him from Latika and acting the role of the Oedipal rival. But he has also been his brother's protector, saving him twice from Maman. We, too, have come to view him ambivalently as a rival and villain as well as the only character powerful enough to stand against the Mamans and Javeds of the world. When Latika, trapped in Javed's household, pleads with Jamal that there is no hope, he says, "Salim will help us," prompting her to retort, "You still believe in Salim?"

But there is no one else to believe in. The police detective is a step in that direction, believing Jamal's story and allowing him to return to the show, but his role is only a foreshadowing of the entrance of a benevolent father.

We also have had a glimpse into Salim's inner world that suggests a deeper moral core. Before leaving to do some criminal work for Javed, possibly murder, we see Salim, dressed in prayer robes, begging forgiveness from Allah for what he is about to do. He too, has a hidden inner ideal.

Jamal, of course, has never learned the name of the third musketeer. Desperate, he uses his final lifeline, the opportunity to phone a "friend." He has called Salim once before, seeking him from a phone bank, clearly shocked and touched when he heard his brother's voice. As if to let us know why he will still call his treacherous brother, he offers the excuse, "It's the only phone number I know." We could speculate that he must seek help from idealized, protective Salim, the only positive male image left him. That wish is gratified.

Salim and Latika are with Javed's gang, somewhere outside of Mumbai, hiding from some unknown danger. Salim sees her watching Jamal on television. Saying at one point, "He'll never give up," he decides to help them and to make right what he has damaged. He quietly approaches Latika and offers her the keys to his car to make her escape. She objects that Javed will kill him, but he tells her, "I can take care of Javed." Finally, he hands her his cell phone and tells her to hold onto it.

And so, when Jamal makes his call to his brother to ask the name of the third musketeer, his brother does not answer. At first, there is no answer. Latika has left the cell phone in the car while she got out to watch the show, providing us with a little suspense as we wonder whether we are watching a true tragedy in which the lovers can never be reunited. Finally she answers, to Jamal's shock and delight.

Of course, she does not know the name of the third musketeer. Jamal must guess and as he guesses "Aramis" (also the third baseman for the Chicago Cubs, by the way), we see Salim, dressed in his ceremonial religious robes, waiting inside a locked room for Javed and his men, standing in a tub filled with his money. As his brother wins the final prize, Salim shoots Javed and is then shot down by his henchman. As he is dying, Salim says, "God is great."

The final piece to the fantasy is not only the re-finding of the mother through Latika, but the re-finding of a benevolent father who sacrifices his own life so that Jamal and Latika can go on with theirs together. He kills Javed as he had killed Maman so that Jamal can have his woman without shedding blood. He sacrifices his own life essentially abdicating his right of seigneur, of the rival father, allowing Jamal the Oedipal victory. In this Oedipal configuration, so common in literature and film, the child wins the mother's love because he, not the father, truly loves her.

The final scene is a reunion of the lovers at the train station, the place at which Latika had been lost and re-lost. Jamal kisses Latika's scar, but she asks him to kiss her on the lips. They kiss, completing the Oedipal fantasy. With this kiss, they meet halfway, Jamal ascending to manhood and Latika returning to childhood innocence, leaving us with a warm feeling that appears to repair the traumatic losses of childhood.

Eternal Sunshine of the Spotless Mind

A MAN COMES TO analysis complaining of strange behavior and large gaps in his memory. "I ditched work today, took a train out to Montauk. I don't know why. I'm not an impulsive person." He discovers that there are two years of entries torn out of his diary, entries he does not remember making.

He has other complaints as well. He describes himself as shy—"If only I could meet someone now. I think my chances of that happening are somewhat diminished seeing that I can't make eye contact with a woman that I don't know."—and needy—"Why do I fall in love with every woman I see who shows me the least bit of attention?" Nevertheless, he has spent a night walking and lying on the iced over Charles River in Boston with a woman he just met on that trip to Montauk, and was about to take her home to his apartment.

The man's name is Joel Barish, and he has not actually entered an analytic consulting room (nor the Twilight Zone), but into a film written by Charlie Kaufman, which is close to the same thing.

The screenwriter, Charlie Kaufman, has made a career of exploring the limits of the human mind by putting it into strange situations. In *Being John Malkovitch*, people could inhabit each other's minds. In *Adaptation*, he shows himself writing the film's script while divided into twin brothers. It wouldn't give him much of a living, but in a sense he is a psychoanalyst's screenwriter. In this film, *Eternal Sunshine of the Spotless Mind*, he allows us to examine the relationship between memory and meaning as it unfolds in the analytic process, and perhaps even gives us a cinematic equivalent of transference.

We soon learn that Joel is the victim of massive repression. Utilizing one of Kaufman's fantasy devices, he has contracted with a company called "Lacuna, Inc." to erase his memories of his former girlfriend, Clementine Kruczynski, the same woman he has met at Montauk after the repression. We see two gawky technicians setting up some kind of apparatus on Joel's head as he sleeps, sedated, in his bed. The main action of the film occurs in Joel's mind as the memories are being erased, with a subplot intertwined as we also watch the neurotic, bumbling memory erasers at work and play during the night that Joel is undergoing the procedure. In fact, the first memories that are erased are Joel's memories of visiting Lacuna and contracting for the repression (demonstrating what Freud discovered on his way to the Structural Theory, that for repression to work, the process must itself be repressed).

In effect, two parallel processes will now emerge moving in opposite directions. The film shows us Joel's memories as the technicians are removing them. At the same time, we, the viewers, are experiencing those memories, in effect gaining understanding as Joel is losing it. We learn about Joel's past at the same time that he is forgetting it.

As Joel's memories unfold, we begin to piece together the dynamic history of his symptoms. Joel's symptoms did not start with repression. On the night before the procedure, he looks severely depressed, in anguish, crying and banging his arms on the steering wheel of his car. As the memories unfold, we learn the source of his depression. His girlfriend, Clementine, has left him abruptly and contracted to have him erased from her memory. He has contracted to repress his memories of Clementine partly out of a desire for revenge—it is a way of killing her intra-psychically by destroying his internal representation of her—and partly as a defense against his painful grief. As viewers and analysts, we are already making excellent progress, having made sense of his use of repression.

As more memory is revealed, we can understand how our patient came to grief. Working backwards, from effect to cause, we can again piece together the underlying dynamics. On the surface, we see a hurt and frustrated Joel confronting an irresponsible, hurtful Clementine.

In his memory, Joel is sitting alone at home waiting for Clementine. When she gets home, dressed for a night out, it is late. She has damaged his car, driving drunk. As the argument heats up, Clementine says, "Face it, Joely, you're freaked out because I was out late without you, and in your little wormy brain, you're trying to figure out, 'Did she fuck someone tonight?'" Frustrated and stung, he hurts her back, saying, "Now, see, Clem, I assume you fucked someone tonight. Isn't that how you get people to like you?" This is the last straw for Clementine. Joel chases after her as she runs out, first apologizing, asking her to come back, sensing that he is losing her both in the memory and with his realization that she is being erased from his life. The scenery crashes and disappears. He screams, "I'm erasing you and I'm happy. You did it to me first."

But this is again a false surface, a compromise formation which, in effect, serves as a defense against a deeper source of anxiety and shame.

The memories move back a few hours to earlier that evening. Clementine dresses to go out. As she is leaving, she says, "I should have left you at the flea market." That association takes us back to still earlier in the day at the flea market where we see a different picture, a very affectionate Joel and Clementine. She reaches towards a baby in its mother's arms. As they resume their walk she says, with a pretty smile,

"I want to have a baby."

Joel says, "Let's talk about it later."

"No, I want to have a baby."

"I don't think we're ready."

"You're not ready."

"Clem, do you really think you could take care of a kid?"

This is where the affect changes. She says, "What?" An argument breaks out. She accuses him of being unable to commit to anything.

We are not usually so fortunate to get to such core material so quickly, but films have to fit years of analysis into about 90 minutes. Our patient is behaving strangely because he has repressed important memories and feelings about his girlfriend. They had broken up over a vicious argument, ostensibly about her irresponsibility (as he saw it), but really about his fear of starting a family, and his fear that she will be unable to care for a child. We are barely into the film and have already seen the importance of memory in constructing meaning and the disruptiveness of repression, a lesson from Anna Freud (1936).

Understanding symptoms is often the opening act for a psychoanalysis, and in this case for a film. As we move on, underlying characterological problems emerge for treatment. We have seen some of the characterological issues for Joel in his opening description of himself: "If only I could meet someone now. I think my chances of that happening are somewhat diminished seeing that I can't make eye contact with a woman that I don't know." "Why do I fall in love with every woman I see who shows me the least bit of attention?" He is inhibited, fearful and needy. His reaction to Clementine's wish to have a baby is a further clue which will prove to be closely tied to the source of his insecurity.

It is not surprising that he is also afraid to reveal himself. In one of the first memories we see, Clementine tells Joel, "You don't tell me things, Joel. I'm an open book. I tell you everything, every damn embarrassing thing." Joel reacts with defensive sarcasm, telling her that "constantly talking isn't necessarily communicating." She takes offense, at the same time pushing him, saying "I want to share things, Joel. That's what intimacy is." He in effect acknowledges the defense, saying, "My life just isn't that interesting." As the night of repression develops, he will, at least in his mind, trust her with his "embarrassing" memories.

In order to have a successful film, you must have sufficient tension, and in order to have a successful analysis, there must be sufficient conflict. The process of repression becomes conflicted as Joel becomes aware of the overly loud and intrusive technicians through his sleep. One of the technicians, a geeky young man named Patrick, had fallen in love with Clementine while they were doing her memory erasure. He had stolen items and information about her relationship with Joel and was using them in a strange form of identity theft, attempting to make her his girlfriend. Joel hears him talking about it and then hears him talking to Clementine on the phone. He is startled to hear Patrick using his pet name for her, "Tangerine", prompting him to turn to the memory of first using that nick name. Apparently stimulated by jealousy and rivalry, he moves to memories of intimacy with Clementine.

As Joel relives those intimate moments, he begins to fight the repression. He calls plaintively in his dream state to Mierswiak, the scientific genius of Lacuna, to be allowed to keep "this one memory" and then to stop the process entirely. He tries to wake up so that he can tell them to stop as he realizes he doesn't want to lose his memories of Clementine. Much of the action of the film centers around Joel's attempt, in alliance with his internal representation of Clementine, to protect his memories and his mental image of her.

The film enlists our allegiance as well by subtly focusing on a dynamic that will prove to be central to Joel's characterological problems. First, the film begins to raise our sympathy for Clementine by juxtaposing two scenes, one outside of Joel's mind and the other within.

Patrick goes to Clementine's house, where she is reacting to her own massive repression of her relationship with Joel. She is frightened and disorganized because of the massive repression. "I'm lost. I'm scared. I feel like I'm disappearing. My skin's coming off. I'm getting old. Nothing makes any sense." We are again reminded of Anna Freud's warning about the disruptiveness of repression. Patrick tries to use what he has learned from Joel's notebooks, even gives her a gift that Joel had bought for her. She anxiously insists that they go to Boston that night. She does not know it but she wants to reorganize herself around a forgotten memory of going to Boston with Joel, a memory we will see in a moment.

Joel's next memory reinforces our sympathy for the lost and frightened Clementine. We see Joel and Clementine lying together under a blanket. She tells him how lonely she felt as a child. "Like you don't matter." She had thought she was ugly growing up, trying to make her ugly doll, named Clementine, be pretty so that she could "magically change, too." As Joel kisses her, telling her she's pretty, she hugs him, saying, "Joely, don't ever leave me," in a way that touches us as well as Joel. With these two scenes, we experience Clementine's vulnerability and fear of loneliness. In a stroke, the film has played upon our own need for intimacy and our own fear of loss. From this point on, we want to reunite the lovers.

It is here, around this memory of vulnerability, loving support and fear of loss, that Joel begs Mierswiak to leave the one memory. Now he recalls loving moments with Clementine, starting with a night in Boston in which she leads him out onto the iced-over Charles River. He is frightened walking onto the ice, but lying next to her, he tells her he is as happy as he can be.

Having tasted loneliness and loving compassion, we are ready to feel Joel's urgency as he now tries to prevent losing his memories of Clementine. The decoders are trying to separate the lovers while we hope against hope that they can be kept together. Joel enlists the aid of his internal representation of Clementine, the Clementine constructed from his memories, in his battle with Mierswiak and his technicians. In a sense, we see them together again trying to fight the repression, literally running from memory to memory in an attempt to keep ahead of the grim memory editor.

Perhaps I am pushing the analogy too far, but I am here reminded of another feature of the analytic process. When the analyst finds herself pulled into a particular emotional issue it is likely to be an important issue for the analysis. In this case, the central issue is attachment and loss, and it will prove to be central to our "patient's" character. But to get to the sources of this conflict, we must find a way to childhood memories.

The suggestion, significantly, comes from Clementine, or more correctly from Joel's internal image of her. She suggests that he take his memory of her to places that the memory erasers won't know to look for her. As Joel takes Clementine to his childhood memories, where she does not belong, he is revealing himself in the way that she had wished he would earlier, in effect allowing us to continue to observe his analysis.

In Joel's mind, Clementine has first pushed him to be more revealing. Now she suggests that he take her to childhood memories. In the context of the film, she is becoming a Virgil for his Dante. As he moves with her to childhood memories, his image of her will take on an additional role.

We see Joel in various childhood situations while Clementine accompanies him, sometimes as an addition to the memory, at one point playing the role of his babysitter. Baby Joel complains that his mother pays no attention to him. The film presents this subtly, but it gives us a likely source for Joel's insecurity and neediness. Clementine does pay attention to him, even pulling up her skirt to reveal her panties, getting a "Yuck" from Baby Joel. Baby Joel is happy when he has his mother's full attention as she gives him a bath in the kitchen sink while Clementine's image keeps him company.

This allows Joel's memories of Clementine to blend into his childhood memories. Of course, we have a concept in analysis that involves the blending of childhood and current memories—transference.

Transferences

This transference image has a particular valence. Unlike his mother, Clementine is caring and attentive. His internal image of her is blending with his childhood memories, with Clementine playing a positive, supportive role. She is becoming a gratifying transference image, a "good" mother.

We are reminded of his anxious accusation earlier, "Clem, do you really think you could take care of a kid?" The question reflects his fear and anger about his mother's ability to take care of him. In the process of having Clementine removed from his memory, Joel is also developing a transference image of her by which she can take care of a kid, better than his own mother, and can undo his childhood fears. We have seen evidence of it in their adult relationship as well, with Clementine leading a frightened Joel out onto ice where he finds he is very happy.

This is further reinforced. As they try to hide his image of her from Mierswiak, Joel takes Clementine to his most hidden memories, experiences of shame. We see her with him as his mother catches him masturbating in his bedroom, then we see him bullied by a group of small children. Clementine rescues him from this encounter, telling him, "They're not worth it" and reassuring him, "It's O.K., you were a little kid." This is like the process of analysis, uncovering memories with their affect so that they can be reappraised in the light of adult understanding. Clementine is now serving as a positive transference figure, helping to guide him through the traumatic memories.

There is further reinforcement from the subplots, involving the decoders who are going through their own difficulties while they work on Joel. These involve a series of love triangles. Howard Mierswiak, the middle aged genius of Lacuna, Inc. is admired and loved by his receptionist, Mary, who is in turn sought after by Mierswiak's chief technician, Stan, a geeky but pleasant young man. Then there is the triangle involving Clementine and her new boyfriend, Patrick, who is Stan's assistant. Only Joel and Clementine are together at the film's end. The immature and phony Patrick makes Joel look like a mature Oedipal winner by contrast.

At the end of Joel's memories, we see him on the day he first met Clementine. She had broken into an unoccupied summer home on the beach at Montauk. He had gone in with her reluctantly, but left her as she began to raid the wine cellar, making him fear that they would be caught stealing, but also backing off as she offered to play that they were a married couple. As the memory is about to be removed, he says that he is sorry he did not stay with her that night, revealing a greater willingness to trust to a commitment with her. As the memory is being taken away, she whispers to him that he should meet her in Montauk the next morning, at last revealing to us why he is driven by a sudden impulse to take the train to Montauk at the beginning of the film.

As the story comes full circle, we again see Joel getting out of bed to start the day. Now, we understand, having uncovered the unconscious memory that makes sense of what was originally so perplexing. We also have a very different feeling about Joel and Clementine's meeting on the train back from Montauk, having seen them together through the ups and downs of an intense relationship. There is something peculiarly affecting when we see two people meet without their consciously knowing that they have been intimate. We experience it in the closing scene of *Here Comes Mr. Jordan* and its remake, *Heaven Can Wait*, as well as in the lesser known popular film, *Sliding Doors*. In each, a man and woman meet by chance, aware of an attraction and an odd sense of familiarity while the viewer knows that they have formed an indelible bond over the course of the film. In each, we expect a happy reunion with a new beginning to the love affair. We are particularly affected by the sense that the lovers knew each other in "another life". We have the experience of a reunion of lovers who have known each other in the unconscious past. That is particularly appealing as a re-finding of a long lost love; transference, or something like it.

The plot takes a final twist as the rejected receptionist, Mary, having learned that Howard had erased from her memory a previous affair with him, retaliates by sending all of his customers their files, including the tape they had made about the memories they wanted erased. (One of the messages of the film, expressed in Mary's attempt to revive the forgotten relationship as well as Joel and Clementine's re-finding of one another is that those who don't know their personal history are forced to repeat it.) First Clementine and then Joel receive their files and listen to their angry description of the other. It is like a massive reconstruction of repressed material, in this case making them aware of the relationship they have had without being conscious of the actual memories.

This last device allows us to experience a resolution to the original trauma. Having listened to enough of Joel's taped complaints about her, Clementine leaves him once again, saying, "It's been nice knowing you and all."

But as Joel stands by the door watching her leave, he hears his own words,

"What a loss to spend that much time with someone only to find out that she's a stranger."

Coming from the tape, it nevertheless sounds like one of his inner thoughts. We are primed to hear it in terms of the wastefulness of letting such an investment in love be lost again. He asks her to wait.

She says, "I'm not a concept, Joel, I'm just a fucked up girl who's looking for my own piece of mind. I'm not perfect."

Joel: "I can't see anything I don't like about you."

Clementine: "But you will. You will think of things. And I'll get bored with you and feel trapped because that's what happens with me."

Joel can now accept this imperfect relationship. He tells her, "OK."

Clementine accepts it as well: "OK."

With this happy ending, as we fade to them playing together on a snowy beach, the trauma is repaired. Joel and Clementine are not merely reunited, they have found a way to overcome the angers, fears and frustrations that caused them to lose one another. They are committed to staying in a real relationship, with all its problems. It is a happy ending for the viewer who has experienced their loss and their intimacy first hand.

The "patient" has benefited from his "analysis". He understands his symptoms, and, more importantly, has made gains in dealing with his character. He is more mature, able to trust the idea of having a family without being troubled by his frustrations with his own mother. He has the confidence to enter into a commitment of intimacy without being certain of the outcome. As so often happens, he does all this without being aware of the influence of transference.

Freud, Anna (1936) *The Ego and the Mechanisms of Defense: The Writings of Anna Freud, Vol. 2.* International University Press, 1966.

The King's Speech

FILM CAN ALSO REPRESENT transference in a clinical therapeutic setting.

The King's Speech was met with a great deal of excitement when it came out. I think this may have been particularly true in the analytic and therapeutic community. It is, after all, about a therapy and more importantly about a therapeutic relationship. Although the therapy is speech therapy, it is very specifically a form of speech therapy that focuses deliberately on personal dynamics and, with less conscious intent, on transference-countertransference dynamics.

For anyone who has not seen the film, it is based on a true story of a very special speech therapy. The patient is "Bertie," the Duke of York who would become king after his older brother abdicated. The speech therapist is an Australian commoner named Lionel Logue. To compound the difference, we learn that Logue is a self-made man, a would-be Shakespearean actor, who has no formal degree in speech therapy.

Logue's approach shows some intuitive understanding of psychodynamics and the role of psychic conflict in physical conditions. He is firmly convinced that dealing with the personal dynamics of his patients is essential to resolving their speech impediments. In fact, that conviction creates conflict between the two primary protagonists, contributing to the transference entanglements that make the film so interesting to analysts, and, I think, to the "lay" viewer as well.

The future king is a severe stutterer. The film opens to a painful scene in which he attempts to give a speech at a crowded stadium in 1926. He begins haltingly while making progress, but after a few sentences, he falters and cannot go on. We can feel the tension and sense the shame as the members of the audience at the stadium frown with disdain or possibly sympathy.

The scene shifts to a painful session with a pompous speech therapist, who forces Bertie to try to speak through a mouthful of marbles. When he attributes the technique to Demosthenes, Bertie's wife, Elizabeth, wonderfully supportive in an intelligent way throughout, pointedly asks, "That was in ancient Greece. Has it worked since?" The Duke nearly chokes on the marbles and angrily cuts the lesson short.

It is Elizabeth who seeks out Logue. We are treated to a cute dance, as Logue does not understand who his prospective patient is.

"Well, we need to have your hubby pop by. Tuesday would be good. He'll give me his personal details, I'll make a frank appraisal and we can take it from there."

"Doctor, forgive me. I don't have a hubby. We don't pop. And nor do we ever talk about our private lives."

It is this last point that will prove crucial to the course of the treatment. In fact, we know that many patients are reluctant to talk about their private lives. In the Duke's case, that defensive reticence is reinforced by a life spent trying to keep the private life private, a special issue for the rich and famous, for whom confidentiality takes on added meaning. When told that his new prospective patient is the Duke of York, Logue shows more understanding of the situation, but still insists on conducting the sessions in his office.

In his own way, he begins using an analytic approach with the Duke in their initial consultation.

"Well, I believe when speaking with a prince one allows the prince to choose the topic."

With hesitation and stuttering, the Duke answers, "Waiting for me to commence a conversation one can wait rather a long wait."

These are actually the first words he has spoken to Logue. We can recognize the Duke's reluctance to speak along with his mildly self-deprecating humor. After a pause, Lionel asks if he knows any jokes and again, with a sharp sense of humor, the Duke answers through his stutter, "Timing isn't my strong suit." Despite his difficulty speaking, we can easily find him engaging, even as he shows us his resistance.

Lionel deals with the resistance by going along with it. He offers the Duke a cup of tea and when the Duke refuses, turns to the fireplace to make one for himself, humming as he does it, in essence provoking his patient by demonstrating his own willingness to wait him out. The Duke takes the bait.

"Aren't you going to start treating me, Dr. Logue?"

"Only if you're interested in being treated."

The message is clear that it is the Duke's responsibility to be an active participant in his treatment, challenging his passive resistance.

He continues, "Call me Lionel."

This has a double meaning. As we are watching it, it appears to be an attempt to establish the relationship on a personal basis, something that the Duke resists strenuously. Much later we shall see that Lionel has a second purpose. He is covering up the fact that he does not have a degree.

The dialogue devolves around the issue of intimacy. (Throughout these dialogues, the Duke's speech is generally halting with extreme stuttering.)

The Duke says, "I prefer 'doctor.'"

"I prefer Lionel. What'll I call you?"

"Your Royal Highness. Then, it's 'Sir' after that."

"It's a little bit formal for here. I prefer names."

"Prince Albert Frederick Arthur George."

"How about Bertie?"

"Only my family uses that."

"Perfect. In here it's better if we're equals."

"If we were equals I wouldn't be here. I'd be at home with my wife and no one would give a damn."

The tension increases when Lionel asks Bertie for his earliest memory.

"What on Earth do you mean?"

"First recollection."

(With increased stuttering and a raised voice): "I'm not here to discuss personal matters."

"Why're you here then?"

(Exploding—stammer free): "Because I bloody well stammer!"

When Bertie is openly angry and cursing, the stammer disappears. (It is reminiscent of Tourette's syndrome.) Throughout the film there will be a suggestion of a connection between aggression and stuttering.

Lionel responds, "Temper."

"One of my many faults."

"When did the defect start?"

"I've always been this way!"

"I doubt that."

"Don't tell me! It's my defect!"

"It's my field. I assure you, no infant starts to speak with a stammer. When did it start?"

"Four or five."

"That's typical."

"So I've been told. I can't remember not doing it."

"That I believe. Do you hesitate when you think?"

"Don't be ridiculous."

"One of my many faults. How about when you talk to yourself?"

When Bertie doesn't answer, Lionel adds, "Everyone natters occasionally, Bertie."

"Don't call me that!"

"I'm not going to call you anything else."

"Then we shan't speak!"

I've given the dialogue in detail to give the flavor of the interaction. Even without hearing the tone, the exchange rings with competition and angry tension. There is interplay of a barely friendly tennis match, with Lionel throwing Bertie's phrase, "One of my many faults," back at him; and, with intermittent outbursts of overt hostility on Bertie's part, in this last instance when he is probed with intimacy. The session ends with the patient walking out, saying this is not for him, but not before Lionel has gotten him to read Hamlet's soliloquy into a recording device while listening to loud music through earphones. As we can guess, the reading was virtually perfect. It will later convince the Duke to return.

We have learned that the Duke's problem started in early childhood, in fact at the heart of the Oedipal period. As if to confirm a dynamic speculation, we next see him with his father, King George V. The king, looking regal, delivers a radio address in a voice worthy of Michael Gambon, who plays him. He then forces his son, Bertie, to read the speech into the (now dead) microphone. As Bertie meets a wall of stuttering, the king coaches him like a horse driver with a whip, throwing out comments such as, "Get it out, boy! ... Form your words carefully ... Relax! ... Just try it! ... Do it!" What began as encouragement ends as sheer bullying, the future king reduced to a whipped pup.

Immediately after that, we see him first listening to his reading of Hamlet and then returning with his wife to see Logue. This time, Logue reluctantly agrees to coach him purely in the mechanics of speech, demanding that they work every day. We see the two of them, and sometimes the three of them, with Elizabeth participating, in a series of manic exercises designed to loosen his throat muscles, strengthen his tongue and tighten his diaphragm.

From our viewpoint, listening for the analytic process, Logue is making a tactical retreat, not directly challenging the resistance while allowing the patient to become engaged.

With Bertie showing some improvement giving a speech, we return to the family dynamics. The entire royal family is gathering around King George's deathbed. Several years have passed and the once imposing king is now dying and suffering from delirium. Bertie's older brother, David, appears to be panicking at the prospect of being king. His problem is that he is obsessed (that is the tone conveyed by the film) with a married American woman who has been divorced. David fears that his ascension to the throne will upset his relationship with Wallis.

Here we get a very different take on that relationship. Many of us remember multiple replays of newsreels announcing the romance of a

Transferences

king who would step down to marry a commoner, an American at that. *The King's Speech* views it from a dramatically different perspective. Through the eyes of Bertie and his wife, David is being irresponsible in having an affair with a twice-married woman. There are also references suggestive of her being a loose woman.

David is portrayed as hedonistic, irresponsible and totally obsessed with Wallis. He ignores Bertie while on the phone with her and describes his pain at becoming king as having to do with how it will affect Wallis.

It is in this context, after the passing of George V, that we witness the next important session in Bertie's treatment. He arrives, possibly at his regular time, but unexpectedly.

"Bertie, they told me not to expect you. . . . Sorry about your father."

"I don't wish to intrude," (gesturing towards the consultation room). "May I?"

"Of course. Please come in."

At Bertie's request, Lionel gives him some brandy. With this natural reinforcement, the session begins in earnest.

Offering an opening for personal reactions, Lionel tells Bertie that he had not been present for his own father's death, and that it "still makes me sad."

"I can imagine so. What did your father do?"

"A brewer. ... At least there was free beer. ... Here's to the memory of your father."

"I was informed, after the fact, my father's last words were: 'Bertie has more guts than the rest of his brothers put together.' He couldn't say that to my face." Bertie continues, stuttering, "My brother. That's why I'm here."

"What's he done?"

"Can't say. I can't .. ."

He stutters severely, becoming totally locked up and Lionel tells him to try singing it to overcome the stutter. Bertie balks at doing this and Lionel adds an incentive, telling him he can work on a model airplane he's been eyeing hungrily if he tries singing to the tune of "Swanee River," "When I was a boy with David ..."

Bertie balks at "crooning Swanee River."

"Try 'Camptown Races' then. 'My brother D, he said to me, doo-dah doo-dah ... .' Continuous sound will give you flow. Does it feel strange, now that David's on the throne?"

"It was a relief... Knowing I wouldn't be King."

"But unless he produces an heir, you're next in line. And your daughter, Elizabeth, would then succeed you."

To the tune of Camptown races, Bertie sings, "You're barking up the wrong tree now, Doctor, Doctor."

"Lionel, Lionel. You didn't stammer."

"Of course I didn't stammer, I was singing! ... Oh!"

Lionel rewards the disclosure by allowing him to work on the plane.

Bertie continues, "David and I were very close. Young bucks ... you know."

"Chase the same girls?"

"David was always very helpful in arranging introductions. We shared the expert ministrations of 'Paulette' in Paris. Not at the same time of course."

"Did David tease you?"

"They all did. 'Buh-buh-buh-Bertie.' Father encouraged it. 'Get it out, boy!' Said it would make me stop. Said, 'I was afraid of my father, and my children are damn well going to be afraid of me.'"

Lionel is watching his patient work the model plane and asks, "Naturally right handed?"

"Left. I was punished. Now I use the right."

"Yes, that's very common with stammerers. Any other corrections?"

"Knock knees. Metal splints were made ... worn night and day."

"That must have been painful."

"Bloody agony. Straight legs now."

"Who were you closest to in your family?"

"Nannies. Not my first nanny, though—she loved David ... hated me. When I was presented to my parents for the daily viewing, she'd ... ."

Once again, he is locked up, unable to go on.

Transferences

Pressed to go on, Bertie answers in a combination of speaking and singing (sung portion in italics): ""She'd pinch me so I'd cry, and be sent away at once, *then she wouldn't feed me, far far away.* Took three years for my parents to notice. As you can imagine, it caused some stomach problems. Still."

Apparently in history taking mode, Lionel asks, "What about your brother, Johnnie? Were you close to him?"

"Sweet boy. Epilepsy ... and ... he was 'different.' Died at 13, hidden from view. Too embarrassing for the family. I've been told it's not catching."

At the end of the session, Bertie tells Lionel that he's the first ordinary Englishman—Lionel corrects him, "Australian"—that he's ever really spoken to. (Nanny transference?)

When Lionel tells him, "What are friends for," Bertie answers with a trace of sadness and sarcasm, "I wouldn't know."

In this first opening up of the therapy, we get a history of a traumatized child, mistreated by his first nanny, made fun of by his siblings and his father, forced to wear metal braces for who knows how long, neglected so that he describes himself as closest to the nannies.

And with that traumatic background, we see evidence of suppressed rage in the stuttering. He locks up trying to describe what the nanny did to him. This may be an expression of fear, but everything we have been hearing suggests fear mixed with rage. When he is able to speak, through the singing, his sarcasm comes through.

We also have suggestions of the Oedipal dynamics played out not only with the father, but also with the older brother, who sounds patronizing and sometimes cruel.

Bertie says that he is relieved that he isn't king, and when Lionel reminds him that he would be next in line if there is no heir, Bertie sings out that he's barking up the wrong tree. He is adamant at not wanting the crown. This will prove telling in the next session that we see.

Before that, we are given a clue in the next scene, when Bertie attempts to confront his brother about his behavior and his plans.

Bertie: "I've been trying to see you ..."

David: "I've been terribly busy."

"Doing what?

"Kinging."

"Really? Kinging? Kinging is a precarious business! Where is the Tsar of Russia? Where is Cousin Wilhelm?"

(Some of Bertie's hostility is ringing through as a displaced murderous rage.)

"You're being dreary."

"Is kinging laying off eighty staff at Sandringham and buying yet more pearls for Wallis while there are people marching across Europe singing 'The Red Flag'?"

David hurries down some stairs to hunt for a bottle of champagne for Wallis in the wine cellar with Bertie following and saying,

"And you've put that woman into our mother's suite?"

"Mother's not still in the bed, is she?"

"That's not funny."

Finding the bottle of wine, David says, "Wally likes the very best."

Bertie retorts, "I don't care what woman you carry on with at night, as long as you show up for duty in the morning!"

"This is not just some woman I am carrying on with. This is the woman I intend to marry.

"Excuse me?"

"She's filing a petition for divorce."

"Good God! ... Can't you just give her a nice house and a title?"

"I won't have her as my mistress."

"David, the Church does not recognize divorce and you are the head of the Church."

"Haven't I any rights?"

"Many privileges..."

"Not the same thing. Your beloved Common Man may marry for love, why not me?"

"If you were the Common Man, on what basis could you possibly claim to be King?!"

"Sounds like you've studied our wretched constitution."

"Sounds like you haven't."

"Is that what this is all about? Is that why you've been taking elocution lessons?"

"I'm attempting t-t..."

"That's the scoop around town. Yearning for a larger audience are we, B-b-b-Bertie?"

"D-don't say such a th-"

"Young brother trying to push older brother off throne ... Positively medieval."

Now, Bertie is completely locked up in his stuttering.

Despite some stuttering, Bertie is relatively articulate, accusing his brother of shirking his responsibilities until David accuses him of desiring to usurp him. The accusation completely locks him up. The implication is clear to a layman, certainly to an analyst. The accusation hits at a central conflict. Lionel addresses that conflict through the transference at the session following this interchange.

"All that work, down the drain. My own brother ... I couldn't say ... I could say ... I couldn't say a word in reply!"

"Why do you stammer more with David than you do with me?"

"Because you're bloody well paid to listen!"

(He spits this out angrily without stuttering.)

"I'm not a geisha girl."

"Stop trying to be so bloody clever!"

"What is it about David that stops you speaking?"

"What the bloody hell is it that makes you bloody well want to go on about David?"

"Vulgar but fluent. You don't stammer when you swear."

"Bugger off!"

"Is that the best you can do?"

"Well bloody bugger to you, you beastly bastard!"

"A public school prig can do better than that."

"Shit then. Shit, shit, shit!"

"See how defecation falls trippingly from the tongue?"

"Because I'm angry!"

The session has moved to the central conflict over anger, the connection between anger and stuttering—we would say inhibition—and all of it in the transference.

"Ah, know the "F" word?"

"Fornication?"

"Bertie."

"Fuck ... fuck, fuck, fuck!"

"Yes! You see, not a hesitation!"

"Bloody, bloody, bloody! Shit, shit, shit! Bugger, bugger, bugger! Fuck, fuck, fuck!"

Lionel's son knocks on the wall asking what's going on. Lionel comments that that's a side of Bertie not often seen and Bertie says, "we're not supposed to really, not in public." Lionel suggests they go outside for a walk, overruling Bertie's objection.

In this part session, we have most of the pieces in place, suppressed anger leading to severe inhibition brought into the transference. What is still not made explicit is the connection with Bertie's older brother, David, the King. This comes together as they resume the session on a walk in the park, but, as we shall see, there is a suggestion of an interpretive mistake on Lionel's part, and possibly a counter-transference reaction.

Lionel begins, "What's wrong? What's got you so upset?"

"Logue, you have no idea. My brother is infatuated with a woman who's been married twice—and she's American."

"Some of them must be loveable."

"She's asking for a divorce and David is determined to marry her. Mrs. Wallis Simpson of Baltimore."

"That's not right. Queen Wallis of Baltimore?"

"Unthinkable."

"Can he do that?"

"Absolutely not. But he's going to anyway. All hell's broken loose."

"Can't they carry on privately?"

"If only they would."

So far, the discussion is relatively neutral.

Now, Lionel brings it back to Bertie's conflict.

"Where does that leave you?"

The answer is very telling: "I know my place! I'll do anything within my power to keep my brother on the throne."

"Has it come to that? But the way things are going, your place may be on the throne."

"I am not an alternative to my brother."

At this point, Lionel makes what could be viewed as a mistake and a counter-transference enactment. Patting Bertie on the shoulder, he says,

"If you had to, you could outshine David."

The entire film has been set up to make us feel that this statement is very true. In it, we can sense Lionel's affection and admiration for his patient. The problem is that it bypasses the conflict. Lionel is now assuming that Bertie disowns any ambitions to take his brother's place out of a lack of confidence; yet, the entire film and all the contents of the sessions to this point belie that opinion. What we have seen unequivocally is that Bertie is conflicted, to put it mildly, over his rivalry with his father and his brother, his rivalry marked by intense rage. It is this Oedipal conflict that appears to be at the heart of his inhibitions. He responds in keeping with this, in a transference reaction that at once expresses his rage while he continues to disown his regal ambition.

"Don't take liberties. That's bordering on treason!" (Displacing his treasonous Oedipal wishes onto his therapist.)

"I'm just saying you could be king. You could do it."

"That is treason!"

Lionel does not see his mistake, but goes on in the same vein.

"I'm trying to get you to realize you need not be governed by fear."

He is of course right and wrong. Yes, Bertie is governed by fear, but not fear of failure. He fears his Oedipal rivalry and rage. He is governed by fear of his anger and ambition.

Bertie responds (in keeping with the dynamics), "I've had enough of this!"

"What're you afraid of?"

"*Your poisonous words!*"

I have italicized this for emphasis. He sees the expression of Oedipal, regal ambition as poisonous.

"Why'd you show up then? To take polite elocution lessons so you can chit-chat at posh tea parties?"

"Don't instruct me on my duties! I'm the brother of a King ... the son of a King. We have a history that goes back untold centuries.

You're the disappointing son of a brewer! A jumped-up jackeroo from the outback! You're nobody. These sessions are over!"

He walks off angrily, having displaced his feelings again. Using the transference, he accuses Logue of being the disappointing son, the accusation he diverts from his brother, David. The treatment is interrupted.

Logue has a very brief "consultation" about his counter-transference with his wife, who points out that he may be confusing his own ambitions for his patient (whose identity she does not know) with the patient's ambitions for himself.

We now watch history taking its course as David makes his abdication speech, saying that he can't discharge his duties without the support of the woman he loves. (The romance of this has been undermined most pointedly by a report that Wallis has been carrying on an affair behind his back.)

Finding himself unable to give his accession speech, Bertie returns to Lionel, somewhat apologetically, supported by his wife, who has told him that she had no ambition to be Queen, but would do so with complete faith in his ability to be a good king. Leaving his wife, Elizabeth, in the Logue family's dining room, he goes in for a session with Lionel, who now comes closer to the correct interpretation. The opening addresses the problem of replacing both the older brother and the father.

"I understand what you were trying to say, Logue."

"I went about it the wrong way. I'm sorry."

"Now here I am. Is the nation ready for two minutes of radio silence?"

"Every stammerer always fears they will fall back to square one. I don't let that happen. You won't let that happen."

"If I fail in my duty ... David could come back. I've seen the placards 'Save Our King!' They don't mean me. Every other monarch in history succeeded someone who was dead, or about to be. My predecessor is not only alive, but very much so. What a bloody mess! I can't even give them a Christmas Speech."

Logue brings it to the paternal conflict: "Like your Dad used to do?"

"Precisely."

"Your father. He's not here."

"Yes he is. He's on that bloody shilling I gave you."

Lionel brings it back to the Oedipal period. "Easy enough to give away. You don't have to carry him around in your pocket. Or your brother. You don't need to be afraid of things you were afraid of when you were five. You're very much your own man, Bertie. Your face is next, mate."

This session, in which Lionel addresses the central Oedipal conflict, is interrupted when Lionel's wife comes home to find the Queen at her table. There is a cordial, respectful and yet warm meeting of the two couples.

The transference comes directly into play in one final dramatic session. They meet at Westminster Abbey for a rehearsal. Bertie confronts Lionel with the fact that he is not a doctor, has no credentials. He accuses him of leaving the country with a voiceless king, compares himself to "mad King George." Then he sees Lionel sitting on a ceremonial chair. He insists that he get up. Lionel says it's just a chair.

"That chair is the seat on which every King and Queen ..."

"It's held in place by a large rock."

"That is the Stone of Scone. You're trivializing everything."

"I don't care. I don't care how many royal arses have sat in this chair ..."

"Listen to me!"

"Listen to you? By what right?"

"Divine right, if you must! I'm your King!"

"Noooo you're not! Told me so yourself. Said you didn't want it. So why should I waste my time listening to you?"

"Because I have a right to be heard!"

"Heard as what?"

"A man! I have a voice!"

"Yes you do. You have such perseverance, Bertie, you're the bravest man I know. And you'll make a bloody good king."

With the Oedipal dynamics and the transference resolved, as they can be so efficiently only in art, the King is now able to assert himself with the Archbishop on the matter of Lionel's coaching him. With Lionel's help, we see Bertie successfully overcoming his speech defect and his now not so unconscious conflicts to deliver a speech to the nation, a nation that he will address through the war years.

Film has generally been awkward in portraying psychoanalysis directly; but, it gives us beautiful depictions of "a good analytic hour" when it uses another vehicle to show it. In *The Sixth Sense*, the ghost of a psychologist treats a haunted young boy, while coming to terms with his own "mortality." In *The Silence of the Lambs*, a psychopathic, cannibalistic psychiatrist controls his own impulses long enough to conduct a transformative, healing session built around a traumatic dream with a young FBI agent. Perhaps most bizarrely of all, in *Rashomon*, a peasant confronts the defenses of a bewildered woodcutter, traumatized by a primal scene experience, freeing him to open himself to forgiveness and relief from his depression.

Now, we can add *The King's Speech* to that collection of barely disguised successful analyses, an analysis marked by Oedipal conflict, Oedipal conflict displaced to sibling rivalry, and an intense transference-counter-transference enactment and repair, resulting in a literal ascension to the throne and a voice freed from conflictual inhibition.

Afterword

I HOPE THAT THESE commentaries have given a clear picture of how I approached these films psychoanalytically. I looked for repeating patterns in the film that suggested a particular aspect of mind, and then looked for corroborating evidence. I looked for direct evidence in a film supporting an idea that I had discovered in the psychoanalytic literature, and then looked for corroborating evidence. I looked for films that gave direct or metaphorical descriptions of particular common childhood fantasies. I sought out strong and surprising emotions evoked by a film and tried to discern the elements of the film that evoked those emotions. I tried to start from the surface and work to understand what underlay that surface. These are all techniques that in one way or another are basic to analytic technique.

I also hope that I have impressed you with the power and scope of art in general and film in particular to reveal the workings of our minds as they capture our hearts. In this small volume we have moved amongst such diverse topics as the fear and magic of a child learning to walk, the turmoil of adolescence, the use of fantasy as a normal part of growing up and as a defense against the horrors of trauma, the tension between narcissism and love for others, the dynamics of twins embedded in a popular fantasy movie, the tensions of a small child seen through a gigantic gorilla, and the transfer of feelings towards a lost loved one onto someone new. This and more awaits you at your local theater. See you there!

About the Author

Herbert H. Stein, M.D. is a psychiatrist and psychoanalyst who lives and works in New York City. He is on the faculty of the Institute for Psychoanalytic Education affiliated with NYU School of Medicine (IPE) and of the NYU Department of Psychiatry. Dr. Stein has published a previous compilation of essays on psychoanalysis and film entitled *Double Feature: Discovering our hidden fantasies in film*, currently published by Open Roads Media as an E-Book, available in Kindle, Nook and other formats.